Grandparent Guide

The Definitive Guide to Coping with the Challenges of Modern Grandparenting

Arthur Kornhaber, M.D.

Contemporary Books

Chicago   New York   San Francisco   Lisbon   London   Madrid   Mexico City
Milan   New Delhi   San Juan   Seoul   Singapore   Sydney   Toronto

Library of Congress Cataloging-in-P

Kornhaber, Arthur.
    The grandparent guide : the defi
modern grandparenting / Arthur Kor
        p.   cm.
    Includes bibliographical referenc
    ISBN 0-07-138311-5
    1. Grandparenting—Handbooks, manuals, etc.   2. Grandparent and child—
Handbooks, manuals, etc.   I. Title.

HQ759.9 .K644   2002
306.874'5—dc21   2002019339

Contemporary Books

A Division of The McGraw·Hill Companies

1 2 3 4 5 6 7 8 9 0 AGM/AGM 1 0 9 8 7 6 5 4 3 2

ISBN 0-07-138311-5

This book was set in Bembo and ITC Officina Sans
Printed and bound by Quebecor Martinsburg

Cover and interior design by Jeanette Wojtyla

McGraw-Hill books are available at special quantity discounts to use as premiums and sales promotions, or for use in corporate training programs. For more information, please write to the Director of Special Sales, Professional Publishing, McGraw-Hill, Two Penn Plaza, New York, NY 10121-2298. Or contact your local bookstore.

The names and places referring to participants in the Grandparent Study and other case examples have been changed to assure confidentiality.

This book is printed on acid-free paper.

To our new granddaughter, Anna-Claire DeWitt,
to her great-great-great-great grandparents and beyond,
and to her great-great-great grandchildren
and after . . . to use with their own grandchildren

Contents

Acknowledgments

My respectful thanks to the many teachers of all ages—family, friends, patients, and colleagues—who have shown me the magic that happens between grandchildren and grandparents.

Since I am a doctor who writes and not a writer who doctors, I counted on the good offices of others to help to make this book happen. Among these many kind and helpful people, I want to especially thank my daughter and editorial assistant, Chantal Marie; my literary agent, Jim Levine; and my friends Betty DeGeneres and Bill Walker. At Contemporary Books, I am grateful to my editor, Matthew Carnicelli, for his guidance and kind manner. I am also grateful to Craig Bolt, editorial team leader, for his work on my behalf, as well as to Michelle Pezzuti. And a special thanks to Laurie Sale and Frances Baggetta at Knowledge Kids Network, where the idea for this book was born.

Together, through this book, I hope we can help many people of all ages light up their lives a bit more.

INTRODUCTION

Modern Grandparenting

As many elders will attest, the old expression "things aren't the same as they used to be" has never been more relevant. Today changes take place with unprecedented speed and scope. Several decades ago, who would have thought that the baby boomers—70 million grandparents strong—would be so long-lived and healthy? Who would have foreseen that divorce and remarriage would be so commonplace in our society, creating legions of serial sons- and daughters-in-law and legions of stepgrandchildren? Who would have thought that laws would need to be enacted just so grandparents would be allowed to see their own grandchildren? Did we have any idea that millions of American grandparents would be the sole caretakers of their grandchildren? Did we dream that we would encounter so many diverse families? Who would have thought so many new grandparents would be created by single parents and gay and lesbian couples?

This whirlwind of change has left in its wake millions of grandparents who feel bewildered about how to be and what to do. Many of us feel overwhelmed, confused, and out of touch about being a modern grandparent.

Being out of touch, however, should not be the destiny of today's grandparents. We are an involved and vital generation. To be effective grandparents in today's turbulent world we *must* adapt to the changes and cope with them effectively. That's what being modern is all about. It means having a positive, flexible, energetic attitude toward understanding, learning, and personal change.

Being modern will enable you to keep up with societal change and live in the same world as your children and grandchildren. Being modern will help you maintain a balance between the joys, privileges, and responsibilities of grandparenting, and help you be the best grandparent you can be. And, most of all, being modern will enable you to reinvent yourself and to adapt to future changes.

To begin this task of modernization and to know where we are headed, we have to know where we have been and where we are now.

Let's begin at the beginning.

History: Where We Were

In the past, grandparents' roles were traditional; they remained more or less unchanged for thousands of years. Not so today. A new breed of grandparent has appeared. And society has not yet fully recognized this new generation of grandparents who are younger, healthier, better educated, and more affluent than any generation of grandparents before. That is, you!

What Is New About Being Old?

Our arrival is the good news. The bad news is that we surfaced into an American society that neither recognized nor was ready for us. The nation was blinded to our arrival because America looks toward the young for what is new and innovative. During the twentieth century, being young became increasingly in; being old was out. Old-granny stereotypes still prevailed. Thus, being a grandparent meant being old. Being old meant having no meaningful role or place in society. Of course grandparenting was prospering (ask any grandchild) but it was hidden, a *private* pleasure between grandparents and grandchildren. The potential of our new generation to function as a public force for good went unrecognized by American society. Grandparents were confused because they didn't look or feel as old as their own grandparents had at the same age. They too were ignorant of what was happening and continued to think and act according to old stereotypes.

Changes

Only over the last two decades of the twentieth century did some members of our new generation begin to understand the importance of what was occurring.

New medical advances have increased our life spans, adding many healthy and vital years to our lives. Some elders, who retired at the mandatory age of sixty-five, feeling hale and hearty with still-active minds and a desire to stay in the workforce, were inspired to start new careers. Others redirected their energies in other ways. They were able for the first time to give attention to the emotional aspects of their lives, and begin to get directly involved with their children and grandchildren, something their schedules had not allowed when they were working. Today, millions of grandparents, who had joined the exodus of retirees to warmer climes, are beginning to rethink this decision. Some are contemplating going home and restoring contact with the family they left behind.

All of a sudden, we became aware of another unprecedented event. Increasing numbers of grandparents are now becoming great-grandparents, and expanding their influence to a fourth generation. A new generation is being added to the family roster.

As these changes finally began to register in the public mind, appreciation for the importance of grandparenting began to grow. Today grandparenting is the subject of more and more books. It's all over the press; it's even making its way into academic curriculums, as well as becoming the subject of scientific research. Grandparent-visitation laws have been passed to preserve the place of grandparents within the family, and to ensure that contact with grandchildren is maintained in case of parental death or divorce. Grandparenting consciousness spawned a nationwide intergenerational movement. Today many organizations are involved in removing the attitudinal barriers separating the old and the young. The foster grandparenting program—grandparents helping other people's grandchildren—brings elders and children together in the schools. My own nonprofit organization, the Foundation for Grandparenting, promotes the importance of grandparenting with various intergenerational programs, including Grandparent's Day in the schools. Hospitals participate in our Expectant Grandparent Program, special birthing classes where parents and grandparents gather to discuss family issues, as well as their hopes and dreams for the coming child. Grandparents Raising Grandchildren groups have sprung up all over the nation to offer respite and support to the millions of grandparents who are raising their grandchildren because of parental need or failure. National recognition of the importance of grandparenting was affirmed by the establishment of a national annual holiday, Grandparent's Day.

The Internet is the latest resource bringing elders and the young closer together. Websites such as www.grandparenting.org and others are harnessing the Internet's new technologies to enhance family connections and to serve as an informational and educational center for grandparents.

Grandparent Power

Fueled by findings from my research and clinical studies, I have made an effort, through my books, articles, lectures, and media appearances, to spread the word about the potential for good this new generation of grandparents can bring to bear on family and society. For this to happen it will be necessary to change our nation's current attitudes about aging. The simple truth is that grandparents are eminently useful and powerful where the criteria are love, caring, support, and understanding.

That's why, for more than thirty years, I have been encouraging people to embrace the concept of grandparent power—to apply the grandparent's unique power of love, wisdom, and lifelong experience for the benefit of the family and society. Unlike the bloom of youth, grandparent power does not diminish with age; on the contrary, it actually increases with the passing years. The concept of grandparent power refutes the notion that aging means a diminution of one's capacities. My experience has taught me that in the eyes of a child, the emotional and spiritual power of a loved one increases with age. That's because children can see beyond the wrinkles and relate to the spirit within a person they love.

Grandparenting for All

I also have learned that grandparenting is a role not limited to biological grandparents. Individuals without biological grandchildren can assume many of the same functions and roles as biological grandparents. Indeed, *any elder* can derive fulfillment in a close relationship with a child. This means that all elders can enact some grandparenting roles for other people's grandchildren and gain the benefits of doing so. Additionally, being a vital grandparent is not restricted by geography. Long-distance grandparents can have a profound impact on the life of a grandchild if they are willing to put forth the effort. So can stepgrandparents and grandparents of adopted grandchildren.

Rising Consciousness

This philosophy, grandparent power, is increasingly resonating with people. Many grandparents and elders are starting to understand how their roles and functions as modern grandparents can provide them with an unprecedented template for living a meaningful later life. One spin-off from this realization is that many of us are beginning to reevaluate our rights and responsibilities concerning our grandchildren and our place in society. With our consciousness thus raised, and our empowerment perceived, we are freed to shed restrictive stereotypes and to begin addressing family and social issues that were hindrances to our relationships with our children and grandchildren. It is beginning to sink in that, although we may be parents for many years of our lives, many of us will also be grandparents for more than half of our lives, and some will even be great-grandparents. We are beginning to realize that there are lots of us too; indeed,

96 percent of persons under twenty have a grandparent (Hayslip 2001). Even people who have put off having children until the age of forty will be grandparents for a long time too because of increased longevity.

All of these sweeping changes have brought their share of challenges with them. These touch every personal, familial, and social aspect of our lives. Read on to find out about a few that are worth thinking about.

Challenges Ahead

The greatest challenge we face is the need to keep abreast of all this unprecedented change. This includes personal change, the changing structure of our families, rapid social change—and the effects of each of them on our identity, self-image, and relationships. The American family continues to evolve. Multiple marriages make for complicated configurations; many grandparents have both biological and stepgrandchildren. More than 30 percent of children today are being born from, or adopted by, single mothers, many of them financially challenged. What impact will this have on us as grandparents? Will we be personally needed to take up some of the parenting slack as eight million of our contemporaries are doing today? What new roles will grandmothers and grandfathers be called upon to play? How will this affect our ideas of psychological and emotional independence and individuality?

Old barriers, stereotypes, and prejudices are toppling like the Berlin Wall. Interracial, interreligious, and interethnic marriages are on the increase. How can we best assimilate these changes, especially when they may call into question the validity of a cherished and traditional belief system passed on to us by our ancestors? How do we deal with grandchildren from other cultures, religions, and belief systems? And what about the millions of gays and lesbians who are starting families, either by adopting or using surrogate mothers? Whatever your personal opinions may be about this situation, the fact is that new grandparents are being created. What adjustments will grandparents in such situations have to make to be the best grandparent possible for the grandchild (and of course, the best parent for their child as well)? How can a grandparent help a gay or lesbian grandchild adjust to the world? How do gay and lesbian grandparents who come out late in life maintain a close attachment to a grandchild when parents may disagree with the grandparent's lifestyle?

If these external changes are not bewildering enough, we have also experienced, and must deal with, internal change, too. We are not only living longer, but are also imbued with increased vitality. Thanks to good genes, good sanitation, better health care, and hormone therapies, we have increased our longevity, prolonged our sexually active years, and improved the quality of our lives in general. How will we fulfill our new roles as grandparents now that the stereotypes we were raised with no longer apply?

As you can plainly see being a modern grandparent is no easy task. You no doubt have plenty of questions. That's only natural, as there are lots of challenges you are going to have to face. Likewise lots of growth opportunities await you. I have written this book to help you answer these questions, address the challenges, and become a modern—informed, up-to-date, educated, knowledgeable, and most of all, effective—grandparent.

How to Use This Book

I have written *The Grandparent Guide* as a resource and an educational tool for you, the grandparent. But as your children will be grandparents one day too, I hope you will share the book with your family members of all ages. You can also use this book as a basic text for grandparent classes to raise grandparenting consciousness among your friends and in your community. *The Grandparent Guide* is structured to be used as a text for a grandparent study group. Each chapter supplies a topic for class discussion.

Many of the chapters also include parents' and grandchildren's feelings and viewpoints; I encourage you to solicit the comments and opinions of your own children and grandchildren on the topic at hand. This serves to raise their own grandparent consciousness, increase their awareness of your experience in the role, and prepares them to be grandparents one day too. This multigenerational presentation of issues will help you to see how parents and grandchildren feel in certain circumstances to give you a broader view of some complicated issues. By looking at this broader view, you can achieve greater understanding, compassion, and wisdom. The more you know, the more you increase your grandparent power.

You can also use this book as an educational tool for grandparenting in general. If you have to deal with professionals concerning your grandchild (teachers, therapists, attorneys, politicians, social service workers) ask them to read this book and discuss it with you. This experience will help them to understand important aspects of grandparenting of which they may be unaware.

You can read the book from cover to cover, in topic sequence, to broaden your general knowledge. Or you can refer to this book on an as-needed basis, as a reference tool for a topic that may be of special interest to you. To further your knowledge in areas of special interest you will find appropriate resources, websites, and organizations at the end of many chapters.

Use the book interactively. Perhaps your son is getting a divorce and is hesitant to open up to you about what he is going through. Suggest that both of you read the chapter about divorce, then discuss together what you read. This can serve as an icebreaker to jumpstart a healthy dialogue and keep the lines of communication open. The knowledge you will gain will also help you to nip problems in the bud or even heal negative situations that you may already be experiencing in your family life.

The Grandparent Guide contains chapters addressing what every grandparent needs to know about modern grandparenting. I chose the topics based on the most frequent issues and questions that grandparents and other family members have wanted addressed during my years of research and work in the field of grandparenting. By reading the book you will be exposed to a broad range of knowledge about grandparenting and how it affects all generations. The length of each chapter depends upon the complexity and level of current interest. For example, grandparent-visitation laws and other legal questions, raising grandchildren, long-distance grandparenting, gay and lesbian issues, divorce, technology, and stepgrandparenting are all forefront issues at this time. Each chapter will contain the latest information available. At the end of most chapters, you will find a listing of guidelines that you can apply to enhance your grandparenting experience or to solve conflicts and problems.

Issues and Topics

The subject matter covers all of the relevant and emerging issues related to grandparenting. Part 1 will help you understand yourself as a grandparent. Here you will learn how your roles as an ancestor, buddy, hero, historian, mentor, nurturer, role model, spiritual guide, student, teacher, and wizard comprise the backbone of your grandparenting.

Part 2 will put you in touch with how grandparents are created. Learning how you come to value the role, act it out, and grow and change over the years can be very helpful. To this end, I will explain the grandparent instinct. I will also show you how specific traits of personality and temperament affect grandparenting. To further your understanding of conditions that affect grandparenting, I will discuss how age and gender affect grandparenting in great-grandparents, young grandparents, grandmothers and grandfathers.

Part 3 explains aspects of the special bond you have with your grandchild. This is devoted to help you have the best relationship with your grandchild. I will explain and discuss how special circumstances such as attention, birth of your grandchild, babysitting, favoritism, spoiling, substance abuse, special needs grandchild, travel, spending and visiting, affect your relationship with your grandchild and his parents and how you can do the best in any situation.

Because parents are the linchpins of your relationship with your grandchild understanding family relationships and how to deal with them successfully is critical to being an effective grandparent. I address this tricky area in Part 4, which includes the chapters "Between Parents and Grandparents" and "Between Grandparents."

Part 5 is devoted to putting you in touch with the critical issues you face today as a modern grandparent. Although some topics may not directly apply to you, the knowledge you acquire in reading this material will broaden your knowledge and help you to help others. I will discuss adoption, cybergrandparenting, divorce of parents, divorce of grandparents, and issues linked to changing family forms leading to family diversity, such as gay and lesbian issues, religious differences (racial, ethnic etc), grandparents raising grandchildren, legal issues, long-distance grandparenting, mediation, mistakes grandparents make, and stepgrandparenting.

Your role as a force in the community and society is not to be underestimated. Therefore, in Part 6, I explain the societal implications of Grandparent's Day as well as show you how to raise grandparent consciousness in your community by starting a Grandparent's Day celebration in your community's schools and/or starting a grandparent class, using this book as a reference text. Finally, I will discuss the ideas of legacy and heritage and supply guidelines on how to make memories, start new traditions in your family, and ensure your legacy for future generations.

Parenting is for life, and so is grandparenting. I hope this book will teach you to savor your role as a grandparent, celebrate the good times, cope successfully with adversity, set the example for your progeny and personally enjoy the wonder of personal growth and change.

Updating *The Grandparent Guide* via the Internet

A unique feature of this book is that ongoing updates will be available in the "Grandparent's Guide" section of the Foundation for Grandparenting's website, www. grandparenting.org. By clicking on "Grandparent's Guide," you will be able to download the most current information available, including grandparent-related legislation, new research, financial information, support information, and more. By printing out this information and filing it with this book, your *Grandparent Guide* will never be out of date.

I have written this book as a useful resource to help you take on the challenges of modern grandparenting, to keep you up to date on the changes, and to allow you to develop your own personal grandparent power. Use it well in your quest to be the best grandparent you can be.

PART 1

Understanding Yourself as a Grandparent

The essence of grandparenthood is rooted in the roles that grandparents play for the grandchild, the family, and the society. This is what you "do" as a grandparent. Your power and effectiveness depends on how well you understand your many and diverse roles and how you act them out. By fulfilling these roles, you will bring great joy, meaning, and usefulness to your own life. In addition, you will set a shining example for your children and grandchildren by illuminating their lives too.

CHAPTER 1

Grandparent Roles

G randparent roles are the foundation of grandparenthood. To be an effective grandparent you have to understand what these roles are all about, and then try to fulfill each of them to the best of your ability. Among the roles I have identified as grandparental are ancestor, buddy, hero, historian, mentor, nurturer, spiritual guide, both teacher and student, and wizard. Through your own application of these roles, you supply a blueprint for the future grandparenthood of your children, grandchildren, and great-grandchildren.

Whether you are a grandparent raising your own grandchild on a full- or part-time basis, a stepgrandparent, a grandparent with an adopted grandchild, or a long-distance grandparent, you pass on your legacy of knowledge, experience, and self to your grandchild by enacting these roles completely or in part.

Different from Parent Roles

As a grandparent, you offer your grandchild a broader range of knowledge, emotions, and experience than you possessed as a parent. Your grandparent roles have different functions. Roles such as mentor, nurturer, teacher, and student are practical and informative. Your roles as ancestor and historian are informative, but offer an added dimension of emotional wonder and connectedness to your grand-child's unseen past. Other roles, such as hero, spiritual guide, and wizard, bring in abundant emotional, psychological, sentimental, and spiritual qualities that you will find as you read about each role in depth.

Roles Are Dynamic

Because you and your grandchild constantly grow and change over the years, the roles you play for your grandchild are *dynamic*—they grow and change too. As the years pass, you will find yourself playing different roles, with different degrees of intensity, for your grandchild at different times. Although your roles of historian and role model will remain fairly consistent, for example, you may play more of a nurturer for your grandchild when he is very young, while your crony and mentoring roles become more important as he grows older. Your func-tion as a role model remains stable and permanent throughout your lifetime.

Circumstances will require you to emphasize specific roles at specific times. For example, if your grandchild is in the middle of a family crisis, you may find yourself being called on to provide some extra nurturing. If you are the primary caretaker for your grandchild, you may be more of a teacher and authority fig-ure to your grandchild than the average grandparent. Most of the time, how-ever, you will find yourself fulfilling at least some aspects of each role at different points in your relationship with your grandchild.

The various roles at your disposal are all opportunities to love, teach, enjoy, and support your grandchild. As you read on, you will learn about new aspects of each role and about how you can expand your own identity, expertise, and activities within it. In addition, you may notice that you have been overlooking some aspect of grandparenting that might bring you and your grandchild more fun and learning.

One thing is certain, learning more about each role will help you in your efforts to be the best grandparent possible, to enhance your own sense of self-worth, and to light up your grandchild's life.

CHAPTER 2

Ancestor

One of the irreplaceable roles you play for your grandchild is that of a living ancestor. In this capacity you represent a living link in your ancestral chain. You are the physical manifestation of your grandchild's origins, a representation of all that has come before. You fulfill the greater part of this role just by existing. Being a living ancestor is intricately intertwined with your role as family historian too. The difference being that your historian role is dynamic and constantly unfolding, encompassing a chronicle of the past, present, and future. Your ancestral role entails a representation of the past embodied in the present. It is the foundation for your role as spiritual guide.

Your role as an ancestor is woven into the depths of your being. To a child, the oldest grandparent represents the head of the family (Rosenthal, 1983). You are his connection to history, the cosmos, and the mysteries of existence that are bound up in this and other roles (see Chapter 9, "Spiritual Guide"). Your grandchild knows, no matter how old she is, that she came from her parents, that one of her parents came from you, and that she has emerged as the most recent generation of a line that reaches back into the past.

Ancestral Power

The power of this ancestral role first dawned upon me in 1974 while I was attending a wedding in a rural community in the South. It was there I met Grandpa Waldo, who was welcoming guests on the reception line. Waldo was "well over one hundred years of age," according to his sixty-year-old grand-daughter Pam. Although Waldo was described in a loving way as being "out of it most of the time," according to a forty-year-old great-grandson, everyone who filed past reverently paid Waldo his or her respects. The children lingered for a while to touch him and trace his wrinkles. When I asked what Waldo meant to Ella, his fifteen-year-old great-great-granddaughter, she said, "We all came from him." When it was time for the blessing Pam raised Grandpa Waldo's hand and placed it on the heads of the newly-weds. Everyone was quiet. Waldo uttered a sound and the celebration began. "Now they will have good luck," Pam said. "Grandpa's blessings are well known for that. The oldest in our family always have the blessing power."

Surprising as it may be, you, as a grandparent, have this power too. You may never have thought about it because our society does not tend to view things in emotional or spiritual terms nowadays. So, it is understandable if it is a bit per-plexing and difficult to appreciate the power and sacredness of your role as an ancestor. Nevertheless, in your grandchild's eyes, you do have that power. For your grandchild, you represent the living incarnation of your family line and have connections with long-gone relatives.

This role is acknowledged and deeply respected in certain cultures where only elders, by tuning in on an ancestral wavelength are allowed to invoke the spirits of the dead (Joseph 1968). Indeed, the ancestor role and function reaches beyond death to convey immortality. Many people in the world today, especially in the Eastern Hemisphere, believe their deceased ancestors are with them every moment in their daily lives. They talk to them, implore their aid, seek to please them, fear their retribution for "shaming" them, and ask blessings from them for the living.

Children Need Ancestral Figures

A child with a strong ancestral role connection experiences himself as part of a larger ongoing entity. He feels secure and rooted not only to the past, but also to the present and the future. This is an important feature of "connected" grandchildren (Kornhaber 1992). Family dynasties are often built on the accomplishments of one outstanding individual who sets the tone for the family philosophy and draws the map for guiding its progeny in the future. Ned, a twelve-year-old descendant of one of the signers of the Declaration of Independence, said that he "will be a public servant, like my grandfather and my way-back 'illustrious' grandfather X [name deleted for confidentiality] because it is what my family does. And I know that grandfather X is watching over me."

Eva, nine, is also aware of her ancestral connection to her grandfather. "My grandpa died last year. But when I go to sleep at night I talk to him. I know he is watching over me. Now he's probably with his mom and dad, his grandpa and grandma, and my uncle Ricky who died two years ago."

Age Confers Magic and Authority

Young children view their elders with an imaginative eye. To a young child, just the fact you are alive, having endured over the years, is a wonder. Every wrinkle is a story; every breath is a sign that it is possible to survive whatever life throws at you. Because you have lived a long life, your grandchild sees you as a living ancestor and a survivor. Perhaps it is because the elders have lived in other times and places that children can sense their experience is different, broader. This radiates a sense of infinite connectedness, a feeling of belonging to something bigger than oneself, and a sense of safety and security (see Chapter 5, "Historian"). It is an important reason why so many frightenend children turned to their grandparents for succor and reassurance after the events of September 11, 2001.

Because children have a strong need for an aged figure in their lives, a stepgrandparent or surrogate grandparent can fulfill some aspects of the ancestor role, even though the element of physical heredity and common past is absent. "Granny Maggie's not my real grandma," said thirteen-year-old Ted. "She's my stepmom's mom. But it's cool, 'cause she's the oldest person I know. She's been around a long time and she does things in an old-fashioned way. But it's mostly that I know I can live long like her too."

For older, more practical-minded children dealing with everyday problems, your ancestor role brings you added credibility. After all, you are an "expert" on life, someone who has surmounted trials and tribulations, including your own childhood, adolescence, and parenting years. Gilbert, seventeen, has a grandfather who is, "almost one hundred. It's amazing. Gramps has been around for *one hundred years*. That's a really long time. A family celebration is not complete until they wheel out Gramps and he gives everyone his blessing. He's like Marlon Brando in *The Godfather*." Gilbert is also aware of his grandfather's historian role. "He represents so many things to me. Like the fact that he remembers when there were no cars, and people used horses and carriages to get around. He saw Babe Ruth play baseball and even shook his hand. When I shake Gramps's hand, it's like I'm touching Babe Ruth. Gramps knew my great-great-grandfather and when Gramps talks about him it makes me feel that I belong to a long line of people, not just Mom and Dad."

A Form of Immortality

Your ancestor role is linked to the mystical and the concept of immortality. You have the power to bring long-gone ancestors to life so they are respected, discussed, and honored by your grandchild. Your personal memories of those who have passed away in your family (as well as your anecdotal memories of the stories you heard about your own ancestors who passed away before you were born) bring these people into the present where you share them with your grandchild.

As a grandparent or great-grandparent, and the oldest living link in your ancestral chain, the way you will be remembered by your descendants depends on the memories you create today and the information you pass on. How to accomplish this is up to you. It may be the family name, genes, traits, talents, titles, a financial legacy, stories, memorabilia, antiques, or even the family business.

"I never met my great-great-great-grandparents," said fourteen-year-old Irma, "because they lived during the Civil War, a long time ago. But I feel like I know them because my family has a trunk that has been passed down through the generations and it is full of stuff from my great-great-great-grandparents. I can try on an old dress, read their letters, or play with a pressing iron. It makes me feel like I am with them. Like I know the stuff they used to do and I'm touching the same things they did. Maybe they wanted this to happen and that's why they saved all this stuff. My grandma doesn't have a lot of space, but she says she would never throw out that trunk. She said she wants me to show it to my grandchildren." (See Chapter 49, "Making Memories: Keeping a Memory Chest.")

Your Grandchild: The Youngest Link in Your Ancestral Chain

Your grandchild is the youngest link in your ancestral chain. Teaching your grandchild the ways of your ancestors is an effective way of keeping the memory of them alive and ensuring that their stories will be heard by unborn generations. Nuala, seventeen, enjoys learning Gaelic from her ninety-three-year-old grandmother. "Learning the language is fun. When she teaches me a word, she usually has a story to go with it. She tells me about the trouble she had in her life back in Ireland. She tells me about her aunts and uncles and cousins and how sometimes they would go for days with nothing to eat. When I'm going through something bad, I think that if Grandma made it, I can, too, because she's my ancestor and I've got her blood in my veins."

How would you like your descendants to remember you? What would you like your great-great-great-grandchildren to know about you? What would you like to leave them to play with and wonder about? Start planning your legacy now (see Chapter 50), and you, too, can become immortal. Someday in the far-flung future, one of your descendants might just refer to you as "illustrious."

GUIDELINES

Here are some step-by-step guidelines to help you effectively fulfill your role as a living ancestor.

- Be conscious of the importance of your ancestral role in the family.
- Know that the ideas of a family philosophy and family image are often derived from belief systems, principles, and practices set by you and your own ancestors long ago.
- Discuss the ancestor role with your grandchild's parents. They are ancestors-to-be!
- Discuss the ancestor role with your grandchild. Ask how she perceives you in this role.
- Establish a place for this role in your family's life. Are the elders at family gatherings acknowledged and honored? If not, make it happen.
- Talk to your grandchild about your ancestors. Make them come alive.
- Promote family connectedness by combining your ancestral role with that of family historian (see Chapter 5, "Historian").
- Keep in mind you need not be biologically related to a grandchild to fulfill many aspects of the ancestor role.

CONCLUSION

Your role as ancestor is important to your family. You function as an ambassador to the past, a powerful figure in the present, and a role model for the future. Your personal level of involvement in the role of ancestor will shape your grandchild's view of family history and of deceased family members. In this role, you can have a direct impact on how your grandchild will remember you after you are gone. Your example will influence the way in which each member of your family will fulfill the role of living ancestor in the future.

CHAPTER 3

Buddy

A | s a grandparent, one of your most enjoyable and sentimental roles (because it's more emotional than reasonable) is probably being a buddy to your grandchild. In other words, a pal, secret confidante, and, at times, even a lighthearted conspirator. You are uniquely positioned to assume this role because, as a grandparent, you are not responsible for the day-to-day worries of your grandchild's upbringing. Without primary responsibility, you are free to indulge in this role to your heart's content. Together you can participate in harmless fun and games that add zest to both your lives and cause the generational barriers between you to dissolve. But you must always be careful to temper your enthusiasm about having fun with your grandchild when it involves going against his parents' wishes.

The Buddy Phenomenon

Grandparents play the role of buddy to their grandchildren in many cultures, especially rural and agrarian societies where grandparents and grandchildren spend a great deal of time together. For example, Denise Paulme (1960) studied women in tropical Africa and described how grandmothers from the Burundi tribe act as their grandchildren's buddy. "Towards her grandchildren, a grand-mother may at least dare to indulge openly in revealing her sentiments, without, however, neglecting practical considerations. Grandparents joke with their grand-children, spoil them, protect them against their parents' anger, and, if they are not believing Christians, they expect their grandchildren will in due course per-form the ceremonies of the Imizimu, the spirits of dead grandparents."

In the United States, researchers have observed that grandparents act as playmates with their grandchildren (Cherlin et al. 1986). Our study has shown that, "many grandparents, especially grandfathers, treat their grandchildren in a more relaxed and permissive manner than they ever treated their own children and do extraordinary things with them, as companions and confidantes" (Korn-haber 1982).

Secret Buddy Rituals

Lettie, thirty-four, recalls, "At my grandma's house I got to wear red nail pol-ish. She had been a very glamorous woman in her day, and even in her sixties, she was quite stylish. She wore big hats and lots of jewelry and perfume. And she had long red nails. I just adored her and I wanted to look like her. When I begged my mom to let me wear make-up, even just a little blush and lip gloss, she said absolutely not until I was sixteen. I was eleven at the time, and I told my grandmother about this when I was over there one afternoon. She just kind of laughed and said, 'A little nail polish can't hurt.' And she did my nails, a whole manicure with cuticle remover and everything. I could have swooned. I was so excited. Anyway, I had to take off the nail polish before I went home, but this got to be our ritual, our secret. Every time I went to Grandma's, I got a mani-cure. She was my special pal when I was growing up."

Harry, twelve, works in his grandfather's garage and describes him as his best buddy. "Grandpa lets me hang out with him and learn about cars," says Harry. "Grandpa said the garage will be mine when he retires. He lets me go to the diner with him and the older guys. They don't treat me like a kid."

Bridging the Generation Gap

When you and your grandchild are buddies, the usual generational boundaries disappear, broadening your grandchild's knowledge and understanding of older people. Indeed, much of the private delight that you and your grandchild take in being buddies comes from relating to one another on the same level. You both can just "let go" (see Chapter 23, "Attention"), bringing fun and spontaneity into your relationship.

Gwen, sixteen, says, "I can tell my grandmother anything—and I mean *anything*. I tell her things I would never tell my parents. She's my best friend." Gwen's grandmother, Fillipa, fifty-seven, says, "Gwen is like a really close friend. She is kind and sympathetic and loves to gab, just like me. We gossip about everything." Such a close relationship can be especially supportive to a teenage grandchild who could use a little extra help and communication while suffering the pains of adolescence (see Chapter 22, "Adolescence").

Maintaining a Healthy Perspective

It is possible that the buddy activities you enjoy with your grandchild might be misconstrued by other family members as *spoiling*. Should you notice this, don't sweep the issue under the rug. Go to the heart of the matter, ask people how they feel and discuss the situation until you arrive at a satisfactory understanding for all concerned (see Chapter 27, "Spoiling Grandchildren").

Another common scenario that can create family problems occurs when a grandparent enjoys a buddy role with a favorite grandchild and neglects a less-favored grandchild (see Chapter 26, "Favoritism"). This can be a source of great pain for the rejected grandchild as well as for other family members. Chris, age seven, knows what it feels like to *not* be Grandpa's favorite buddy. "Grandpa always wants to play baseball with my brother because he plays better than me and I always get left out." When Chris's grandfather was informed about Chris's feelings, he made an effort to be a buddy to Chris too. Now Chris is his grandfather's "airplane model building buddy."

Keep It Harmless

There may come a time when your grandchild may want to take advantage of your status as his buddy and use your clout with his parents to bend a rule or two. If this happens, it is best to set very clear boundaries concerning family rules and regulations. There are, of course, times when a grandparent may look the other way when a grandchild breaks a minor rule, but it's important to let your grandchild know that you respect the guidelines his parents have set for his behavior.

Joe, a sixty-six-year-old grandfather, got into trouble with his grandson's parents when he allowed Vince, fifteen, to talk him into giving him driving lessons and was found out. Joe thought Vince's parents were being too strict when they would not allow Joe to take driving lessons until he could maintain a C average in school. In Joe's opinion, the happier a child was, the better he performed in whatever he did, so he gave in to Vince's pleas. Although Joe apologized for his transgression, the family emotional climate was frosty for quite a while. In hindsight, Joe agreed that it would have been better to discuss Vince's plight openly with his parents rather than go behind their back as he had done. Regarding discipline, it is important for you and the parents to present a solid front to your grandchild. No matter how you may feel about a certain disciplinary issue, it is a good policy not to contradict parental rules or regulations, especially in front of your grandchild. If you feel a particular rule is too strict, discuss your feelings about the rule with the parents *before* you allow your grandchild to break it. If you do not respect the parents' policies, you can expect them to interpret your behavior as a challenge to their authority.

If you happen to be one of the many grandparents who are raising or caretaking a grandchild on a regular basis, the buddy role will be a bit more complicated. After all, if you are caring for your grandchild full-time, you are also the full-time authority figure. This can limit the conspiratory aspect of your fun. But of course, you can still have spontaneous fun and press the limits when appropriate (see Chapter 41, "Raising Grandchildren"). If you are caretaking your grandchild part-time, and you are deferring to the parents' authority, you will have an increased opportunity to be a buddy.

Distance Is No Obstacle

You can have a buddy relationship with your grandchild even if you do not live nearby (see Chapter 43, "Long-Distance Grandparenting"). One great tool for establishing closeness is finding a common interest—for example, a hobby you both enjoy and can talk about. Having something in common that is ongoing and necessitates contact can make the distance between you seem smaller and keep you up to date with one another.

Vishnu, a fifty-six-year-old San Francisco computer scientist, lives thousands of miles from his grandson in India. To bridge the distance they have become pen pals, and they share a common hobby in stamp collecting. They write letters and exchange stamps once a week. They search out stamps, explore stamp-related websites and communicate daily via E-mail. They refer to one another as "stamp buddies." Vishnu travels home to India twice a year and hopes to bring his grandson to the United States one day. "Of course we are much more than stamp buddies," he says. "We talk about a lot more than stamps."

Stepgrandparents and grandparents of adopted grandchildren have the same opportunities of becoming a buddy to their grandchild as biological grandparents. In fact, when children already have biological grandparents, it's a great opportunity for a stepgrandparent to come into their stepgrandchild's life as a buddy. Children always have room for buddies.

GUIDELINES

Here are some guidelines to help you maximize your role as your grandchild's buddy.

- Spend as much time as you can with your grandchild or maintain regular contact via E-mail or snail mail. Engage in mutually enjoyable activities.
- Share your feelings and life experiences with your grandchild.
- Learn about your grandchild's world. Visit his school; or invite his friends over to your house.

- If your grandchild wants to talk about other family members, listen and validate his feelings, but refrain from commenting or judging.
- Let the parents and other family members know how much you enjoy your role as your grandchild's buddy.
- Be a buddy to the parents as well. You don't want them to feel left out.
- Enjoy!

CONCLUSION

One of the most pleasurable relationships of your life can be as a buddy to your grandchild. Having a younger person as a crony can be a great deal of fun, and this role allows your grandchild to see you in a joyful and sometimes frivolous way. Enjoy this role to the fullest, but be alert to how parents view your antics.

CHAPTER 4

Hero

In mythology and legend, a hero is often of divine ancestry, endowed with courage and strength, celebrated for bold exploits, and favored by the gods. Although most grandparents do not fit this description exactly, grandchildren need heroes, and grandparents often can fill the role pretty well. Children need someone to look up to, someone they can model themselves after, and someone to inspire them. Of course that's what parents do; they are on-the-spot heroes for the child. But grandparents, because they are a bit more removed and have a broader range of experience, can be heroes with an added dimension, one that is a bit more connected to the mythic.

These days a grandparent's heroic role is needed more than ever because public heroes are in short supply. Everyone's favorite politician, sports figure, or movie star eventually seems to get involved in a scandal. This leaves a dearth of heroic figures in your grandchild's life. That is where you come in.

Your Heroic Past

Chief among your most heroic qualities (in your grandchild's eyes) is your epic past. The fact that you have lived in times and places so far removed from your grandchild's own everyday experience imbues you with heroic qualities. Grand-parents who were born in foreign lands and speak foreign languages, who wit-nessed events that grandchildren can only learn about from history books, who had exciting jobs and adventures, or who traveled to exotic places can be far more exciting to children than the plastic superhero dolls they play with.

For example, one grandfather told his granddaughter of the time he was attacked by a grizzly bear and how he escaped in one piece. To this six-year-old, he sounded like Superman! Children love to hear stories of grandfathers who fought the good fight in foreign wars, or tales of grandmothers and great-grandmothers who had many children and took care of the house on little or no money, or crossed the ocean to come to America. "My grandmother's my hero," said eight-year-old Gary. "She marched across Hungary and Poland for two whole months during the Second World War to escape being killed by the Nazis. She ate roots and vegetables and even animals she killed herself. She told me she joined the 'Partisans' and shot at German soldiers. So when she tells me to do something, I do it. And no one messes with me because Grandma taught me to take care of myself. If anyone tries to mess with me, I'm going to sick Grandma on them."

Your grandchildren feel free to brag about your heroic qualities. Nan, eigh-teen, said she was proud of her grandfather who was stationed at Pearl Harbor on the day the Japanese attacked and went on to fight in many of the major Pacific sea battles. Nan wrote a book report for her high school English class on Tom Brokaw's book *The Greatest Generation*. On the day she read it to her class, she invited her grandfather as a surprise guest, "He was a hit," she said, "and the school 'hero' for a day. And I was so proud when he showed off his medals."

Your heroic qualities have become especially relevant since September 11. Today's grandparents have lived through many wars. Many young people have never experienced a war. They feel frightened and bewildered; they yearn to know how to think and act in such a time. That's why it is especially important for grandparents today to share their past experiences and pass on the lessons they learned to the young—lessons like persevering in the face of danger, courage, living a life as normal as possible, and being able to laugh at the same time the bombs are falling, like the British did in the air-raid shelters during the Second

World War. Only those who have experienced war first-hand can give young children the perspective, courage, and support they need in troubled times. To a child this is true heroism.

Everyday Heroism

How you see yourself, and how you believe the world sees you, can be quite different from how your grandchild sees you. To understand this fully you have to understand the workings of your grandchild's mind.

For a child, the fact you have lived a long life is already a spectacular achievement. Even your infirmities can be intriguing and inspiring to your grandchildren. Keep in mind that every bump, wrinkle, and scar you possess has a story. Swollen joints, missing teeth, and the stories that go with them, are fascinating to children. Furthermore, you are setting an example that shows your grandchild that, in spite of infirmities, one can still live a meaningful life. Grandparents who have had tuberculosis, malaria, black lung disease, or other exotic illnesses are a wonder to children. So are grandparents who have overcome adversity to win success or fulfill a dream.

You can also be a hero by coming to the rescue in a crisis. Offering financial help or intervening with parents during a family conflict can be important acts of heroism that can have a direct impact on your grandchild's life. When fourteen-year-old Anna's parents were tied up with work obligations and could not take their daughter to a national three-day debating contest across the country, Anna's stepgrandmother Roberta paid her airfare and even chaperoned Anna to the competition. Anna won second prize and said, "I couldn't have done this without Roberta. She's my hero."

GUIDELINES

Your role as a hero is intricately linked to your other roles as ancestor, family historian, spiritual guide, and role model. Here are a few guidelines to help you identify specific aspects and responsibilities of this role, understand the status you are accorded, and, of course, enjoy it to the fullest.

- Your grandchild needs heroes and wants to cast you in that role. Be prepared for this and remember that events or experiences that may seem unremarkable or uninteresting to you may seem very remarkable and interesting to your grandchild.
- Your heroic status gives you a bully pulpit from which to teach values and morals and set standards for your grandchild.
- The potential range of your heroic activities is endless, from feeding the hungry to starting a successful family business that becomes a dynasty.
- Your heroism can be taught through deeds or tales.
- On a lighter note, try to refrain from exaggerating your experiences or telling "fish stories" Doing so takes away from the credibility of your real achievements and experience. (One grandfather who had been a company clerk during his military service regaled his grandson with battle stories. The grandson ended up thinking his grandfather had won the Korean War single-handedly.)
- When the opportunity arises, act heroically! Your grandchild is watching.

CONCLUSION

Your grandchild most likely already views you as a heroic figure. The role is there for you to fill. So don't be surprised if, when you recount your past exploits to your grandchild, you gain a new perspective on your life, or even attain heroic status in your own eyes!

CHAPTER 5

Historian

O ne of the essential roles that you can play for grandchildren is the role of historian. Although this role overlaps in some ways with the role of ancestor (see Chapter 2, "Ancestor"), as a historian you are not only the living embodiment of generations past, but you are also a living witness to the history of your own times as well as those of your ancestors. By sharing your memories and stories of days gone by with your grandchild, you bring the past alive, embody the present, and ensure your grandchild's future role as a historian.

If you have a stepgrandchild or an adopted grandchild, your role as historian is especially important. You can tell your grandchild about your ancestors and what life was like when you were growing up, and even help your grandchild find out more about her own ancestors. In this way, you ensure your grandchild's awareness of the historian role (Kornhaber 1981).

Grandparents Are Natural Historians

Throughout human history, grandparents have served as the repositories of wisdom and history. Your role as the family historian is as important today as it was back in the time when *all* information was verbally passed on from the old to the young through stories. The fact that we now live in the age of an information explosion by no means renders your homespun yarns and family stories obsolete. Today's youth has access to a vast amount of history via the Internet, but this cannot replace the excitement of learning history from a person who has firsthand experience of events.

Children love hearing stories about how their grandparents immigrated to the United States, or what it was like to fight in a war, to give birth, to live through the Depression, to have seen Elvis Presley perform live when he was just starting out, and so on. Piggy-backing on your own experience, your grandchild can mentally and emotionally travel through time. Your accounts of famous places and events transport your grandchild beyond his or her immediate existence.

Children Are Curious About the Past

Children naturally question their elders to learn about what life was like in the old days. I believe that elders and children are biologically programmed to give and receive information in this manner and thus pass it down to unborn generations.

Terry, twenty-one, tells of visiting his eighty-nine-year-old grandmother during a college spring break. "Grandma has a really neat little house on a lake in Michigan. I stayed with her for two whole weeks, just me and her. We cooked together and listened to music and talked almost constantly. She actually lived through a lot of the American history stuff I learned about in school. She told me how her family had a Model T Ford, and about the radio shows and how when they came on it was such a big deal to everyone. She remembers hearing about Lindbergh flying across the Atlantic and how exciting that was to her. She also told me about my grandfather who I never knew. Her stories about him made him seem like a real live person to me. I can't wait to go back and stay with her again. I wish she'd live forever."

A Common History Means Being Connected

When you provide a sense of history and family roots through this role, your grandchild will begin to think in terms of "we" not just "I." A child who thinks in terms of "we" feels that he is part of a historical continuum. With that continuum comes a sense of belonging, safety, and security.

Davina, fifty-five, has made an effort to foster this feeling of family identity and continuity in her grandchildren. "When my three grandchildren come to visit, we tramp down to the basement and go through the boxes of family heirlooms that I inherited from my parents. Some of the stuff is over 150 years old. We look at the pictures and I tell the kids the stories about their ancestors that I heard from my parents and my grandparents. They love it and so do I." This experience of connecting with his family's past makes Davina's grandson, Gregory, twelve, feel connected to his ancestors. "She even has some of their clothes and pictures," he says. "My great-great-grandfather was a general in the Civil War. He got killed, but he was a hero. Granny has one of his medals. When we learned about the Civil War in school, I got an A on my paper because of Granny telling me all that stuff about my great-great-grandfather."

Keeper of the Family Archive

As a grandparent, you have a responsibility to be the curator of your family archive. Creating a historical archive for your grandchildren and family members will teach them about your life and your family's past. It will give them the marvelous sense of belonging to an entity larger than themselves. Your historical archive will preserve your precious family memories for posterity and will continue to grow as new family members make their own contributions. Your archive is only limited by your family's imagination.

As a modern archivist, you have an enormous advantage over grandparents in the past because you can avail yourself of the wonders of modern technology, digital cameras, video cameras, and tape recorders to document family happenings. Preserving memorabilia like report cards, a lock of a child's hair, wedding invitations—or birth announcements, all touching reminders of life's milestones—is easier than ever before. A pressed flower, a newspaper clipping, or a football trophy, each with their own story, make deceased relatives seem vibrantly alive to young children. Everyone loves looking at photographs, of course, and an audiotape or videotape of you talking about your family history and life experience can be a powerful memento for the generations to come. Make sure to remind family members on an ongoing basis to send material to add to the archive.

In addition to chronicling past events by means of your family archive, you can share current events with everyone in your family via a family website (see Chapter 43, "Long-Distance Grandparenting"). It's a great way to keep your loved ones up-to-date on the latest family happenings.

You can take your grandchild to visit an important site in your family's history. In fact many families today are visiting Ellis Island, the place where millions of European immigrants set foot on American soil. (To find out more about family members who may have come through Ellis Island, go to www.ellisisland records.com.) Does your old neighborhood or school still exist? The old ball field, riding stable, cinema? The site of your first job? Where you got married? Take your grandchild to visit the family gravesite. Go through your photo album with your grandchild and, as you point out people in each photo, tell a story about them. Construct a family tree with your grandchild and get as many family members involved as possible.

GUIDELINES

Every family needs a historian. Here are some guidelines to help.

- Think about the family historians in your past that taught you about your family history. What relics from the past do you possess?
- Create a historical archive for your family.
- Ask your grandchild to help you create the archive.
- Make your family's history come to life by bringing your grandchild to visit places where family members lived, played, worked, studied, or are buried.
- Have your family regularly send you items to include in the archive.
- Create a family tree.

- Create a family website to share your archive and stories with family members who live far away.
- Above all, teach your grandchildren the most important lessons you have learned from the past.

CONCLUSION

Your role as historian is extremely important to your grandchild and your whole family. Sharing your own life experiences as well as those of your ancestors will give your grandchild a sense of continuity and belonging. By creating a family archive, you are creating a legacy for the unborn generations of your family to enjoy. By means of the archive, unborn generations will appreciate your efforts, and come to know you. They in their turn will pass that knowledge on to their descendants.

RESOURCES

- Hampton Inns offers a free booklet entitled "Making Memories" on its website, www.hamptoninns.com, that contains information and examples on creating a family memory archive.
- nara.gov/genealogy will give you access to the National Archives to research your family history.
- www.ellisisland.org lets you search passenger records for relatives who passed through Ellis Island.

CHAPTER 6

Mentor

A s most involved grandparents come to realize, it's not only what you teach your grandchild that matters, it's *how* you teach her. That is the magic of your mentor role. As your grandchild's mentor, you go beyond your basic teaching role (see Chapter 11, "Teacher") and accomplish much more than simply transmitting your knowledge or skills to her. Indeed, you are a cheerleader firing her imagination, inspiring her dreams, nurturing her spirit, and encouraging her intellectual growth while giving her a sense of self-worth. As a mentor you provide your grandchild with learning, inspiration, and motivation that will last her whole lifetime. Mentoring your grandchild is a way of offering yourself to her so that in helping to shape her mind and spirit and offering knowledge and skills to be used in the world, she absorbs *your* spirit as well.

Grandparents as Mentors

Most accomplished people report having a significant mentor who encouraged, even inspired, them in their interests and lifted them up when they got discouraged. In Greek mythology, Mentor was Odysseus's trusted counselor. Nowadays, we have disconnected the mentor's link to the gods, but the meaning of the word carries pretty much the same connotation: a wise and trusted counselor. However, it is more than that.

Isaac, fifty-eight, made his fortune creating a national chain of bagel bakeries. "I owe it all to my grandfather; Zadie, I called him. He was a Talmudic scholar and made a living as a tailor. He loved bagels and made them in the old country. I loved bagels too. So, since I showed an interest, he would spend hours and hours with me teaching me how to make bagels. 'Bagels today are too light' he said. 'The secret is dense, like matzoh balls, heavy.' He taught me how to boil them in water, and dip them quickly in and out of hot oil before baking. I had to get it just right, just right. Timing between the boiling, the oil, and the baking was critical. He showed me only twice and then it was up to me. He would taste a bagel I made and say 'Phooey, too light,' and throw it to the birds. 'I hope this doesn't kill them,' he would say. He knew where the line was between pushing and lifting. I knew all the time that he loved me so I took the flack from him. When I got fed up because I couldn't make the kind of bagel he wanted, I wanted to quit. Then he would be the nice guy. He would smile and tell me I could do it. Then one day I got it right and he kissed me and bragged all over the neighborhood. 'This is dense,' he said. When I went to college I got a part-time job in a bagel bakery but I didn't like their bagels. 'Too light,' I said. So I went in one night and made some dense ones and they sold like gangbusters. And the rest is history. And I know my Zadie is smiling down on me."

A Special Way of Teaching

Mentoring a grandchild involves a unique way of teaching. Parents' style of teaching possesses a judgmental quality because they are understandably very emotionally involved with their child's performance. A mentoring grandparent, on the other hand, is an effective teacher because *unconditional love* makes the grandchildren feel safe and comfortable, accepted for who they are, not just how well they perform.

This observation is supported by a recent multigenerational study examining the reactions of parents and grandparents to a child's completing designated tasks. The study showed that the parents were more judgmental about their child's performance than were the child's grandparents (DeWitt 1997). Because grandparents' teaching methods are often less judgmental than those of parents, the child's performance is often enhanced. As Jaime, eleven, puts it, "I'm not good at math so my grandpa helps me with my homework. Grandpa is really nice to me so I do better with him because I am not nervous when I screw up. I can learn from him easy because he uses things I know. He helped me learn addition and subtraction with eggs from his chickens. And I don't feel as bad when I get something wrong like I'm disappointing him . . . the way I feel dumb when I blow it with Dad."

To be an effective mentor, you must spend time alone with your grandchild and give her your undivided attention. That's when the magic happens, when you and your grandchild are focused on being together. That's when she is totally open to receiving the wisdom that is your legacy (see Chapter 23, "Attention"). Your classroom is everywhere, your lessons ongoing. Your curriculum is a living encyclopedia of human experience, knowledge, skills, and wisdom. You provide insights on issues such as family heritage, ethics, values, long-lost skills, crafts, philosophy, and religious matters; and you do it all with a personal, loving touch.

As you know, children spend most of their time in school taking tests, being graded, and learning from a cast of teachers that usually changes from year to year. School is a place where learning requires effort. Grandparents teach an ethos of "being" and play, where learning is allowed to happen effortlessly. Some of the subjects you are capable of teaching your grandchild—heritage, ethics, values, philosophy, religion, fishing, sewing, and household repair—are not readily available to children from other sources.

Occasionally, a child will find a special teacher, but most often in the average school environment there is no sense of continuity or permanence. Each fall, a child must prove himself anew, and in this highly competitive world, it's easy for a youngster to question his own value. A consistent one-on-one relationship with parents and grandparents can help ameliorate this problem.

Many children report that the knowledge, skills, and attitudes they acquired from their grandparents stayed with them much longer than did the information they acquired from other sources.

A Special Way of Learning

From a psychological point of view, children may be particularly open to learning from their grandparents because they do not feel the need to challenge their grandparents' influence. This is the opposite of what happens during the psychological processes of separation and differentiation from parents (see Chapters 22, "Adolescence," and 23, "Attention"). So subtle is this process that in later years adults usually cannot distinguish exactly how they learned what they learned from their grandparents.

Maureen, thirty-two, claims, "My grandmother never gave me any baking lessons; I just helped her in the kitchen for many years. Then one day, she was ill and asked me to bake the pies and cakes and breads for Christmas and I did it without a second thought." Her twin sister Caitlin reports a similar experience with her grandfather, a glazier. "I can fix any kind of glass windows or mirrors because I tagged along with my grandfather on Saturdays and watched him do it."

Accentuate the Positive

Your grandchild can learn from you whether he is gifted or average, disabled or fit. The combination of talents and abilities your grandchild possesses are his alone. You can help him recognize his uniqueness and inspire him to strive to fulfill his potential. Indeed, accentuating the positive is perhaps the most important function of your mentor role.

Jerome, sixteen, describes his grandmother as a special teacher. "I'm dyslexic, and I had to repeat first grade. I thought I was dumb, and I felt so bad in September when all my friends were in second grade and I was with a bunch of babies I didn't even know. Then at Christmas, my grandma came to visit and she became my special teacher. She had been a kindergarten teacher herself, and she brought some picture books and had me tell her stories from looking at the books. I didn't have to read any words. I did it all with my imagination. She got really excited, and she wrote the stories down. I did pretty well reading them back to her, because I knew what I had said. That felt so good. She told me a boy with a mind like mine was very special, a genius even. I believed her. And she told me never to forget that she was my biggest booster. Every time I got a report card, I discussed it with her and she gave me ideas to help me, like sitting in the front row of the class, and reading aloud when I was studying so I would not get sleepy. When I got older, I eventually learned to read, although I still can't spell too well. Then my grandmother gave me a computer for my twelfth birthday, with a spell checker, and I wrote a whole novel. I read it the other day and it's really good. Maybe I'll polish it up and get it published. Who cares if I can't spell? Any computer can do that!"

Like Jerome's grandmother, you can be an even more meaningful mentor when your grandchild needs special help (see Chapter 29, "Grandchildren with Special Needs"). The best approach is to focus on your grandchild's strengths, not his weaknesses. You can pass on your skills and talents, or learn something new together with your grandchild.

Time and Distance

The opportunities to be an effective mentor to your grandchild are limitless. For example, at the grandparent-grandchild summer camp that my wife, Carol, and I started in 1985, grandparents who only see their grandchildren infrequently teach them outdoor skills such as canoeing, fishing, hiking, or wood carving. Some grandparents teach their grandchildren to swim or dance. (For more information about our camp, see www.grandparenting.org.)

You can mentor your grandchild by using the telephone, E-mail, or regular mail. Jed, sixty-two, taught his grandson how to use a digital camera; now Jed and his grandson send each other pictures via the Internet on a regular basis (see Chapter 43, "Long-Distance Grandparenting"). Using the Internet, you can correct your grandchild's term papers, discuss new programs and games, and give advice. No matter how far you live from your grandchild, you can still find ways to fulfill your role as her mentor.

Mentoring Other People's Grandchildren

Mentoring by elders is now generally recognized as being so valuable that it has been adopted—and adapted—by many organizations and programs across the country. Many corporations sponsor programs where their employees read to children in local schools. Some elders are involved with programs that help mentor children from single-parent homes (see the resources listed on the next page).

Mentoring is a function of grandparenting that *all* elders can participate in. Stepgrandparents and grandparents with adopted grandchildren can mentor their grandchildren just as well as biological grandparents. In addition, elders who do not have grandchildren can mentor children within their communities. The rewards of mentoring a child are deeply satisfying. "Mentoring gives my life meaning," said Sal, seventy, a four-time grandfather who mentors children in a local school. "One of the kids I mentor has no men in his life. When I walk into his classroom and he sees me, his face just lights up. I take him to the library and we work on his lessons. It keeps my mind sharp, too. I know what I'm doing means a lot to these kids. It's a joy and a privilege."

GUIDELINES

Here are some guidelines to help you mentor your grandchild.

- Find out what your grandchild *needs* to know.
- Find out what your grandchild *wants* to know.
- Teach your grandchild your top two skills.
- Find activities you both enjoy and can do together; for example, painting, reading, playing music, and discussing issues.
- If you are a long-distance grandparent, communicate with your grandchild on a regular basis.
- Establish a mentor relationship with other children in your community.

CONCLUSION

Mentoring your grandchild will enable you to have a positive and long-lasting impact on your grandchild's life, while enriching your own life as well. Your stable, nurturing presence can be an extremely effective teaching tool for your grandchild, especially in today's turbulent society. In addition, being a mentor to your grandchild will reinforce your vital connection.

RESOURCES

Write for information on mentoring programs.

Creative Grandparenting
609 Blackgates Rd.
Wilmington, DE 19803

Foster Grandparent Program
330 Independence Ave. SW
Washington, DC 20201

Generations Together
University Center for Social and Urban Research
600A Thackery Hall
University of Pittsburgh
Pittsburgh, PA 15260

CHAPTER 7

Nurturer

The role of nurturer is perhaps the most basic and necessary role you can play for your grandchild. Nurturing as a grandparent is an extension of your parental nurturing role into another generation, with some added dimensions. When you nurture your grandchild, you not only express your love, but you also care for and protect her. The role of nurturer offers you the opportunity to foster her growth and development.

An effective grandparent nurtures from the moment the grandchild is born until the moment when the grandparent leaves the earth. Nurturing is one role in which grandparents and stepgrandparents can have great impact.

Like other grandchildren, your grandchild most likely is acutely aware of being the recipient of your nurturing attention. While I was studying how children perceived their grandparents (Kornhaber 1989), one question I routinely posed the children was, "What does your grandmother do?" The majority of children thought their grandmothers *worried* about them and took care of them. Eight-year-old Sybil told me, "Whenever I'm late, or I hurt myself, or I don't go to the bathroom every day, my grandmother is worried." In other words, children perceive their grandmothers as nurturers, people who care deeply about their welfare. The same holds for grandfathers. Children see grandfathers as perhaps worrying a little less but still very concerned about helping and supporting them. "My parents take care of me," said eleven-year-old Heather, "and my grandparents take care of all of us when we need them."

Nurturing Is Forever

Your nurturing role can begin before your grandchild is born when you provide support to the expectant parents. You might start by attending a childbirth training class with the parents. Sit down with them and discuss how much you would like to be involved with nurturing your grandchild. Ask the parents what they expect from you as a grandparent (see Chapter 24, "Birth of a Grandchild"). It is extremely helpful to new parents to have you by their side as part of their support network. Most grandparents love caretaking a newborn and can give exhausted parents a welcome reprieve.

Grandparents who baby-sit their grandchild have an exceptional opportunity to develop a close bond with them (see Chapter 25, "Baby-Sitting"). Cooking meals together, shopping, taking walks in the park or teaching your grandchild to ride a bike, for example, are nurturing activities that create enduring memories.

Bunny, thirty-three, remembers the Saturday afternoons she spent with her grandfather when she was a child. "My grandparents were like second parents. Both my parents worked on Saturday so my grandparents would come over and make breakfast for my brother and me. Then Grandma would pack a lunch and Grandpa would take us somewhere, usually to the park, for the rest of the day. When my parents weren't there, my grandparents were."

Adolescents usually need extra doses of care, understanding, and tenderness from their grandparents because of the tension they are experiencing with their parents (see Chapter 22, "Adolescence"). Many grandparents give their grandchildren a leg up in life with financial assistance. That's nurturing too. Mason, sixty-five, bought his grandson a new car for a wedding present. "He can't afford a car and he needed a new one," says Mason. "He had such a piece of junk. Now I know he and his wife are safe in a car with dual air bags."

Grandparents who have been strong nurturers to their grandchildren may find their grandchildren nurturing them in their later years. In fact, I have come across quite a number of grandchildren caring for their elderly grandparents. Tonetta, thirty-five, refuses to let her grandmother go to a nursing home. "When I was young, Gram always took care of me. I don't work and am home with my children all day. I can't bear to think of her in a nursing home. I'll take care of her. It's good for my kids to share in her care. She took care of me. Now it's my turn."

Backing Up the Family

Your support and caring provides an emotional and social safety net for the parents of your grandchild. When you back up your grandchild's parents, you expand your grandchild's support system, thus making your grandchild feel secure. Twelve-year-old Toshi says, "When my mother got very sick and my father was traveling, Grandma moved in and took care of me and my brother and sisters and my mother, too. With her and Grandpa, I never worry about anything because they're there and they make me feel good." After Larry's dad was killed in the World Trade Center attacks, he and his family moved in with his grandparents. "I guess my grandpa has to take my dad's place now," said Larry, who is nine.

You can help early on if something goes wrong with your grandchild's birth. Nowadays, many professionals urge grandparents to be part of a family-centered care system when a newborn is in intensive care.

Today's world makes your role as your grandchild's nurturer especially important due to heavy work responsibilities, the high divorce rate, and other factors that can erode a family's support system. During divorce, for example, parents often are so consumed with their own pain and legal battles in addition to their regular daily responsibilities that they spend less time with their children (see Chapter 37, "When Parents Divorce"). Dorian, thirteen, said, "Having no brothers or sisters, I felt like I was alone when my dad left. Mom was at work all the time and neither of my parents knew how scared I felt. Then my grandparents started to come over to the house every day and I visited with them over the weekend. During the week I could stay overnight whenever I wanted to. They came to get me at school when Mom couldn't. They took care of me and we had fun together. I feel like they saved me."

When Nurturing Cannot Be Expressed

The nurturing role seems to include a built-in "worry" factor within grandparents that monitors the grandchild's health and well-being. Unfortunately, this instinct can be frustrated in cases when parents are causing problems for the child. For example, in cases of child abuse, close grandparents will sense something harmful is going on with their grandchild. Because many children see their grandparents as their first line of defense they may let their grandparents know, in one way or another, about the abuse they are suffering. This makes for a delicate situation; if the grandparent's personal efforts on behalf of the grandchild are frustrated and it is necessary to go to the authorities for help, the parent will often seek retribution by denying the grandparent access to the child (see Chapter 42, "Legal Issues").

When parents falter, grandparents may have to come to the rescue and be full-time nurturers for their grandchild. This situation is increasingly common today because of the disintegration of the traditional family system (22 percent of children are born out of wedlock, one-third of them to teen-age mothers) and social problems. This has resulted in increased numbers of abandoned children and reports of child abuse. According to the United States Census Bureau, currently there are more than eight million grandparents raising their grandchildren. As a response, Grandparents Raising Grandchildren organizations have sprouted up around the country. One grandmother raising her grandson said, "When my grandchild is in danger, I am there for him. The only way he's going into a foster home is over my dead body" (see Chapter 41, "Raising Grandchildren").

Long-Distance Nurturing

As many long-distance grandparents know, nurturing can be done from a distance (see Chapter 43, "Long-Distance Grandparenting"). No matter how far away from your family you live, make sure your grandchild and family know you are there to be called upon in time of need. And if you are called, be sure to respond. Your grandchild will appreciate it forever. Of course, maintaining regular contact with your grandchild and family via telephone, E-mail or regular mail is very important to keep you in one another's mind and heart (see Chapter 36, "Cyber-grandparenting").

GUIDELINES

Here are some guidelines to help you fulfill your role as nurturer.

- Help the parents prepare for your grandchild's birth.
- Nurture not only your newborn grandchild, but the parents as well.
- Ask the parents if you can help obtain supplies for your new grandchild (a high chair, crib, stroller, etc.). Financial assistance is a form of nurturing too.
- With the parent's permission, have as much direct contact with your grandchild as possible. Change her diapers, feed her, etc.
- Monitor your grandchild's health and well-being.
- If help is needed for your grandchild, consider supplying it yourself.
- Be available to baby-sit. If you don't live nearby, visit your grandchild as often as feasible.
- When adversity strikes, offer your support to the parents and your grandchild.

CONCLUSION

In your role as nurturer, you may be called upon to nurse your grandchild through an illness, give advice to family members in times of stress, or provide financial or emotional support. Throughout human history grandparents have nurtured their grandchildren. Our modern-day society challenges grandparents to find new and creative ways to continue fulfilling their role as nurturer. If you need more information about this role, ask your grandchild for a job description.

CHAPTER 8

Role Model

A s a grandparent, you are a role model. Your actions show your children and grandchildren how they should behave as grandparents of the future. Their level of involvement and much of their success as future grandparents will depend on the trail you blaze for them. The image of grandparents they carry inside of them is based on their experience with you and the example you set for them.

Living Example

Clark, eighteen, is profoundly impressed by his eighty-nine-year-old grandmother's good health, active lifestyle, and vibrant sense of living each moment fully. The vital image of his grandmother has helped to bring about Clark's positive perception of the elderly and has also provided him with a positive model for his own aging. "My grandmother has had such a huge impact on my life. She will live inside me forever," says Clark. "Just because of her I think that I will live a long time, and that I will just get better and better at whatever I want to do with my life. Look at Grandma. She started playing the piano when she was seventy-five."

Keiko, thirty-five and a mother of three, admires her father's dedication. "He is a good father, a wonderful grandfather, and a family leader. When he makes my children happy, he makes me happy. Because I am so busy with work, I can't spend the amount of time I would like with each child. By following my father's example, I know I'll get a second chance when I become a grandmother."

"My grandfather had *guts*," recalls Frieda, twenty-seven. "He had Parkinson's disease and had to spend the later years of his life in a wheelchair. His speech was slurred, but he was sharp as a tack and he never lost his sense of humor. He loved to have me sit and listen to his jokes and stories, and I could understand him better than I could understand anyone. I admired his courage so much. I miss him right this minute just as much as I did the day he died ten years ago. I'll never forget him, and I hope I'll be as funny and brave as he was when my own end is near."

Defying Ageist Stereotypes

Although children of all ages are acutely aware of their parents' aging process, they often do not notice their grandparents gradually growing older. So, in your grandchild's eyes, you are pretty much the same at age forty as you are at seventy. Unless bad health causes rapid physical change, your grandchild's perception of you is relatively fixed because your aging process is slow compared to the rapid growth a child experiences. Your status as an older person always remains relatively stable for your grandchildren.

The more in-depth knowledge your grandchild has about you, gleaned from one-on-one time spent together (see Chapter 23, "Attention"), the more immune your grandchild is to the negative ageist stereotypes peddled by the media. Because children tend to generalize one specific experience to the broader world, the more your grandchild has a positive connection with you, the more likely she will be to have a positive perception and connection with other elders.

Investigators Bekker and Taylor (1966) examined how the number of generations in a family can influence a young person's perception of age. In one study, they found that students with living great-grandparents perceived grandparents as having fewer characteristics of old age than did students with no living great-grandparents. In a study of high school students, researchers Ivester and King (1977) reported that those who had contact with their grandparents had a more positive attitude toward older people in general than those who had little or no contact.

Grandchildren who enjoy positive relationships with their grandparents look forward to being grandparents themselves. Those with exceptionally close relationships with their grandparents often express the willingness, or even the desire, to care for their aging grandparents in their own homes. In an informal study conducted by the Foundation for Grandparenting (Kornhaber 1988) at a senior center in Texas, one out of seven grandparents was living with an adult grandchild. One woman described caring for her grandmother as "only paying back what she did for me. She took care of me when I was helpless. It's only natural I do the same. What goes around comes around."

Family Relationships

Grandparents also provide examples of positive leadership when they set a positive context and emotional tone for the family. Grandchildren who observe their grandparents and parents communicating freely and working to resolve conflicts are likely to develop a positive image of both parenting and grandparenting. In such an environment, children learn that multiple generations can make for a happy, harmonious family. They then go on to model this behavior in their own families when they become parents and grandparents.

Awareness

Being able to profoundly affect your children's and grandchildren's future grand-parenthood is an awesome responsibility. Being aware of this responsibility on a day-to-day basis is the first step in becoming the best role model possible. Understanding that your words and actions are noticed, examined, and remembered by your children and grandchildren is very important. Every role you play well as a grandparent enhances your status as a positive role model. Of course, the opposite is true as well; grandparents who are not mindful can also send out negative signals.

Keeping a Grandparenting Journal

Keeping a journal can be a very effective tool to help you reflect upon your status as a role model for your grandchildren. I highly recommend this practice. To start, purchase a well-bound journal consisting of high-quality durable paper. If possible, set aside a regular time each day that you can devote yourself to writing with no distractions. Before you know it, keeping your journal will become a very enjoyable habit.

In your journal, make a list of what you do that serves as a positive role model for your children and grandchildren. Which of the grandparenting roles do you most enjoy? Which do you naturally do best? Which do you least enjoy? What areas of your grandparenting do you think could use improvement? What steps must you take to bring about this improvement? For example, if you are a long-distance grandparent, perhaps you could make an effort to contact your grandchildren more often. As time passes, evaluate your progress toward your goals. Ask your children and grandchildren for their feedback and include their comments in your journal as well.

One benefit of keeping a grandparenting journal is that someday you will be able to share it with your children and grandchildren. It will become part of your legacy to the unborn generations to come.

GUIDELINES

Here are some guidelines to help you in your striving to be a strong role model for your grandchildren and family.

- First, finish reading this book and relate what you read to your own life.

- Take some time to think about the kind of grandparent you want to be for your grandchildren. How do you want to be remembered?
- Identify the differences between what you are presently doing, and what you would like to do.
- Reflect on what kind of role model you currently are for your children and grandchildren. How do they see you today and how will they remember you in the future?
- Reconcile all of the differences between what you are presently doing and what you would like to do.
- Keep a grandparenting journal. Add to it on a regular basis. Treat it as something that unborn generations of your family will read. Chronicle your hopes, dreams, and experiences—your successes and failures. Your family will cherish this emblem of you for all time.

CONCLUSION

Your thoughts, feelings, and actions supply a living example and a psychological blueprint for your children and grandchildren. The way you act, and what you do as a grandparent will affect future generations of your progeny. Not only is a journal a useful tool for self-improvement, but it can also serve as a roadmap for your progeny as future grandparents.

CHAPTER 9

Spiritual Guide

One of your most important roles as a grandparent involves cultivating your grandchild's spiritual development. This is the role of spiritual guide, a powerful position that can have a profound impact on the moral path your grandchild will take.

Spiritual Aspects of Your Relationship

The specific nature of your role as spiritual guide does not lend itself to description in clinical terms. We need another language to describe it. That's because the spiritual aspects of the grandparent-grandchild relationship reach far beyond the biological, psychological, and social dimensions of human experience. It is easier to describe the bond in emotional, sentimental terms, or in poetry or literature.

Acting as a spiritual guide involves teaching your grandchild to harvest such fruits of the spirit as love, tolerance, compassion, reverence, joy, peace, gentleness, faith, and kindness. These intangible qualities are related to the deepest and most mysterious dimension of your relationship with your grandchild.

You can teach your grandchild to weave qualities of the self with the world beyond the self. Character traits such as honesty and reverence are of the self. Gazing at the heavens while contemplating the awesomeness of existence is an activity beyond the self, as is seeing more in life than meets the eye, the numinous dimension of existence.

You may wonder why this role as spiritual guide is especially important to grandchildren. After all, parents cultivate their children's spirits too, teaching ethics, morality, and religious values. The answer is that grandparents' teachings have a quality that supplements a parent's teachings (see Chapter 11, "Teacher"). This quality is less purposeful and relates more to the numinous because it has its roots beyond the everyday in wisdom, experience, a long view of life, and an ever-increasing awareness of one's mortality.

As Carol, a sixty-nine-year-old grandmother says, "When I was a young mother, I looked at my children from a practical, protective, didactic point of view. Were they dressed correctly for the weather? Did they finish their spinach? Why was someone coughing? As a grandmother, I look at my grandchildren with wonder and see them as little human beings with their own unique characters. I wonder about what kind of human beings they will be when they grow up. I guess I am more philosophical now. These moments of observing from a distance were hard to come by when I was a busy parent. As a mother I was more concerned with the safety of their bodies and now as a grandmother I am more aware of their happiness and their souls."

In a Similar Place

Elders and children are closer to birth and death than the middle generation. They share a curiosity about a universe that the one has just entered and the other will shortly leave. In addition, grandparents and grandchildren inhabit a similar place in society, which reinforces their special spiritual connection, especially older grandparents and young children. Because they may be less involved in the purposeful everyday world and have less responsibility, they potentially are freer to focus on the spiritual nature of their existence.

As their physical abilities ebb, elders and grandparents become more relaxed and contemplative, their spiritual capacity expands to contemplate life's mysteries. These are the same issues that children are preoccupied with. They believe in angels and monsters and are able to live in their imaginations. Grandparents can make their grandchildren's dreams come to life. The stories that grandparents tell their grandchildren often contain themes of wonder and fantasy, and transmit spiritual awareness and knowledge of the meaning of life's mysteries, of worlds beyond everyday life (Timberlake 1992, Joseph 1968). Grandparents' life experience accords knowledge in the ways of the world, enabling them to deal openly with issues such as life's meaning and our mortality. They have the time, attention, and natural inclination to savor their grandchildren as sacred (see Chapters 2, "Ancestor," and 5, "Historian").

Illumination and Transformation

Simply put, the spiritual aspect of the grandparent-grandchild relationship is about giving meaning to one another in a way that busier people don't have time for. When connecting spiritually, a grandparent and grandchild illuminate and transform one another. Although perhaps sentimental, this description, is founded upon years of observing interactions between the young and the old.

As part of an intergenerational study to gauge how the young and the old affect one another, I brought a group of elementary schoolchildren to visit a nursing home. One of the children involved in the study was a perky seven-year-old named Annie. When we entered the nursing home's sitting room, Annie noticed a wheelchair-bound woman slumped in the corner of the room. The woman seemed utterly unaware of what was happening around her.

"Look at that granny over there," Annie said. "She looks lonely." A nurse suggested that Annie go over and talk with the woman, whose name was Mrs. Boyce. We approached Mrs. Boyce, and Annie squatted down in front of her, tilting her head so she could look into the woman's eyes. "Hi!" Annie said with a smile.

Mrs. Boyce shifted in her chair. "Hello, child," she whispered.

"I like your dress," Annie said. "It's cute." She straightened Mrs. Boyce's collar. "And this is pretty."

A nurse called me away to ask for some advice about her patients. When I returned from the nurse's office I noticed that Annie was not in the recreation room. A nurse told me that Annie had wheeled Mrs. Boyce back to her room. I hastened to the room, and there I found Mrs. Boyce sitting straight up in her chair combing Annie's hair, the two of them chatting away. Mrs. Boyce's affect and level of physical activity, indeed her very essence, were completely altered.

This is an example of how spirit works between the young and the old. I know it defies scientific explanation. Nevertheless, it happens. While Annie was clearly enjoying herself, Mrs. Boyce had undergone an amazing transformation. There was now life in her movements, her eyes were bright, and she was full of energy. Something within her had been "transformed" by Annie. There is no medical explanation to explain Mrs. Boyce's transformation, although studies conducted on intergenerational social programs show increased health, attention, and vitality among elders who mentor children (Bower 1991, Caren 1991, Cerrato 1990, Ozer 1992). This mystical power, generated between the young and old, illuminates and transforms them both.

Tending the Spirit of Your Grandchild

Your spiritual communion with your grandchild means teaching the way to goodness, tolerance, kindness, and understanding. This role is often ignored or overlooked; yet it is a vital countervailing force to toxic social teachings that fill children's minds with messages of violence, hate, and intolerance.

Children, especially in today's de-spirited times, need to experience the spiritual dimensions of life. The grandparent-grandchild relationship is ideally suited to the discovery of this dimension.

Spiritual Language and Spiritual Action

You guide your grandchild in matters of the spirit with thought, language, and action. When talking to your grandchild, use a language of the spirit. Words such as *kindness, compassion, understanding,* and *selflessness* evoke spiritual thoughts and open your grandchild's mind to another plane of existence.

By acting in a moral, ethical, and honest manner, you are setting the example of a spiritually evolved lifestyle. Your grandchild will notice if you make a point of paying the correct admission price at the movies, for example, or sticking to the speed limit posted on the highway. Such seemingly simple things send powerful messages to a child.

Involve yourself in spiritual activities. Knowing that you volunteer at a hospital, attend a place of worship, respect religious traditions at home, demonstrate reverence for nature, help others who are less fortunate, and demonstrate kindness and compassion toward others helps your grandchild recognize you as a guardian, and example, of spirituality in action.

If you are religious, show the positive aspects of your beliefs. Many grandparents in our studies allude to the strength they derive from their religious beliefs. With the parents' consent, use the philosophy, language, and rituals of your religion so that your grandchild may carry your religious torch on to the next generation. Discussing your own spiritual views and experiences serves to heighten your grandchild's spiritual consciousness.

A 1993 survey I conducted with one hundred middle-class Caucasian grandmothers found that 73 percent had learned religion from their grandparents, and 49 percent reported teaching religion to their grandchildren. Another 16 percent said that their children had chosen a different religion but allowed the grandparents to teach their own religion to the grandchildren. Only 4 percent said their children are of different faiths and do not want them to talk about religion with the grandchildren.[1]

Michael, a forty-year-old American Indian, said he saw his grandfather "talking to God," after Michael's father was killed in action in Vietnam. "I was a child when we found out that my dad was killed. One night I was playing out back and I heard my grandpa singing and talking to the Great Spirit, what you would call God. Grandpa didn't know I was there. He was talking and crying

---

1. Kornhaber, A. *Contemporary Grandparenting* (1996). Thousand Oaks, Calif.: Sage Publications, p. 102.

and he was talking to my dad up there too, hoping he was well. I was a little scared but I thought, 'Wow! My grandfather is talking to the Great Spirit.' That night I looked at the sky and tried to find my dad and I talked to him, too. I talked a lot and it felt good."

Even though hard science can't explain it, some researchers attest to the value of a spiritual connection. In a study examining grandparent caregiving (Minkler, Roe 1993) the authors noted that "prayer, reading the Bible, and turning to God were the most frequently cited means of coping" for grandparents raising their grandchildren. The Grandparent Study has also found that spiritual activity, especially prayer and meditation, is an often cited source of support for many grandparents. This is especially true for many of those involved in the grandparents' rights movement who were deprived of access to their grandchildren. Many say they find their strength and perseverance through their spiritual and religious beliefs.

Many grandparents show a grandchild how to connect with the numinous in times of stress. When Rosie, sixteen years old and three months pregnant, was abandoned by her boyfriend Manny after the doctor advised them that she would soon lose the baby, she was devastated. Soon afterward, she began to experience abdominal pain and bleeding. Her parents thought it would be good for her to get away for a weekend and visit her grandmother Consuelo in an adjoining town. Consuelo was known as a *curandera*, or healer, and was often called upon to minister to the sick. She took Rosie to early mass at the local church and told her to light a candle to Our Lady of Guadalupe, Consuelo's special saint. "You are never alone," she told Rosie. "There are guardian angels that watch over you." They lit another candle on Sunday morning, although she was in pain and still bleeding. Rosie said she felt better about her situation and was no longer in as much anguish over Manny. Sunday afternoon she miscarried her baby. Rosie returned home, went back to school and resumed her life. "Manny and the baby—that was not to be. I learned from my grandmother that I'm never alone, and that is forever."

Even if you do not follow a religious belief system, or you have no spiritual beliefs at all, you can still guide your grandchild's spiritual development.

Take reverence, for example. Eloise, fifty-five, is a painter and an atheist. When she is stressed she takes walks in the woods and sketches flowers. "The forest is my church," she tells her five-year-old grandson, Felix. One afternoon she took Felix out for a walk. He was throwing rocks against a tree. "Don't do that, dear, you'll hurt it," she said. "The tree don't feel anything," said Felix. "Yes it does," Eloise said. "The tree is alive." Eloise walked over to the tree and hugged it. "Come on, Felix," she urged, "hug me, and hug the tree." Felix hugged Eloise and then proceeded to hug the tree as tight as he could. "I hear a sound." Eloise answered, "It's the tree's heart, dear."

Blessing Power

There is a natural tendency for the young to give credence to what I may term as the supernatural, or spiritual powers of the very old. I have seen this in many individuals, in many cultures. For example, the American Indians I worked among believe deeply in the power of blessings from grandfathers and grandmothers. Many cultures and religions have accorded elders the power of blessing, which assures health and success.

Children know the power of blessings. Dr. Rachel Naomi Remen, author of *My Grandfather's Blessings*, is a physician who treats people with chronic and terminal illnesses. In her lovely book, she describes how her grandfather blessed her when he finished praying.

When Grandpa finished talking with God he would turn to me and say, "Come, Neshume-le." Then I would stand in front of him and he would rest his hands lightly on the top of my head. He would begin by thanking God for me and for making him my grandpa. He would specifically mention my struggles during that week and tell God something about me that was true. Each week I would wait to find out what that was. If I had made mistakes during the week, he would mention my honesty in telling the truth. If I failed, he would appreciate how hard I had tried. If I had taken even a short nap without my nightlight, he would celebrate my bravery in sleeping in the dark. Then he would give me his blessing and ask the long ago women I knew from his many stories—Sarah, Rachel, Rebecca, and Leah—to watch over me.[2]

Although the power of blessing may be driven by a specific belief system it nevertheless remains that, as a grandparent, your own approval (in the form of an invocation of God by a blessing) can carry significant clout for a child. Kami, twenty-eight years old, would not marry until she could return to India with her fiancée to obtain her grandparents' blessing for her marriage. "They are older and wiser," she said, "and I believe they know what is best for me. Ever since I was a child they would bless whatever I did if they agreed that it was good. My grandfather and grandmother would place their hands on my head and we would pray together. They blessed my idea of coming to the United States to study. Now I want their blessing so I can get married to an American and live in the United States permanently. With their blessing I know that I am protected."

Spiritual Disconnection

When the spiritual connection between grandparent and grandchild is ruptured, it can cause great pain and suffering for all concerned. These wounds go deep, affecting the spirit as well as the psyche. The rupture of a close grandparent-grandchild relationship not only results in upsetting both parties, but it can go deeper, penetrating the spiritual layer of the person's being. This, as I mentioned in a previous book, has a "de-spiriting" effect, which often leads to mourning and clinical depression. Yoki, fifty-five, said, "My heart is gone," after she was told that her grandson and his parents were moving to the other side of the country. She knew that she would no longer see her grandson every day. The spiritual wounds are especially severe when parents intentionally separate grandparents and grandchildren (see Chapter 42, "Legal Issues").

---

2. Kornhaber, Arthur. *Spirit* (1986). New York: St. Martin's Press, pp. 152–153

Viewing the grandparent-grandchild relationship from the spiritual point of view offers compelling reasons why a close relationship should be protected, honored, and respected. To be an effective spiritual guide, take the time to ask yourself the following questions: What does spirituality mean to you? How do you use your spiritual beliefs in your daily life? What specific spiritual values, beliefs, or rituals do you want to transmit to your grandchild? How are blessings related to these efforts? Are there any impediments to transmitting your spiritual values? If so, what can you do to overcome them?

GUIDELINES

Here are some guidelines to help you celebrate this special aspect of your relationship with your grandchild and to better serve as your grandchild's spiritual guide.

- Take time to think through your own attitudes and philosophy concerning this role.
- Decide how you will implement this role in the most authentic way possible in the light of your own values, philosophy, and experience.
- Make known in the family your beliefs and your intention to act as a spiritual guide.
- Coordinate what you intend to do concerning your spiritual or established religious practices with the parents.
- Spend time alone with your grandchild in nature.
- Engage in a charitable activity with your grandchild.
- Share your own spiritual experiences with your grandchild.
- Listen to your grandchild's conceptions of the meaning of life, nature, and God.
- Discuss the "fruits of the spirit" mentioned above with your family.
- Demonstrate spiritual values in action and language.

- Transmit religious beliefs when appropriate and with the parents' consent (see Chapter 40, "Religious Differences").
- Even if you profess no spiritual beliefs you can teach goodness. Set an excellent personal example; teach generosity, kindness, and concern for others by engaging in charitable activities with a grandchild.

CONCLUSION

As a spiritual guide, you show your grandchild how to cultivate the fruits of the spirit by teaching ethics, morals, and values and by leading a spiritually conscious life. Because you are uniquely suited to connect with your grandchild in a contemplative state of mind, you both are naturally primed to marvel and evaluate the mysteries of the universe in a profound manner. By so doing you will illuminate and transform yourselves.

CHAPTER 10

Student

G randparenting involves life-long learning—first as a grandchild, then as a parent, and finally as a grandparent and great-grandparent. As a student of grandparenting, you may read books, join grandparenting groups, or do other things to raise your grandparenting consciousness. But by far the greatest teacher you will ever have in this endeavor is your grandchild.

Although it seems that elders are typically the ones teaching their juniors, the other way around is equally true, though not as evident. Learning, especially when it is transmitted in the relationship between grandchild and grandparent, is definitely a two-way street. For your grandchild you are both a teacher (mentor) and a student. Your grandchild can teach you to keep up with the world. Just as you teach and inspire your grandchild with your knowledge, she can teach and inspire you with her knowledge of contemporary times across the generations and motivate you to jumpstart your capacity to grow and change.

Lifelong Learning

To be a good student of your grandchild you have to allow yourself to be open and receptive to new ideas. (You don't have to agree with them—just be open to them.) Take technology, for example; let your grandchild take you by the hand

and lead you into the technological present and future. Computers, modems, fax machines, video games, DVD players, palm pilots, the latest research in science and math—whatever seems intimidating and beyond your grasp can be made comprehensible and fun if you allow your grandchild to teach you about it. If you are already up-to-date, share your interests.

"My grandma was terrified of the ATM at the bank," said Melissa, seventeen. "She is a smart lady, and has managed her own money since my grandpa died seven years ago, but you couldn't get her to go near those machines. She did not want to apply for an ATM card, but would stand in long lines, waiting for a teller, just for the simplest transaction. One day Grandma reluctantly agreed to go to the machine with me. I kind of teased and challenged her and so on, and she started getting into it. Then she saw how simple it was and she was really getting a kick out of it. So, she got herself a card and a touch-tone phone. Now she loves to use the phone to do her banking right from home. She's seventy-four and a real whiz. My parents and I are all going to chip in and buy her a computer for her seventy-fifth birthday so she can bank on-line!"

One of the most touching stories I know of a grandparent/student is that of a grandmother who had been illiterate all her life. Her three-year-old grandson went to a Montessori nursery school where there were special tactile letters of the alphabet made from sandpaper. To learn the shapes the children traced the letters with their fingers. On visiting day, this grandmother tried the technique with her grandson, and "suddenly it began to make sense." Inspired, she enrolled in a literacy-tutoring program, and learned to read at last. "Now I read to my grandson and he reads to me," she reports. "Learning to read has changed my life, and I have Johnny to thank for that."

Being a student of life means keeping up with your grandchild's world (see Chapter 21, "Effective Grandparenting," and Chapter 23, "Attention") so you can discuss a common reality. Make sure to visit your grandchild's school and your children's workplace. See what they are watching on television and what they are doing with their friends. Flip through their magazines. This way you will always be able to learn new things—about the world and about your family. Grandparent power means growing power.

Allowing Your Grandchild to Be a Teacher

By sharing in the fun of allowing your grandchild to teach you new things, you are also empowering him and helping to build his self-esteem. Your attention and receptivity contributes to his sense of himself as someone who has something of value to give and someone who possesses information and skills that are transmittable to others. With this comes a respect for old age and lifelong learning. By being a permanent student, you set a great example of how to remain open to learning new things at any age.

Grandparent Classes

It is up to you to keep yourself informed about the latest personal, social, and political information concerning grandparents. Keep up with the latest books. Stay current with breaking news and issues via our website (www.grandparenting.org). Keep a lookout for grandparenting classes in your area; better yet, start one in your community. Standard courses are being developed to raise grandparent consciousness (Strom and Strom 1992) and increasing grandparent effectiveness.

GUIDELINES

Here are a few tips to help you become your grandchild's best student.

- Never believe you are too old to learn. We evolve and grow until the day we die. New knowledge is generated at every moment.
- Allow your grandchild to teach you new things. It will be a positive experience for her and expands your own knowledge.
- Set a positive example for your grandchild by the pleasure you take in learning new things from him—whether it's a new dance, a new school subject, or mastery of a new gadget or idea.
- Discover something new together with your grandchild.

- Keep up with the latest in grandparenting news via www.grand parenting.org
- Start grandparent classes in your community.

CONCLUSION

Your grandchild is a source of lifelong learning for you. Stay interested and involved. Your grandchild's life experience, successes, setbacks, interests, and hobbies are his curriculum to teach you. He can teach you what's going on in his contemporary world, and you can teach him more classic knowledge. Being a student will keep both of you vital and involved.

CHAPTER 11

Teacher

T he role of teacher is one of the most essential and enduring roles you have as a grandparent. Even though you influence your family by your example, you can also teach your grandchildren in a more conscious and active way. Your grandchildren naturally expect to learn from you and it is your right to teach your grandchildren what you know, whether or not what you teach is in vogue. As a grandparent, you have the right and the responsibility to run your own classroom about life, to develop your own curriculum, and to pass on your wisdom, knowledge, and life experience.

Your Curriculum

In your role as your grandchild's teacher you impart general information and skills. Everything you know and have learned over the years comprises your curriculum. Therefore you can freely teach whatever your specialties may be—baking, whittling, singing, speaking a foreign language, playing chess, gardening, knitting, skiing, swimming, diving, even braiding hair. The more classic your skill, the more important it is for you to pass it on. Did your own grandmother teach you how to tat or cross-stitch? Then don't let the lessons die with you. And remember: there are no books, no lesson plans, and no videotapes that will ever be as effective as personal coaching, particularly when teacher and student are linked by love.

The things you can teach are things your grandchildren won't learn anywhere else. One twenty-year-old granddaughter, Ludi, told me, "I took ballet lessons when I was a little girl, and my grandmother was the one who chauffeured me. She had been a dancer in her youth in Russia and before my first lesson, when I was eight years old, she taught me how to do the right hairstyle, with looped braids caught up in colored ribbons. I practiced and practiced until I got it smooth and perfect. My teacher was so impressed. Then over the years, my grandmother taught me how to make a bun and a twist—the more grown-up styles. She showed me pictures of herself as a girl with exactly the same hairstyles. I loved that, especially since I look so much like her."

Your grandchild is primed to benefit from what you teach. Because your grandchildren usually view their time with you as pleasurable, and because your emotional attachment is so strong, your grandchild learns from you effortlessly, even unconsciously. As one precocious grandchild said, "It's like osmosis." There is no need for pointers and chalkboards when you are teaching. Your love and dedication make your lessons stick in your grandchild's mind.

In fact, a number of adults have reported that what they learned from their grandparents "stuck" better than what they learned from their parents. This is because children do not feel the need to oppose their grandparents as they do their parents thus they accept, and absorb, information from their grandparents much more easily.

Take advantage of this natural situation. By becoming your grandchild's active and involved teacher, you will be passing what you know on to future generations. By teaching your grandchildren and influencing the kind of people they become, you will achieve a very real kind of immortality,

When Your Curriculum Is Censored

Sometimes your grandchild's parents may worry about what you are teaching her. This situation is not uncommon in families of new immigrants coming to

America who want to discard the old ways and start over in their new country as quickly as possible.

Li, a Chinese grandmother, had a conflict with her daughter-in-law Ellie. Li wanted to teach her granddaughter Connie, age ten, about her Chinese heritage. Connie was fascinated by what her grandmother taught her—family history, special family recipes, the stories behind old family costumes, and memories from Li's childhood.

The problem started when Li told Connie that it was important to cook well in order to attract, and please, a husband. When Connie's mother, Ellie, heard what Li had said she was livid. "My mother-in-law is brainwashing my daughter," she said. "She's teaching Connie to be submissive. I want her to be a liberated woman, not like the women in the old county who were nothing more than slaves. Li still thinks that pleasing a man's palate is the highest calling in life for a woman."

Li couldn't understand why Ellie was so vehement about her teaching Connie to please a husband. "What's wrong with teaching my Connie to be a wife and mother?" Li lamented. "If Ellie paid more attention to that my son would be happier." Since the conflict was not getting resolved, I suggested that everyone sit down and talk things over. Li pointed out to Ellie that she was not teaching Connie "submissiveness" at all. She only wanted to teach Connie about her ancestors and give her a sense of rootedness and continuity. "I am teaching Connie to know me, and to know our ancestors, who are with me every day," Li said. "And for a woman to take care of a home is not submissiveness; it's working together with the husband for the family. It's being a family."

Together, we decided to allow Connie to determine if there was a problem. "I am not being 'brainwashed' by my grandmother at all," Connie told me. "I love most of the stuff she teaches me. Some of the ancestor stuff, well, I do not really understand, but she is very serious about it. She does have old-fashioned ideas, but they are interesting. I love to listen to her. All we are doing is having fun. Besides, I hate to cook. My husband will have to cook his own food."

If your children are having difficulty with what you are teaching your grandchild, talk this problem over with them. Discuss the issue openly and come to an appropriate compromise (see Chapter 33, "Between Parents and Grandparents"). Generational differences in attitudes, values, and outlook are to be expected, especially in a society that changes as rapidly as ours does. If you use the family council for discussing conflicts and problems, you'll be able to reach a meeting of minds that will benefit everyone. Here again, the crucial issue is to avoid needlessly alienating the middle generation. Your access to your grandchildren depends on their goodwill.

GUIDELINES

Here are some hints to help you to be the best teacher possible for your grandchild.

- Take a moment to think about what you would like to teach your grandchild.
- What you teach does not have to be relevant to today but must have an enduring relevance (traditional manners, for example).
- Make sure to teach in a relaxed and informal manner (see Chapter 23, "Attention").
- Ask your grandchild if there is anything special he would like to learn from you (recipes, carpentry skills, arts and crafts, etc.). Showing what you can do may stimulate your grandchild's interest in a certain activity or skill.
- If any conflict about your "curriculum" occurs with your grandchild's parents, make sure to identify the issue and resolve it satisfactorily.

CONCLUSION

One of the most important roles you have involves teaching what you have learned throughout your life to your grandchild. Know that *you* are the curriculum and teach effortlessly. Be alert to what your grandchild wants to learn from you. Also understand that what may seem banal and insignificant to other adults may be wondrous in your grandchild's eyes. So tailor your teaching appropriately and ask your grandchildren for periodic evaluations of your curriculum.

CHAPTER 12

Wizard

Your role as a wizard for your grandchild is one of the most enjoyable, freewheeling, and free-spirited roles you will ever play. It is also one of the most wondrous for your grandchildren, especially the young ones who still live in a magical world. When you take on the role of wizard (although adults in the everyday world are blind to your transformation) your grandchild will view you as a mystical person. Whether you are a biological grandparent, a stepgrandparent, or an adoptive grandchild, you have the same potential to fly with your grandchild to life's more mysterious and mystical places.

As a wizard, you provide a playful, imaginative counterpoint to your grandchild's task-oriented everyday world. Unlike parents and teachers, you need not be as vigilant about enforcing many of the concepts of duty and discipline with your grandchildren (although you may exemplify these concepts). Consequently, you are free to indulge your grandchild's fantasies in a way that other authority figures in his life cannot. This can be fun—and also serious.

Grandparents and Magic

Age and magical powers have been inextricably linked throughout human history. Like Don Juan, the mysterious Yaqui sorcerer in the books of Carlos Casteneda, the old have the power to shape shift—to assume different physical forms and become different people. To your grandchild your talents and gifts can seem wondrous. You can be different people, because you were different people at different stages of your life and have accumulated different powers. Even the super-rational Jean-Paul Sartre marveled at his grandfather's "magical" ability to recite what was written in any of the books in his library.

In the Tupian tribe of South America, the grandfather is associated with thunder. Among the Yurok Indians, every grandmother has her own song that has the power to drive away evil spirits. Fairy godmothers have special powers, too. Indeed, a child might think that her grandfather and the Wizard of Oz have plenty in common. Although their "real" power may differ, he can make seemingly impossible things happen and encourage her to believe that dreams can come true.

Nan, twenty-five, remembers taking walks with her grandfather when she was a little girl. He would encourage her to let her imagination soar. "As we walked, we would make up stories. We saw a hawk in the sky and made up poems about him. I once saw a woodchuck and grandfather asked me what it would be like to be a woodchuck and for me to make up a story about where the woodchuck lives and about her family. I did and he loved it. The next day he took me to the woodchuck's den and showed me where she really lived and her babies. He told me that my imagination could be more interesting than reality. We imagined beings in the forest. He told me about leprechauns. And we used to watch for them. I swear I saw them peering out from behind trees. We would make sure to find a four-leaf clover before we looked for the 'fairy people,' as he called them."

Wizardry and healing powers are linked. Lois, forty, lived on a farm when she was a child. She remembers that all the farmers in her town would call upon her grandmother whenever their livestock fell ill because she had the power to heal sick animals. Lois's sideline is finding water for well diggers. She learned this skill from her best friend's grandfather, Ike. When Lois was thirteen he spent an afternoon teaching her. "Grandpa Ike showed me how to cut a willow branch, and how to hold it when I walked. And when I almost jumped out of my skin when the point of the willow jerked to the ground he said, 'you've got the gift.' And I was very proud. Then he told me that I could never take money or a gift from anyone that I found water for because it would break the spell. And I never did."

Anton, a sixty-five-year-old medical doctor, feels he inherited a gift for healing from his grandmother while growing up in Haiti. "She was a priestess and as soon as I was old enough to walk she would take me when she went to help the sick. I watched how people respected her and saw her do amazing things, like talking to animals. She told me that I have the gift, too. Sometimes, when I've done all I can for a very sick person with traditional medicine, and it doesn't work, I'll think about my grandmother and call on her to intervene. She will come and tell me what to do."

The Necessity of Fantasy

For children fantasies are not luxuries—they're necessities, particularly for children between the ages of four and five. Most child-development experts acknowledge that there is a deep human need for fantasy throughout life and that young children especially benefit from imaginative play. From a psychological point of view, magical thinking is a common mode in children until they attain the alleged "age of reason" (approximately seven years). That's why many children believe in ghosts and have imaginary friends. That's also why they sometimes weave tall tales that get them into trouble with their more logic-minded parents. On the other hand, "wizardry-minded" grandparents may know exactly what the children mean.

Sellie, five, had an imaginary friend she called Tabatha. When Sellie came for an overnight visit with her grandparents they set a place at the table for Tabatha, made a bed for her, and even placed a toothbrush for her in the bathroom. Sellie's grandfather, Carter, fifty-right, said "It was fun and innocent, and I knew Sellie would grow out of that phase. We just let her enjoy herself. When I was a kid, I had a make-believe dog that looked like Lassie. It never bothered my parents 'cause there was no mess and no vet bills!"

Young children do not lie. They believe their fantasies. Lying is a conscious act that older people do. Enlivening a child's imagination doesn't necessarily mean lying. As Ed, sixty-seven, says, "A bit of blarney never hurt anyone." Besides, studies have shown that children who are adept at make-believe prove to have enhanced intellectual skills, are more complex thinkers, display above-average verbal skills, and are more emotionally balanced. Armed with this knowledge you can freely facilitate and nurture your grandchild's magical thinking and your own wizardry.

Wonder and Wizardry

With magical thinking, children's capacity to appreciate wonder is infinite! Even such seemingly mundane tasks as letting dough rise for a loaf of bread or making a garden grow can be magical for small children. For young children, pulling a fish from the water is magical. Making a sweater from a ball of yarn or watching a chick hatch is magical, too. And the one who does it is wizard-like!

Tyrone, seventy-two, describes a game he plays with his grandson in which he operates the car headlights, windshield wipers, and horn with "magic from his fingertips." He points at the instruments with one finger while he secretly switches them on with his other hand. His delighted four-year-old grandson, Tommy, squeals with joy when the windshield wipers turn on or the horn sounds. Tyrone hasn't told his amazed grandson his secret yet and is waiting for him to figure it out. "Then I'll have to find something else to convince Tommy I'm magic," he says with a chuckle.

To this day Gilda, sixty-six, gets up early on Christmas morning before her family arrives for their traditional dinner together. She places half-eaten cookies and a half-filled mug of cocoa on the fireplace hearth. Then she dusts flour on the bottom of an old pair of slippers and stomps around on the floor making "Santa's footprints." "It looks so real my twelve-year-old grandson jokes that he believes Santa really was here."

When your grandchildren see you as a magical person, it further solidifies you as unique and distinct from their parents. With your tricks, your talents, and a twinkle in your eye, you can transport your grandchildren to a wonderland.

GUIDELINES

Here are some guidelines to help you enhance your role as wizard.:

- Get in touch with your own hopes, dreams, and fantasies.
- Reach back into your childhood and rekindle some nonrational memories and dreams.
- Join in with your grandchild's imagination and magical thinking.
- Enter into your grandchild's fantasy world. Draw together and make up stories about the people in your drawings. Read stories to your grandchild, have a tea party, build a dollhouse, have a car race with sound effects, camp out in tents and pretend you're in the Amazon, write a play together and act it out.
- Be creative and fun; make an effort to let yourself go.
- Share your gifts and talents with your grandchild. Artistic abilities are especially wondrous to children.
- Feel free to push the borders of reason and reality if you are having fun!

CONCLUSION

When you play the role of wizard for your grandchild, you are nurturing his fantasy life and thus helping him grow intellectually and emotionally. You are also, for a moment, helping him escape the pressures of purposeful reality that he inhabits most of the time. Remember that you are a magical figure to your grandchild. Travel with her on the wings of fancy. When you use your imagination, the sky is the limit. Activate your own wizardry and be your grandchild's companion in the preternatural world of make-believe and illusion, of dreams and surprises. Fly together on the wings of fancy and enjoy the flight!

PART 2

The Making of a Grandparent

The making of a grandparent starts at birth and continues throughout life. Understanding this process will make you a more understanding and effective grandparent. The first step is to know what your grandparent identity is all about. This means you must become familiar with the emotional, physical, and psychological factors that affect the quality of your grandparenthood.

In the following chapters, I will explain some of the important factors affecting your natural instinct and identity as a grandparent, and how they develop through the years. I will also explain how other factors, such as temperament, gender, and age affect you in this role. Finally, I will show how to apply this knowledge to become the most effective grandparent you can.

CHAPTER 13

Grandparent Development

Y our attitudes, hopes, dreams, and expectations for yourself as a grandparent develop throughout your life. Your grandparenting skills are both innate and learned. They are continually influenced by biological, psychological, interpersonal, and social forces that ultimately determine your feelings about what being a grandparent means to you; your identification with the role; the value you place on being a grandparent; how you grow, change, and develop as a grandparent; and how you teach your children and grandchildren about grandparenting.

Understanding how this process of development works will help you become a more assured, happy, and effective grandparent.

A Lifelong Process

You began your grandparent development as a grandchild. It started from the very first moment you saw and related with your own grandparents. From that point on, the various psychological and behavioral dimensions of your grandparenthood began to unfold over the years.

- From being nurtured as a grandchild, you learn to nurture your own grandchildren.
- From listening to stories as a grandchild, you learn to tell stories to your grandchildren.
- From assimilating knowledge from elders as a grandchild, you learn how to pass on knowledge.
- From watching how your parents and grandparents related to one another you learned how to do the same.
- From the change and growth you experience as a child, parent, grandparent and great-grandparent, you learn what life is all about, and accumulate wisdom.

These factors form your grandparent identity that grows and develops through the years.

Your Grandparent Identity

Both nature and nurture affect the development of your grandparent identity (Kornhaber 1996). Here is how it works. Your experience as a grandchild impresses upon you what grandparenting is all about. This happens on both a conscious and unconscious level. These early impressions and experiences are stored in your memory as part of your latent grandparent identity. This is a mental idea or image of grandparenting that is essentially dormant in your mind until a grandchild comes along (see Chapter 14, "The Granparenting Instinct"). This latent identity, created in your pregrandparent phase, prepares a blueprint for your future grandparenthood. You can see now why it is so important for grandparents to understand how their example affects their children and grandchildren who are in the formative stages of creating their own grandparent identity.

Nature

Your latent grandparent identity is colored by your nature. Nature is nothing more than aspects of a grandparent's personality that serve to increase (altruism and generosity, for example) or decrease (narcissism and selfishness) his or her affinity for this role. Nature is reflected in personality characteristics such as temperament (see Chapter 15). When all of these nature and nurture factors are considered, you will have established many of your attitudes, hopes, and dreams concerning grandparenting before you actually become a grandparent. That is why those expectant grandparents who have very positive latent grandparent identity cannot wait to become grandparents.

Experience

Your personal experience as a grandchild can color your perception of grandparenthood in a positive or negative way. Having a wonderful grandparent builds a strong foundation for future grandparenthood. "My grandmother is so great that I want to be just like her when I grow up," says seven-year-old Justin. "But I'll be a grandfather, of course."

On the other hand, a negative grandchild experience can create trepidation about becoming a grandparent. Gladys, fifty-two, a kind and gentle person, says, "I didn't like my grandmother. She was always criticizing me. I worried about what kind of grandmother I would be. I wondered if my mother, too, would be like her mother and nag my kids to death." Because Gladys is a kind and tolerant person, her grandchildren love her. Even though she had a tenuous latent grandparent identity, she turned out to be an effective and loved grandmother. The lesson here is that grandchildren of dysfunctional grandparents may have a negative bias toward their grandparenthood (see Chapter 45, "Mistakes Grandparents Make"). Fortunately, for Gladys, her positive personal characteristics overcame her negative experience.

After your first grandchild is born, your natural instinct or biological urge to be a grandparent brings to life your latent grandparent identity. Then you become a real-life grandparent. (I explain this phenomenon in depth in Chapter 14, "The Grandparenting Instinct.") Simply put, after the first grandchild comes along you stop dreaming about being a grandparent and *become* one.

Positive Grandparent Identity

Effective grandparents have a positive grandparenting identity. The more positive the identity, the better the grandparent. Following are some organic and psychological factors I have identified that contribute to a positive grandparent identity.[1] Although experiencing these factors contributes to becoming an effective grandparent, it is not absolutely necessary to have experienced *all* of them. Fortunately, you can create some of these circumstances as an integral part of your grandparent development; by doing so, you can help your children and grandchildren establish a positive grandparenting identity too.

As a Child
- Have a positive relationship with a grandparent.
- Experience love, joy, security, and fun with a grandparent.
- Have an elder or grandparent encourage your intellectual growth.
- Have a grandparent point out genetic linking, physical similarities in the family. ("I have my grandmother's eyes, my grandfather's throwing arm.")
- Experience a sense of being able to count on grandparents when adversity strikes.
- Have a grandparent who is available and responsive to you.
- Have a spiritual connection to a grandparent or elder.
- Be exposed to examples set by your grandparents of family connectedness, family continuity, and family rootedness.
- Be exposed to grandparents who play a range of roles within the family.
- Identify with a grandparent in a positive way. ("I want to be able to paint like Grandma.")
- Observe grandparents supporting parents.
- Experience intergenerational harmony.
- Observe parents and grandparents working through conflicts and problems.

---

1. Kornhaber, Arthur. *Contemporary Grandparenting.*

- Observe the positive behavior of grandparents and elders from other families, the outside community, and society.

As a Parent
- Value the grandparent-grandchild relationship.
- Observe and positively experience how your own parents act as grandparents.
- Cultivate the bond between your own parents and children; and actively serve as the linchpin of the grandparent-grandchild relationship.
- Observe the positive experience of your child as a grandchild.
- Embrace the potential positive ethnic and cultural influence of grandparenting.
- Observe your parent "rehearsing" future grandparenthood.

These factors may or may not have been present in your own development. Whatever the case, they intermingle with your own personal characteristics, such as your temperament and health, as well as your life situation (marital status, financial situation, where you live, etc.) and determine the quantity and quality of your grandparent identity.

A Work in Progress

You are still growing and changing; therefore your development is a work in progress. There is a lot in the past, but there is also a lot to come because you will spend a great deal of your life as a grandparent—and a great-grandparent too! Every challenge you face is an opportunity to continue your growth and development as a grandparent (see Chapter 10, "Student"). Be especially aware of the fact that you supply the example for the future grandparenthood of your children and grandchildren. How you respect and enact your role becomes an important part of the latent grandparent identity they are currently building. By serving as an excellent role model you will positively influence the way in

which many generations of your descendants will deal with their own grandparenthood.

GUIDELINES

Here are some guidelines to think about during your own development while
you are setting the stage for your child and grandchild's positive grandparent
identity.

- Understand that grandparenting is a growing and ever-changing
  experience.
- Try to be a positive influence in your grandchild's life.
- Try to be a positive influence in the parents' lives.
- Communicate to your family the fact that you enjoy being a
  grandparent.
- Share the origins of your own grandparenthood with them.
- Let them know that you are still growing as a grandparent and
  you are open to positive suggestions and change.
- Share your growth and change with them.
- Keep up with the times.
- Discuss the idea of grandparent development with your peers.
- Make your children and grandchildren aware that they are
  constructing their grandparenthood of the future.
- Be the best grandparent you can be.

CONCLUSION

Your development as a grandparent is an ongoing process. Monitor your personal
growth and change in this area. Ask your children and grandchildren how they
feel about you as a grandparent. Enjoy their compliments and listen to their suggestions about how you can be a more effective parent or grandparent. And
remember to nurture their grandparent identity by being the best grandparent
you can.

CHAPTER 14

The Grandparenting Instinct

O ne of the most important factors affecting your involvement in grandparenting, as well as your growth and development as a grandparent, is your natural instinct for the role. Yes, I said *instinct*.

The idea that a grandparenting instinct might exist came to me as a result of my studies. The more I looked into grandparenting, the more people told me they experienced a natural urge to grandparent. Some even reported feeling such an instinct when they were very young.

Further inquiry taught me that this instinct initiates action as a drive to feel, think, and act as a grandparent. This drive has certain unique characteristics; it is manifested in different ways in different people; it can grow and change over time; and its strength is influenced by personality, life experience, and culture. Furthermore, grandchildren seem to have a mirror image of this grandparenting instinct—in other words, an instinct to be grandparented.

The Need to Grandparent

George, seventy-six, was one of the many grandparents I interviewed who expressed a lifelong, deeply felt desire to grandparent. As George described it,

"I'm George the first. My son is George the second. My grandson is George the third. Now we have just welcomed George the fourth into the world. I feel happy and fulfilled because ever since I was young I dreamt of having lots of grandkids to enjoy who would carry on the family name and tradition. Now it's a reality."

Before I ascribed the kinds of feelings George expressed to an instinct, I asked myself many questions. Why did George feel so strongly about being a grandfather his whole life? Was this due to a particular characteristic all his own or did other grandparents feel the same way? Was George's drive to grandparent something that went beyond a universally acknowledged instinct to perpetuate the species by mating and parenting?

The answers to these questions may be of great practical importance to you in understanding aspects of your own grandparenthood.

Instincts and Drives

To help you to understand the grandparenting instinct fully, I have to get a bit technical and explain the deference between an instinct and a drive. An instinct is an inborn pattern of behavior, a hereditary hard-wiring that initiates certain behaviors necessary for survival. Common to all animals are instincts for self-preservation, feeding, mating, certain parenting behaviors, aggression, and so on. Instincts can be strong or weak, depending on the individual. A drive, however, is the active expression of an instinct. For example, the instinct to reproduce is manifested as a sex drive that leads to mating. The stronger the instinct, the stronger the drive can be.

This said, an instinct is hard-wired in our being, built into our genetic makeup; a drive is a behavior that can be modified. For example, in humans, as in all animals, there is an instinct to reproduce and rear one's young, and most people are physically equipped to do so. Nevertheless, for a number of personal reasons, the instinct may not be expressed as a strong drive in some people. As a result, some people, for whatever reason, may choose not to have children.

On the other hand, instincts and drives may not be able to be fulfilled and have to be compensated for or satisfied in other ways. Using the example above, people who are physically unable to have biological children but have a strong parenting instinct can adopt them. In this way, they fulfill their parenting instinct and drive. Others who can't, or choose not to have children for one reason or another, may get involved with other people's children.

Moira, seventy, has a single adopted daughter, forty-one-year-old Clara. Clara adopted one-year-old Shelby. "Because my daughter wasn't married, I had resigned myself to the fact that I might never be a grandmother," she said. "But as soon as I saw Shelby, I thought, 'this is my granddaughter,' and all my hopes and dreams about having a grandchild to love were fulfilled."

The instinct and drive to grandparent can be fulfilled by a step-grandparent (see Chapter 46, "Stepgrandparenting") too. Lettie, a sixty-seven-year-old stepgrandmother, said, "I have no children, but my grandmother hormones rushed out when I met my two stepgrandchildren." Grandparenting other people's grandchildren is yet another way. Sara, eighty-two, has been a foster grandmother for more than thirty years and has "forty-four grandchildren who are as close to me as they could be."

In my questioning of 120 grandparents about their awareness of a grandparenting instinct, 5 percent of the people reported never being aware of any grandparenting instinct, 40 percent said they felt they were aware of such an instinct before they became grandparents, and 55 percent said they were not aware of an instinct until they had a grandchild (Kornhaber 2001).

Energy and Drive

The grandparenting drive is powered by the grandparenting instinct. To understand how they operate together, it is necessary to understand how energy affects our instincts and drives. All human instincts that are manifested as drives are imbued with energy. The intensity of a given drive varies from person to person (some people are more or less aggressive, sexually active, socially active, etc.). An individual with a high-energy aggressive drive makes an excellent warrior or football player. A person with a low-energy aggressive drive would do better at chess.

A strong grandparenting instinct packaged with an abundance of energy fuels the grandparent drive, which creates an active and involved grandparent.

On the other hand, a grandparent with a low-energy drive may be content with minimal grandparenting effort.

Drive and Grandparenting

This idea may help explain some perplexing situations in your life. For example, why do young grandparents usually treat their grandchildren the same way they treat their children? If we view this situation in terms of energy and drive, and we know that energy is finite and has to be allocated to a number of drives, we can understand that a young grandparent who is still raising her children and holding down a job might not have much energy left over to devote to grandparenting. In this instance, her primary parenting and self-preservation instincts consume all her energy and her grandparenting instinct and drive can be selectively de-energized. A grandparent in such a situation will then treat her grandchild like one of her own children.

Fay, for example, who became a grandmother at thirty-eight, admits that she does not differentiate between her four children and her three-year-old grandchild. "I treat them all the same. I feel like I have five children. My daughter Betsy is my grandson's mom. I treat her like she is his older sister. I'm all mother and very little grandmother as yet."

However, when a person is ready to grandparent, there is amply energy available to power the grandparenting drive. After a person has already raised children to maturity and is psychologically ready to grandparent, nature provides energy to fuel their grandparenting instinct. Those who are ready for grandparenthood hopefully have more time to devote to grandchildren because they may move out of the social mainstream. They may be retired from their job or have an easier, more time-flexible occupation. Their other drives, such as self-preservation, aggression, ambition, and sexuality, which were previously working in high gear, might now be satisfied

Unexpressed energy can cause discomfort. An unfulfilled sex urge is one example. This idea can be applied to grandparenting too. It explains why a grandchildless grandparent-in-waiting, ready and willing to be a grandparent, can feel so frustrated and thwarted.

The concept that a grandparenting drive may be energized differently from person to person, also answers the question of why some grandparents are so attracted to their grandchildren. Mel, sixty-five, is a high-energy grandparent. "My wife and I have moved three times just so that we can be near our son, his wife, and our four grandchildren. Since I am retired with a good pension, I am fortunate to be able to do this. Nothing else is more important to me at this time in my life than being a good grandfather and helping my son and his wife. For some reason, I feel I have a very strong urge to be a grandfather. Perhaps an even stronger urge than I had to be a father."

How Grandparents Perceive the Instinct

My experience shows that people become conscious of their grandparenting instinct at different times in their lives. Some perceive the presence of a grandparenting instinct early, even before the first grandchild arrives. Rosalie, sixty-five, says, "I always had a very strong desire to be a grandmother. This desire is the fuel of my grandmotherhood. I couldn't wait until my first grandchild was born."

A majority of people in my study reported feeling a grandparenting instinct, and an accompanying drive that involved feeling, thinking, and acting as a grandparent, only after the grandchild arrived. However the drive is perceived, it is expressed in a highly individualized way that depends on factors related to both nature and nurture. Among them are the strength of an individual's instinct, the individual's personality, and his or her personal and social experience.

Cynthia McGreal (1985) examined the expectations of 146 grandparents before and after the birth of the first grandchild and found evidence of a pre-grandparenthood rehearsal process. The study also noted (and was confirmed by my subsequent studies) that women anticipated the role before men did. As Corinne, a fifty-six-year-old grandmother of six, says, "I wanted to have children, and I wanted to have grandchildren. I am a good grandmother because I just naturally am. I always looked forward to being a grandparent even though all my grandparents died before I was four years old." Her husband Otto noted that he only became interested in being a grandfather after the first grandchild came along. "I never thought much about being a grandparent before the grandkids came along. Corinne, however, often talked about it. When the grandkids arrived I knew what she was talking about."

Like Otto, the birth of a grandchild puts many grandparents in touch with their grandparenting instinct. Bridget, seventy-five, reports her grandparenting instinct was triggered when she bonded with her new grandchild. It took Bridget a while to understand that she had a grandparenting instinct at all. "When I was younger, I really didn't care if I had children or grandchildren. I had no particular longing for them. But once my children and grandchildren came along, I loved them. Now I couldn't bear the thought of not having them. But if you asked me before the children came along if I had an instinct to parent or grandparent I would have said no. I grew close to them over time."

Like Bridget, many people who never gave much thought to grandparenting before their grandchild was born reported experiencing an undeniable urge to grandparent as soon as they saw and held their new grandchild.

When people are conscious of an urge to grandparent they describe their experience in emotional and spiritual terms. They use expressions such as "personal meaning," "spiritual meaning," "a need to be a grandparent," "joyfulness," "the meaning of life," "a need to protect my grandchild," and "it feels good to continue the generations." One grandmother, a psychologist, believes her instinct was "related to emotion, continuity, meaning, and role fulfillment."

Learning and the Grandparenting Drive

For better or worse your life experience impacts your grandparenting drive. Positive examples set by grandparents, resulting in a happy grandchildhood, establish positive grandparenting awareness. "I'm naturally a devoted grandfather," says Norbert, sixty-seven, "but I also learned a great deal by example from my own grandfather, and the example of my father who was a wonderful grandfather to my kids." Like Norbert, children who have been well grandparented usually look forward to the day when they will become a grandparent. Seth, twelve, says, "I want to be a good grandpa to the grandchildren I will have because my grandpa and I have so much fun together."

On the other hand a negative experience can impact the grandparenting instinct negatively. Jim, sixty-six says he was completely turned off by the grandparenting idea because he was badly treated by his own grandmother. Many people with negative experiences concerning a grandparent have a negative bias toward the role until they live it themselves.

Parenting experience is important too. For some, grandparenting is a continuation of a natural instinct to parent. These people report being sensitized to the presence of a grandparenting instinct because they have experienced a strong parental instinct and were happy and fulfilled as parents. An individual's enthusiasm for the role of grandparent is further reinforced if his or her own parents and children have a good relationship. In fact, parents who understand the importance of the grandparent-grandchild relationship usually go out of their way to support the relationship of their child with their child's grandparent. Tom, forty-two, brings his children and parents together as much as possible. "It's not easy sometimes to drive my son Charlie to his grandparent's house for the day, but I make sure I do it come hell or high water. Hopefully Charlie will go out of his way to drive his kids to my house one day. Then I can enjoy the perks of being a granddad."

Evolution of the Grandparenting Drive

The more "ready" a person is to be a grandparent the more palpable the instinct. For example, the phrase "I can't wait to be a grandparent," uttered by many grandparents-in-waiting, signals the stirrings of an instinct and drive waiting to be energized into action. Before the first grandchild is born, the instinct can reach an individual's awareness emotionally and intellectually in terms of longing to care for a grandchild, or daydreaming about what it would be like to play with a grandchild. One grandmother expressed her latent instinct in terms of fantasizing about shopping. "I can't wait for my daughter to have a baby. I walk past these cute children's clothing stores and I have no one to buy for. When my first granddaughter comes along, buy stock in those stores because I am going to buy everything in sight!"

The latent instinct emerges into a grandparent's consciousness with the birth of the first grandchild (even in cases when the grandparent is not present at the birth) and becomes a drive to action. When the grandparent first sees and holds a new grandchild a powerful bonding experience ensues; it is reinforced with continued contact (see Chapter 24, "Birth of a Grandchild"). The birth of a child induces what developmental psychologists call "approach and caretaking behavior" in its parents and grandparents. This brings grandparenting thoughts, feelings, and actions into the conscious level. That is why I feel it is so important for grandparents to be physically present when their grandchild is born.

That said, the feelings about becoming a grandparent can transcend distance. Even when grandparents cannot attend their grandchild's birth, they nevertheless are profoundly moved. Some have told me that they knew the exact moment when their grandchild was born without being told.

Mannie, sixty-two, is a long-distance grandfather who was unable to attend the birth of his first grandchild. One evening after dinner he told his wife, "The baby's here!" A little while later his daughter called him from the hospital. He was elated. He asked her to hold the phone near his grandchild so he could hear her. "I felt wonderful," he said. "I wanted to do something, to hold the baby. 'I am a grandfather!' I told myself. How pleased I was, but also very frustrated that I couldn't be near them. So I walked around in circles and called everyone I knew to give them the news. I was like a car going fifty miles an hour with the brakes on. The next day when I walked outside, I looked at babies differently. I just couldn't wait to see my new granddaughter." When I asked him how he knew the baby had come without anyone telling him, he replied, "I just know these kinds of things."

Grandparent Drive and Grandparent Identity

When a grandchild is born, the new grandparent's latent (inactive) grandparenting instinct becomes functional (active). Frances, fifty-one and a new grandmother, explains, "I used to spend a lot of time thinking about one day having a grandchild [this is the rehearsal process that indicates a latent grandparenting identity]. I was really looking forward to my daughter becoming pregnant. When

I saw little Patty being born my heart soared [activation of grandparenting drive]. I knew that I would do anything to be close to her, help protect her, help her parents raise her and see her grow up. I knew that being a grandmother was going to be the most important part of my later life." At the point when her grandchild was born, Frances started functioning as a grandmother [I call this her "functional" grandparent identity].

Frances's enthusiasm is supported by Myra, sixty-six, who "went crazy with joy" when her daughter, who was six months pregnant, invited her to see her unborn granddaughter on an ultrasound in the doctor's office. "I immediately went shopping," she said.

Factors Affecting Grandparenting Drive

Having a drive is one thing. But as Percy, fifty-four, will tell you, "Wanting to be a good grandparent is one thing. Doing it is another. To be a good grandparent means being available and spending time with your grandchild. Finding the time and energy to do the job with all that's going on today is tough." As Percy knows the grandparenting drive can be reinforced, diminished, or frustrated by external circumstances. For example, Mannie, the long-distance grandfather mentioned earlier, experienced a sense of frustration from living so far away from his grandchild when she was born.

Society's attitudes toward grandparenting can strongly influence how individual grandparents value themselves in the role. Juana, forty-six, is aware that she possesses a high-energy drive to grandparent. Fortunately she lives in a culture where grandparents and grandparenting are valued and respected. "I know how to be a good grandmother and I have a strong urge to do so. I also know that I will be important and honored by my family, my community, and my church for being a grandmother, as my mother and grandmother are. This is a wonderful part of life that I look forward to with all my being."

On the other side of the coin, Bill, a sixty-four-year-old grandfather of three, lives in an adults-only retirement community in southern Florida. His neighbors are all long-distance grandparents and not very involved in their grandchildren's lives. Grandparenting is devalued in this subculture, and Bill accepts the notion that being a grandparent means being old. "There are not many grandkids around here, except for sometimes during the holidays. I see mine from time to time. Don't get me wrong; I love my grandkids, but being called a grandfather means being old to me. That is why I told my grandkids, 'whatever you do, don't call me grandpa! Especially in public.' So they just call me Bill." Bill's attitude arises from a low parenting and grandparenting instinct. Although he is willing to assume his grandparent role from time to time, he does not place much value on the role. His wife, Bess, calls him a perpetual adolescent. His grandchildren are not close to him, but they report that Bill can be fun to be with. At this moment, Bill's role with his grandchildren is limited to that of an occasional pal with little serious involvement. In terms of the theory of an instinct to grandparent, one would say that Bill has a weak grandparenting instinct and a low drive. Therefore, his involvement as a grandparent will have a tendency to be minimal and tenuous.

The grandparenting instinct and drive can be frustrated or blocked when willing grandparents have no grandchild, or when family conflicts or geographical distance interferes with access to grandchildren.

Grandparents-in-Waiting

There are many grandparents-in-waiting who are anxiously counting the days until they have a grandchild. Blema, sixty-eight, is one of them. Her unmarried daughter Julie, forty and twice divorced, has decided to stay single and to adopt a child. "I am keeping a hope chest for my new grandchild and am very excited about her arrival. But I must admit that I wish I had had a grandchild earlier. I feel I have wasted so many years. However, it is not in my hands. Julie's career always came first, even now. I know it always annoyed her, but maybe it also helped when I used to say the clock was ticking. But I really meant it was also my grandmother clock that was ticking! Now I'm happy and looking forward to being a terrific grandma."

When grandparents-in-waiting can't contain their impatience it can be hard on potential parents-to-be. Too often they are subjected to their own parents nagging them to deliver the goods. "My mother is driving me nuts. Every time I see her she asks me when I'm going to get pregnant," says Matisse, thirty-seven. "Mom had four kids when she was my age and none of my brothers and sisters are even married yet. My husband and I have only been married four years and we don't want to be tied down with a child yet."

When potential parents are unsure about if and when they want a child, it is better for them to make this clear and for grandparents-in-waiting to accept their decision and to be understanding and supportive of their wishes. In this sensitive area putting pressure on potential parents usually creates more problems than it solves. One thing grandparents-in-waiting can do until a grandchild comes along is to be surrogate grandparents to other people's grandchildren. This is a great way to give expression to a grandparenting instinct.

Technological advances in the field of fertility and the broadening of parameters defining who can adopt children, have led to an increase in the number of gays and lesbians starting families (see Chapter 39, "Gay and Lesbian Issues").

As a result, formerly frustrated grandparents-in-waiting are now thrilled grandparents. Stella, sixty-six, never thought she would be a grandmother. When her only son, Fred, thirty-three and gay, first mentioned adopting a child she was taken aback. But after Fred and his partner adopted a little girl, Pier, Stella became quickly involved in caretaking her granddaughter (in other words, her grandparent drive became quickly activated). "I now have a grandchild and that's all that matters," Stella enthuses. "Fred is happy because he has given me something I never thought I would have." Fred agrees. "One of the greatest worries I had about being gay was that I was ending the family line and wouldn't be able to give my mother a grandchild. Now she is so happy. Pier is going to have a hell of a grandmother."

Family Problems

Having a grandchild is one thing; having access is another. That is because the parents' support and cooperation are always necessary. When these things are withheld because of problems among family members, the loving bond with grandchildren can be interfered with, or even severed completely. This situation is all too common today. Divorce and remarriage, personality conflicts, illness, drug abuse, and many other personal and social problems cause conflicts between parents and grandparents. When problems spin out of control, estranging parents and grandparents from one another, the grandparent-grandchild relationship becomes a casualty.

There are millions of grandparents in the United States today who suffer this type of grandchild deprivation. These grandparents love their grandchildren dearly (and vice-versa), but are forbidden to see them. Although the circumstances surrounding this issue are complicated (and are dealt with in depth in Chapters 33, "Between Parents and Grandparents," and 42, "Legal Issues"), many grandparents whose grandparenting instinct is stifled by parental action suffer intense frustration and even clinical depression. When this happens the children and parents also suffer. That is yet another reason why it is so important to work out family problems.

Geographical distance can adversely affect grandparent-grandchild relationships. However, attention and effort can do much to minimize the damage. For more on this topic see Chapters 43, "Long-Distance Grandparenting," and 36, "Cybergrandparenting."

GUIDELINES

Now that you are aware of your grandparenting instinct and how it relates to the way you think, feel, and act as a grandparent, here are some guidelines to help you use this information to enhance your grandparenting.

- Remember, your grandparenting instinct is a feeling; your drive entails feeling, thinking, and "doing."
- Try to get in touch with the strength of your instinct to grandparent. When did you become aware of it? Is it weak or strong? Did it feel stronger when your grandchild was born? How has it changed over the years? How do you express it now as a drive?

- Share with the parents and your grandchild your personal experience as a grandparent. Discuss the idea of drive and instinct.
- Be aware of what fulfills or frustrates the expression of your grandparenting instinct and drive. What increases and decreases its energy?
- Try to identify obstacles that affect the expression of your grandparenting drive. Then deal with them.
- Discuss your grandparenting instinct with your peers.
- Do your best to attend the birth of your grandchild.

CONCLUSION

The grandparenting instinct is the biological engine of grandparenting. Our studies demonstrate that most people experience it in one way or another. It is important that you become aware of how your own grandparenting instinct operates and how it is expressed in a grandparenting drive. When the instinct is thwarted, everyone suffers. When the instinct is allowed full expression and is recognized, validated, and celebrated by society, everyone benefits.

CHAPTER 15

Temperament and Personality

Y our personality and temperament profoundly affect your growth and development as a grandparent and your relationship with your grandchild. It is common knowledge that people with similar personalities and temperaments typically get along best. This certainly holds true for the relationship between you and your grandchild (see Chapter 26, "Favoritism").

Temperament is a quality of character that determines the emotional and psychological behavior. How your temperament fits together with your grandchild's will be a major factor, for better or worse, in determining how seamlessly the two of you get along. This applies whether you are a biological grandparent, stepgrandparent, or have adopted grandchildren. And it holds true whether you live near or far from your grandchild.

All About Temperament

Your temperament can be best described as your typical pattern of thinking, behaving, or reacting. There are many different types of temperament. Observe the personalities of your family and friends. Notice how some seem full of life and enthusiasm, while others are more laid-back or even lethargic. Some talk incessantly, others rarely speak unless spoken to. You may have a friend that is a reserved intellectual and another who hates to read. Maybe someone in your family is a party person and others are happier by themselves. All of us possess specific traits that drive our attitudes and behavior. These traits make up our temperament.

Temperament comprises an important part of what we describe as our "personality." For example, people described as having an outgoing personality usually possess the temperamental traits of an extrovert; in other words, they are usually verbal, like to socialize, and have a good sense of humor. Those with a more introverted personality prefer solitude and limited social activity. All of us possess a unique mixture of temperamental traits that influence us in a variety of ways. And each type of temperament can be an asset or a liability depending on the circumstances.

Temperament affects us intrapersonally and to some extent determines how we deal with ourselves internally—personally—through our thoughts, feelings, and actions. It also affects us interpersonally, determining the mechanisms by which we get along with others, either individually or in groups.

People who share similar temperaments tend to attract one another and get along well. People with dissimilar temperaments may rub each other the wrong way or even antagonize one another. The adage that "opposites attract" is appropriate only if someone is looking for a good brawl.

Types of Temperament

Psychiatrists Alexander Thomas and Stella Chess (1968) have described the qualities of nine different types of temperament. Answering the following questions related to each type of temperament they describe will show you a bit more about your own temperament and your grandchild's.

- Activity Level: How active or passive are you? Are you a morning person or a night person? Are you full of pep or somewhat sedentary?

- Regularity of Patterns: Are your work, feeding, sleeping, and other habits orderly or chaotic? Are regularity and consistency important?
- Approach or Withdrawal: Do you respond to new situations with hesitancy and reluctance or with enthusiasm?
- Adaptability: Are you resistant to change or easily adaptable to new situations?
- Threshold of Responsiveness: Do you react quickly to new situations or does it take a while for you to respond? Do you hide your feelings?
- Intensity of Reaction: Are you highly emotional?
- Quality of Mood: Are you an upbeat person—optimistic and cheerful—or pessimistic and slow to warm up to people?
- Distractibility: Does your mind bounce from subject to subject or can you stay focused long periods of time? Are you highly organized or laissez-faire?
- Attention Span and Persistence: Do you have difficulty listening to others without losing attention? Do you have trouble sticking with a task until completion?

From this constellation of traits, three temperamental "clusters" are used to categorize individuals as easy, difficult, and slow to warm up. The categories describe people who are easygoing, those who are hard to get along with, and those it takes a long time to get to know. For example, people who are approachable, relate easily, and are full of energy and optimism fall into the "easy" category. Others who are shy, pessimistic, agitated, or always moving or talking may be considered difficult. Those who are slow to adapt to new situations, do not like change, and have a low level of responsiveness are deemed slow to warm up. Of course, these general categories have nothing to do with being a good, kind, and loving person.

These categories can be helpful, however, in understanding what is going right and wrong between you and your grandchild. First, take a moment to consider how you would categorize your temperament. Now think about your grandchild's temperament. Are they at all similar? Are you easy with one another or do you tend to rub one another the wrong way from time to time? Do your personalities fit with one another?

Fit

You and your grandchild will automatically get along well if your temperaments are a good fit. As Ossie, a seventy-two-year-old grandfather said. "I'm an early riser and so is my granddaughter, Leshawna. When I stay at my daughter's house and go down to make coffee early in the morning, there is Leshawna with her little shining face. She always pours out the orange juice for both of us 'cause we're the early birds in the family."

Clara, forty-nine, recognizes her fit with her grandson. "Me and my grandson Sonny are two peas in a pod—same interests, same way of looking at things."

The concept of fit extends beyond temperament. Sometimes an exaggerated dose of a particular personality characteristic can cause trouble. For example, an overemotional grandparent (tending toward the "hysterical" in psychological terms) may tend to overreact or worry too much in the eyes of a grandchild. A slightly paranoid grandparent, expressing fear and caution too often, may frighten a child. A highly organized grandparent might upset a grandchild with an obsession for manners, order, and neatness to the point where the child will not enjoy spending time together because he can't do anything right in the eyes of a compulsive grandparent.

On the other hand, when balanced in a healthy way, the same traits can offer positive lessons to a grandchild. An emotional grandparent can be a lot of fun and teach spontaneity, openness, and imaginativeness. A cautious grandparent teaches alertness to danger. A compulsive grandparent can teach orderliness, thrift, and neatness.

Similar personality types tend to have similar interests. Good athletes will play together. Singers will sing together. Emotional people will emote together. Nature lovers will enjoy being out in nature together, and so on. A passive grandparent and grandchild may play cards together for hours. A compulsive grand-parent and grandchild might enjoy cleaning house together or playing with a computer. Artistic grandparents and grandchildren will draw or design clothes together.

Mix and Match

If there is a personality, temperament, or personal interest mismatch, watch out for trouble. Elvis, sixty-two, is an easy, active, and aggressive grandfather. He was a very active athlete in his day and still tries to play sports whenever he can. Although Elvis has continually tried to get his ten-year-old grandson, Josh, involved in sports, Josh is "slow to warm up," shy, and not athletically inclined. "I hate baseball and soccer," Josh says. "I'm afraid of getting hit in the face by the ball. In fact one day I did and my nose bled really hard. I am not a good ath-lete." Elvis admits being turned off by Josh's lack of enthusiasm. "I love Josh and I thought I could share my love of sports with him. He is kind of, I hate to say it, but he's kind of a chicken." Fortunately Elvis made some adjustments in the activities he shares with Josh. These days they fly kites and play computer games together.

Rowena, fifty-nine, has a problem with her grandson who "never sits still. I'm losing weight trying to keep up with him. It's just constant. He never stops. I'm not the most energetic person. I am waiting for a nice calm grandchild."

Acknowledge the Differences

Having a difference in temperament from your grandchild does not necessarily mean you are going to have problems. Once you acknowledge and understand the nature of the temperamental differences, you have made the first and most important step in finding your middle ground.

It is also important to understand that the fit you share with your grand-child is dynamic and will change as your grandchild matures. You might fit each other better at one age than another. An imaginative grandfather might be a big success spinning outrageous yarns for a magical-thinking four-year-old grand-child. But he'll have a bit more difficulty convincing a literal seven-year-old of the veracity of his stories; the child's relentless rational questioning may even anger him. A compulsive grandmother might have trouble with a rebellious two-year-old whom she sees as disrespectful, yet she may take excellent care of compliant infants or older children. An adolescent may relate with greater interest to a working grandparent actively involved in the world than one who is isolated and uninvolved. In fact grandchildren who end up working in the family business usually fit well with the parent and grandparent who work there. The ones who do not fit usually move on—the stuff of which drama is made.

Blending Temperaments and Personalities

If your grandchild's temperament is different from your own, you have to find a middle ground to reach her. One "hard-livin'" Mississippi grandfather, self-described (and proudly, I might add) as a "loud redneck," solved this problem by taking his very shy granddaughter fishing. "She don't have to say a thing when we're sitting out there waiting for the catfish to bite," he said. A sedentary grand-mother found a way to have fun with her hyperactive grandson by playing, in her words, "knock-down, drag-out card games. We also go to see action movies together. That seems to hold my grandson's attention."

Finding the middle ground can sometimes be difficult if you are going against your own nature. Understand that it's not necessarily personality differences that cause relationship problems. It's the way they are handled. There is no right or wrong when it comes to temperament. We are not responsible for the way we are made. We are, however, responsible for what we do about it.

One mistake many people make is to criticize one another for their differences in temperament instead of accepting the person the way they came into the world. Criticizing the other person will most often drive them away and set a bad example. Harry, sixty-eight, learned this the hard way. "We had a great time together when my granddaughter Flo was a baby. When she got to be five I found that I was nagging her because she always kept forgetting stuff and leaving stuff around. Sometimes she didn't pay attention. I started to poke fun at her sometimes because she just seemed to not be thinking. Actually I nicknamed her 'airhead' but I didn't say it in a mean way. One day my daughter-in-law came to me and told me Flo was unhappy with me. She told her mom that I was mean. Well, I was floored, let me tell you. Sick to my stomach was more like it. I did something about it quick. I love Flo. I took her on a long walk and we talked. I told her I wanted to know what she thought of me and she told me I hurt her feelings and she didn't like to be called airhead. So, I apologized for hurting her. I told her I wasn't the most sensitive person and that she was teaching me to be more sensitive. I said I would not call her airhead anymore. And I stopped all the nagging. I can tell she's much happier now when we're together."

GUIDELINES

I have tried to highlight some of the important points about how personality might affect your relationships with your grandchildren. Here are some guidelines to help you to have a better fit.

- Know thyself. Assess your own temperament in terms of its assets and liabilities. See the categories above.
- Know your grandchild. What type of temperament does she have? How do you fit naturally? Are you both an easy fit? If not, where are the differences?
- Make adjustments in the light of this new awareness. Find the temperamental middle ground and spend lots of time there.
- Children grow and change rapidly. You grow and change too. Be alert to the fact that your fit might change, too.
- Serve as an example. Teach everyone in the family about temperament, announce your own temperamental liabilities, and let your family know how you manage its challenges. That way you will set a great example.

Conclusion

Be conscious of your own temperamental makeup as well as that of your grand-child. If you "fit" with one another, so much the better. If not, do some detective work. Identify your differences and make an effort to find a common ground where you are both at ease. Set the example and watch your relationship blossom.

CHAPTER 16

Young Grandparents

A lthough the age can affect the roles a grandparent chooses to emphasize (for example, an eighty-five-year-old grandmother may be more a family historian than a buddy), it impacts little on the quality of grandparenting. The primary influence that age has on grandparenting is in terms of one's readiness to be a grandparent. Readiness to grandparent depends on finishing the hands-on parenting of one's own children. Young grandparents, who are in the middle of parenting, will naturally find it difficult to gather the time and energy necessary to grandparent a new generation when they have their own young children to raise.

On the other end of the age spectrum, the expanding generation of great-grandparents also finds differences in the way they behave as great-grandparents and the way they handled things as grandparents. If you are a young grandparent, or a great-grandparent (now or in the future) the next two chapters will explain how these permutations of grandparenting affect you, your grandchildren, and the rest of your family.

Although grandparenthood is often considered a mid- to later-life phenomenon, that is not always the case. Many people in their thirties and forties are grandparents. These often reluctant "young" grandparents face a very special, and sometimes overwhelming, challenge in balancing the new role of grand-parent with other consuming roles (parent, child, spouse, worker) before they are developmentally and socially ready to do so.

I define a young grandparent to be about age forty-five or under. I use the age of forty-five because it is an average time when most parents have children who are socially (although not financially) self-sufficient. Although being a young grandparent is certainly not a new phenomenon (when the human lifes-pan was shorter people became grandparents at an earlier age), it nevertheless poses many difficulties concerning role boundaries and family logistics—espe-cially in today's hectic times. Young grandparents (unless someone married an older person and inherited a grandchild) were young parents. Take Katia, who was thirty-two when she became a grandparent. Her mother was 50-years-old, her grandmother 66-years-old and her great-grandmother 82-years-old. Katia's granddaughter, Sonya, became the youngest member of six living generations. Imagine what Katia has to go through to fulfill all of her roles for her biologi-cal family, her husband, and her part-time job! How much time and energy does she have available to be a devoted grandmother?

Like Katia, the majority of young grandparents, are usually still fully involved in parenthood and therefore have little time or energy to devote to grandparenting. In other words, they are not emotionally, or socially ready to be grandparents. They are out of step with normal development because, as we know, grandparenthood comes more naturally when one has emerged from par-enthood and acquired the skills and qualities normally associated with grand-parenting (see Chapter 13, "Grandparent Development").

A Welcome Event . . . Maybe

To a young mother, the arrival of a new grandchild may or may not be a wel-come event, depending on the circumstances and the culture. For example, Ella, thirty-eight, was unperturbed when her sixteen-year-old daughter got pregnant. "It's always been like this in my family," she said. "We have our babies young and over with by the time we're twenty. I had four before I was 21." On the other hand, when Barb found out her seventeen-year-old daughter got pregnant she was furious. And even more so when her daughter decided to get married and keep the baby. "I am caught off base. Heck, I am only 39," Barb said. "I've got three children and a full-time job. My husband and I are not ready to be grandparents."

A Reluctant Grandparent

Among the most common emotional and psychological problems young grandparents experience is the lack of readiness for grandparenthood and family role blockage. Those who resent their young child having a baby initially may not welcome the baby as enthusiastically as they would a grandchild they were longing for. Young grandparents may get upset when they find out their child is pregnant, and they may find themselves disturbed when they have to make major accommodations to deal with the event in a constructive way. Through no fault of their own, their lives are suddenly very different.

If a person cannot adapt to these changes, his or her grandparent role is blocked. Such a person does not proceed into the next generation, but rather becomes more of a *parent* to the grandchild. The family remains two-generational. When such blockage occurs, the new baby ends up being treated as just another child in the family, and a sibling to its young parent.

"I have a grandchild," said Lupe. "But I am not a grandmother because I'm only thirty-five years old. I don't act like a grandmother at all. My grandchild is just like one of my children and Aria, her mother, is still my child in high school. I have no grandmother feelings because I am still a mother." Clearly Lupe's step up to grandmotherhood—beyond in the biological sense—has been blocked by her daughter's youth and the family configuration.

Some of the grandparent magic is lost when children view their grandparent more as a parent (see Chapter 41, "Raising Grandchildren"). However, if the adults cope well with such circumstances, the children will too. Reggie was raised by his grandmother, who was "more a mother than a grandmother" to him. Although his single unwed mother "did the best she could," Reggie recognized that his grandmother played the mother role, and his great-grandmother acted like a grandmother. "Mama" was his grandmother and "Celia" was his mother. "Grandma" was his great-grandmother, and "Grandpa," his great-grandfather. Like many other children raised in a similar family configuration, Reggie was far from unhappy. "My mother and grandmother fought a lot about who was going to do what with me, but I got a lot of attention so I didn't complain." Experience shows that children raised in similar family circumstances certainly do not seem the worse for it, especially when there are men in the picture.

Generational Continuity Established

It poses less of a problem for a young grandparent when the parents are married and/or live independently in their own household. In this situation, generational progression isn't blocked. Therefore, the roles and functions of grandparenthood remain clear and intact with perhaps some extra emphasis on helping to support the new young parents.

It is especially important for young grandparents to be aware of the idea of family blockage and to try to maintain as strong a grandparental a role as possible. Isayo's daughter gave birth at age fifteen. Isayo took care of her grandson while her daughter attended school, but she gave him over to her daughter completely at the end of the school day. "I am not going to become a mother to my grandson," she said. "I want to be his grandmother." Although it was difficult to juggle the two roles, especially considering her young daughter's need for a social life, she was successful. As her daughter said, "My mother takes over a lot, but it's OK because she knows more than me. But she also respects that I am the mother, and my son calls me Mom and my mother Grandma. That's the way it should be."

GUIDELINES

If you are a young grandparent, it is important to take time to reflect carefully about how this role affects your life. Whether you relish the role or not, you can certainly make the best of it. Remember your grandchild will never know the difference and will love you whatever your age. Here are some guidelines to help.

- Understand your feelings about being a young grandparent. If you are not happy, talk about it with someone and work through your feelings. Be sure to identify specific issues and take steps to remedy them.
- Understand that your family situation will be different depending on whether your child is married and where they live.
- Realize that the younger your child, the more generational blockage is likely to exist. It is important to recognize how this affects the family and to deal with it. You will most likely have to act in a parental role, at least some of the time, with your grandchild.
- Be sure to let your grandchild know that you are the grandparent and not the parent. This will greatly support the parent-child relationship and give a positive message to the young parent. Furthermore, it will leave you plenty of room to be a grandparent.
- Remember your grandchild will love you all the more if you are a young grandparent because you will have a longer lifetime together.

CONCLUSION

Being a young grandparent brings many opportunities as well as challenges. The most important thing a young grandparent needs to know is that the grandchild is not even aware of the difference—a grandparent is a grandparent. The main advantage to being a young grandparent is that you can revel in the role for most of your life. The point is to make the best of the situation, accept the burden or joy (however you look at it) of the extra years of child care, support your grandchild's parents, and, in so doing, create an enduring and loving three- and four-generational family.

CHAPTER 17

Great-Grandparents

T oday's increased longevity is expanding the family's vertical lineage and swelling the worldwide ranks of great-grandparents. Because this is such a recent development, the Census Bureau does not yet have reliable statistics on the population of great-grandparents in the United States. Only during the last decades of the twentieth century did researchers focus attention on this phenomenon. The completion of the first phase of the Human Genome Project pointed out our increased longevity. Grandparents will be around for a longer time and therefore will have an increased opportunity to become great-grandparents. Investigators Roberto and Stroes (1992) pointed out that 50 percent of all older adults with children could become great-grandparents. This means that the odds are pretty good that you will have a serious chance of becoming a great-grandparent one day.

Although the rise in the population of great-grandparents is beginning to stimulate widespread study, there currently is sparse information about this stage in life. Nevertheless, I will point out some unique aspects of this role and highlight issues that should be explored in greater depth; for example, the difference between grandparenting and great-grandparenting, and the effects of age.

Grandparenting and Great-Grandparenting

The great-grandparent role is an extension of the grandparent role, and, like grandparenting, is played out differently according to each individual and their life circumstances. Like grandparenting, involvement and satisfaction in the role are affected by age, vitality, personal characteristics, and family structure.

Great-grandparenthood is essentially a continuation of grandparenthood in that all the roles are the same, but they are enacted differently (see Chapter 1, "Grandparent Roles"). The younger the great-grandparent the more this holds true. Many of the same issues—distance, divorce, etc.—confront both generations of grandparents and great-grandparents today.

The longer great-grandparents live, the more family members they can accumulate. Because longer life spans increase the chances of remarriage, great-grandparents can often be step-great-grandparents for a great-grandchild and great-grandparents to an adopted great-grandchild. Some great-grandparents complain about being overwhelmed by the number of grandchildren. As ninety-two-year-old Eva says, "I've got great-grandchildren all over the country. Over thirty of them, some I have never even seen. But I never miss a birthday so I'm probably a main support of the greeting card companies."

Roles

For the most part, great-grandparents continue playing their traditional grand-parental roles; the difference is that some of the roles take on an added dimension that age confers. This occurs most often with the more symbolic roles, such as ancestor, historian, role model, and spiritual guide. These are also roles that do not require a great deal of physical health for implementation. In fact, increased age means increased time to mature and accumulate family history, and to serve as a living ancestor for more people. The roles of teacher and student are enhanced as one ages too. The older we are the more we can teach, and learn. If a great-grandchild is physically available, a great-grandparent can be an especially able mentor for a child. My research findings to date also hint that the more passive the great-grandparent, the more her symbolic roles expand. The converse holds true as well. The active roles, such as hands-on nurturer and buddy, are negatively affected by increased physical limitations of the great-grandparent, but not always. Sarah, ninety-five, still plays bridge regularly with her great-great-granddaughter as her partner (buddy).

Family Response

When a grandparent becomes a great-grandparent, there is a generational shift in family relationships. The new great-grandparent relinquishes her former primary grandparenting role to the next generation. People respond to this shift differently. The way they handle the shift depends on the specific family and how well they get along. Some great-grandparents report feeling disempowered, nudged a bit to the family outskirts by the younger generations. Sometimes this is welcome, sometimes not. It all depends on the individual's vitality and desire. "I'd rather leave things to the younger folks," says one ninety-four-year-old great-grandfather. Other great-grandparents enjoy maintaining their role in the family. "The more people in the family and the more involvement I have, the better," as Celia, a ninety-two-year-old great-grandmother, puts it. "I am a great-grandmother, grandmother, and mother, all at once. I've got lots to do."

Most families seem to derive intense satisfaction from their vertical extension. And most new grandparents do not seem to have any problem with their parent becoming a great-grandparent. Leonard, eighty-nine, had a party when he became a great-grandfather. "The family photo we had taken with all of us, with me right in the center, was one of the proudest moments of my life," he said. His son, William, sixty, said he was happy his dad was a "patriarch." "I'll be in the middle of the family photo one day, too," William said.

Age

Since the age of a great-grandparent can vary, other factors such as culture, the age of parenthood, and family size affect how the individual accepts and enacts their role. Some families contain thirty-five-year-old grandparents, fifty-five-year-old great-grandparents, seventy-five-year-old great-great-grandparents, and hundred-year-old great-great-great-grandparents. In such families—and they are on the increase—individual variations of personal vitality, sometimes even more than age, will determine the quality of great-grandparenthood. For example, I know a great-grandparent who assumed many of the grandparents' roles because both grandparents were debilitated, while the great-grandparent was physically fit and in good health.

Vitality

I use the term *vitality* to refer to the health of an individual's spirit. The vitality of the great-grandparent is the engine of involvement in the life of the great-grandchild. The more vital the great-grandparent, the more active she is and the broader the roles she plays for her family. Six-year-old Nicole's vital great-grandmother, Mamie, is still able to climb the five flights to the apartment where Nicole lives. She visits daily and even baby-sits on occasion. "I've climbed stairs all my life," she says, "I'm not going to stop now, especially when Nicole is waiting for me."

One eighty-one-year-old great-grandfather, a retired physician, took his great-grandson Phillip to visit his native village in Greece. "I never thought I would ever do such a thing at my age," he laughed, "but I'm in great shape, so why not?"

Vitality is not necessarily limited to a physical state. On the contrary, physical limitations do not have to impair spiritual or emotional vitality. Emma, twelve, is very close to her wheelchair-bound great-grandmother because, "Great-Grandma is so much fun. She's always making jokes and teaching me something. We are sewing a quilt together. Her hands are kind of shaky, but she can still tell me how to do it."

The Emergence of a New Characteristic?

For the most part personality affects the quality of great-grandparenting in the same way that it affects grandparenting. However, I have noticed one way that great-grandparenting can affect personality. It concerns a newfound sense of adventurousness, almost a devil-may-care attitude on the part of some great-grandparents.

Here is one example: Preston, a formerly conservative seventy-five-year-old, planned to take his grandchildren and great-grandchildren on a trip into the Grand Canyon. "What have I got to lose?" he said. "If I collapse doing it, it'll be a great way to go." Livia, seventy-six, has a sum total of forty-two children, grandchildren, and great-grandchildren. She recently fulfilled a longtime dream. "I always dreamed of going windsurfing. So I did it, not as good as I would have done it fifty years ago, but I did it." The whole family got a kick out of it, especially her great-granddaughter Heather, twelve: "My great-grandma does what she wants and doesn't care what anyone thinks," she said.

Some great-grandparents do things they never dreamed of doing even when they were grandparents—and with flair. This attitude may indicate the emergence of a new characteristic in members of this generation who are surprised to find themselves so healthy at such advanced ages. Perry, eighty-six, says, "Heck, I never thought I would live this long, so I just do whatever I want. What do I have to lose? Would you believe that I play tennis twice a week with a bunch of guys my age? Sometimes a partner complains when he makes a bad shot. Then I tell him stop complaining. At least we're out there on the court and can hit the ball! That's my scorecard. If I'm standing on my own two feet, I'm already ahead of the game!"

Grandparent Emeritus

We are currently witnessing the beginning of a new and different type of great-grandparenthood and setting new standards for this expanded stage of life. Many of today's great-grandparents seem to know this. Kiki, an eighteen-year-old college student, calls her ninety-one-year-old great-grandmother, "Grandma Emeritus." Kiki says, "My great-grandma is kind of retired, but my relationship with her is easy and fluid. It's different from my relationship with my grandmother, which is more intense. Great-grandma is so laid back and since she can't do too much physical activity, we usually spend time talking or watching TV. She's amazing. She can name all the old actors, even in the silent films! I love to hear her talk about her life. My mother and I like to visit her together because it's her grandmother. It's like we have a grandmother in common."

In the grand design of the traditional three-generational continuum, we know that parents are directly responsible for their child's immediate safety and security, and grandparents are the second line of defense. So, what happens with this new generation of great-grandparents? This raises some intriguing questions: What is the new emeritus role about? Where does it fit in? Will today's great-grandparent replace the old grandparent stereotypes of the last century while the new generation of grandparents carves out new roles and responsibilities? Will great-grandparents serve as a grandparent backup system, as grandparents do for parents? For example, millions of grandparents are raising their grandchildren today. If one of these grandparents should falter in this role, might not a great-grandparent help? This happened for Ephrain, eighty-eight. When one of his great-grandchildren's parents and both grandparents were killed in a car accident, he took over the grandparent role. "I never thought I would have to be as involved as I am, because the children had so many other people to care for them. But now that one parent and the grandparents are gone, I have had to step in and take care of them. I pray to God for the strength to do it."

An Exciting Future

Great-grandparenting has an exciting future. With their storehouse full of wisdom and experience, great-grandparents have an even greater potential positive influence than they had as grandparents. Being a great-grandparent for a child of an adopted grandchild lends more credence and power to the family connections of the child. When a stepgrandparent becomes a step-great-grandparent (or a great-stepgrandparent), she deepens and strengthens her ties to her stepfamily and enhances her sense of attachment and belonging.

So much is to be learned about this new and expanding role. All we can state with authority today is that great-grandparenting is in its infancy. There is a lot to look forward to.

GUIDELINES

If you are a great-grandparent or soon will be one, here are some guidelines to follow to do your best in this role.

- Assess your expectations in this role. Consider role models you might emulate.
- Assess your physical condition and vitality. Do the best you can to be as fit as possible.
- Do not be discouraged if you are limited by your physical condition. You are still capable of being a vital spiritual and emotional force in your family's life. Identify your grandchildren and great-grandchildren's needs and see which you can satisfy.
- Keep in mind that your advanced age translates into deeper wisdom and experience for your family to draw on. Make sure they know that.
- If a grandparent falters, and you are fit, do not hesitate to step into that role for as long as necessary. Your grandchildren will thank you.
- Fulfill as many grandparent roles as possible. Be especially aware of roles you can fulfill with a computer (see Chapters 36, "Cyber-grandparenting" and 43, "Long-Distance Grandparenting").
- Enjoy the respect and status that your great-grandparenthood has earned. If you've got it, flaunt it!

CONCLUSION

The study of great-grandparenting and its impact on the family and society is in its infancy. As an involved great-grandparent, you experience a new phase of development. With this gift, you have an opportunity to enrich the lives of your children, grandchildren, and great-grandchildren beyond anything you have ever done as a grandparent. Never forget that you are making history in pioneering the new relevance and abundance of this life stage and paving the way for the legions of future great-grandparents.

CHAPTER 18

Grandparents and Gender

G ender is an important characteristic that affects many aspects of grand-parenting style and grandparent-grandchild relationships. As humorist Saul Turtletaub explains in his book *The Grandfather Thing*, "The most important thing to realize when the baby [grandchild] is born is that you are not gaining a grandchild, you are losing a wife. If you ever thought you would be the most important person in the world to her, you will learn that is not true. Her grandchild now has that title. She will think about the baby all of the time and will be with it every minute possible."

Although grandparents of both sexes do many of the same things, there are important gender-related differences in how and when they do it. Even expectations for playing the role can be different (Somary 1998). Of course, these differences are not cut in stone. Generally speaking, however, gender influences how a grandparent's roles are prioritized, grow, and change through the years. Grandmothers, for example, may tend to be more involved in the early years (Pashos 2000). Grandfathers tend to get more involved as the child grows older, and are free to offer child-rearing advice to parents.

Of course, the strength of gender characteristics (physical appearance, sexual characteristics, aggressiveness, hormones, activity) varies from person to person. Most studies show that satisfaction in the role is relatively equal for both sexes (Peterson 1999). Therefore, the following observations are not absolute; instead they indicate tendencies.

Beyond Gender

Where grandparents are concerned, children tend to blur gender boundaries. They view their mothers and fathers as more sexually differentiated than they do their grandparents (Kornhaber 1983). The older the grandparent, the more this holds true. One benefit of this arrangement is that it offers young children the opportunity to relate to grandparents in a nonsexual manner. This explains why boys, for example, have less modesty in front of grandma (especially where her ministrations are concerned) and why adolescent girls may loll comfortably on grandpa's lap.

Grandfathers also supply their grandsons a more relaxed and contemplative role model for manhood than is typically found in the father–child relationship. This was best described by a youngster who likened his gentle and considerate grandfather to a "male grandmother." Because gender affects grandparenthood along with other factors such as vitality, interests, and personality it does place restrictions on grandparenting style.

Scientific investigators have learned a lot about gender-related differences in behaviors and attitudes by parents toward their children. For example, child development experts point out (DeWitt 1997) that fathers engage more in rough and tumble play with young children, and tease and instruct them more than mothers. On the other hand, mothers challenge children less, and have intuitive and protective mechanisms at work that facilitate caring and readily sense threat or discomfort in the child. I recently witnessed an incident that illustrates such a difference. A young father was having a tough time putting on his two-year-old child's shoes. The child was squirming and uncomfortable but the father finally got the shoes on. When the child started toddling around, the mother immediately noticed that the child was not walking correctly. To the father's bewilderment, the mother exclaimed, "The shoes are too tight, she's outgrown them." The father answered, "They fit fine last week."

I suggest that you read the next two chapters in one sitting and discuss them with your spouse or peers. It might also be a good idea to let your children read both chapters, and get their feedback as to how gender-related changes (menopause, decreased aggressivity) have affected you over the years. This can be quite entertaining and illuminating.

CHAPTER 19

Grandmothers

I n many cases, grandmotherhood can be thought of as a seamless continuation of motherhood with expanded joys and responsibilities. While a woman's biological capacity to reproduce wanes with increasing years, her ability to nurture others, now enriched by emotional growth and knowledge honed by life experience, becomes more powerful than ever. So do her influence, teaching ability, and power to be useful to her family and especially her grandchildren.

This has always been true but something new has happened to modern grandmothers. The stereotype of a rickety old grandma hobbling along with a cane has been replaced by the reality of grandmothers who are longer-lived, better educated, physically vital, and more financially secure than any generation of grandmothers before.

Remarkable Changes

As a grandmother, you are going to have to deal with these remarkable changes under your own skin, as well as external changes in social attitudes and family life. As a modern grandmother you must find a way to balance your own personal expression, creativity, work life, and leisure time. Unlike your own grandmothers, you may find yourself still working full-time. You might be living near your family or in a retirement community, cut off from family and young people in general. You may be widowed, divorced, single, or remarried. You may have stepgrandchildren and/or adopted grandchildren too. You might even have a gay or lesbian child who has decided to start a family of his or her own.

Certainly, you will find it challenging to be an effective grandmother when your children are divorced or if your grandchildren live thousands of miles away. Whatever your situation, rest assured you are well qualified for the job. After all, you have honed your parenting skills by raising your children. You have paid your dues. Now you are qualified to oversee your children do the same. Most of all you can enjoy your relationship with your grandchild. To do so, however, you will have to deal with the many changes in attitudes, social structure, and even in your own self-concept that you have been exposed to in your lifetime. On the other hand, many things have remained the same too. These traditional factors, including grandmother consciousness, form the bedrock of your grandmotherhood.

Grandmother Consciousness

To understand the importance of being a grandmother in these times it is necessary to ponder your own thoughts about being a grandmother. This process is what I call grandmother consciousness. This involves reflecting on the importance of the grandmother role in your life, integrating it into your personality and identity, and living it to the fullest (see Chapter 13, "Grandparent Development"). Many of the powerful qualities that grandmothers possess are intangible and thus hard to pin down. They are often apparent only to children; together these qualities make up the characteristic, as twelve-year-old Celia describes it, of "grandmotherliness."

Dr. Naomi Ruth Lowinsky, author of *Stories from the Motherline* (Jeremy Tarcher Press), writes, "Grandmothers loom behind parents, casting shadows, evoking the mysteries. Less familiar, less everyday than the mother, a grandmother is a woman of another time, telling stories out of long ago, when she was a child, when Mommy or Daddy was a child, when we of the present generation had not yet been dreamed of." Dr. Lowinsky relates grandmother consciousness to the generational continuum. As she explains, "The psychological meaning of the grandmother is an aspect of an archetypal pattern that I call the motherline. A woman's psyche arranges itself around a core connection to female continuity and the birth-giving capacity of the Feminine. The woman who is mother and daughter, grandmother and granddaughter, carries in her lived experience this central mystery of the Feminine. Women are the carriers of the species, the entryway to life. A woman's soul, her sense of the sacred, is, as Irene Claremont de Castillejo said, "imbedded in . . . her very body. . . ."

Grandmother's Power

Grandmother's power is rooted in a life expertise that extends beyond the practical to the mystical. Because she is a natural guardian of the family as well as its biological source, a grandmother is a natural teacher, one who shares—indeed, implants—her wisdom and experience with her family and community. The unique power is recognized and given expression in many cultures, from lullabies to mystical chants. For example, in the Kikiyu tribe in Africa, every grandmother has her own song. This grandmother's song is imbued with magical qualities that comfort, soothe, and heal when she sings it to others when they are hurting. The content of her songs relates her life experience, her own personal pain and sufferings, and the ways in which she has endured through time.

Grandmothers are the recognized *metteurs en scene* of rites of passage and family traditions and have established roles and duties within the culture. The Bororo tribe of Africa deems grandmothers *umufasoni*, or "noble," and the moment when a grandmother is given this title is one of the most important moments in her life. In Haiti, grandmothers are accorded mystical powers and are called upon to help when family members fall ill. In many European and American Indian cultures, a grandmother's blessing can ward off evil spirits, confer legitimacy to social arrangements such as marriages, or ensure good health and success (see Chapter 9, "Spiritual Guide").

In France people even celebrate Grandmother's Day!

Challenges

Unfortunately, strong as they may be within the family, American grandmothers have lost their public influence. This is a situation that needs correcting. Creating a revered and respected place for yourself in society as a grandmother is one of the greatest challenges facing you and other American grandmothers today. To do this will require a great effort from the new generation of grandparents. It requires keeping ahead of the social curve and keeping up with the times so you can be an effective grandmother. You will have to cultivate an ability to consider and change if necessary. You will have to adapt to new attitudes, social structures, family changes, and even in the way that you see yourself. One of the most important changes you will have to make is in the way you think about getting older.

Your Aging Program

The way you were programmed to think and act as an older person by our society meant experiencing a tailspin of physical, mental, and social decline starting at menopause. You were taught to look forward to diminished vitality, vanishing sexuality, social uselessness. You supposed that you might be regarded by your children and society as a burden. In the past researchers have noticed and fully documented these attitudes. "Cross-cultural studies reveal connections between a society's attitudes toward women and menopause. In the West, old women are perceived as crones, and women are symptomatic at menopause and afraid of aging. In the East, women gain respect and power as they age. There is no term for hot flashes in Japan" (Stotland 2001).

Today the crone designation is an outdated stereotype. Yet, in spite of looking and feeling good, many older women still carry the stereotype in the back of their minds.

It's long past time to discard the old program for aging that is still in your mind. Do not allow yourself to "think old." Make it a priority to evaluate what being old means to you and then discard all ageist thoughts and attitudes you may have. Irma, sixty-three, says "every time I get an ache or pain in my knees

I think, 'Uh-oh. I'm getting old. I'll never be able to hike again.' But then I rest a little and usually in two days, I find I can hike again. So, when I start to think that I'm old and falling apart, I stop and tell myself that those are just negative thoughts. Because that's exactly what they are. Thoughts, not reality."

Of course, we physically decline as we age. However, because we have been brainwashed about the aging process, many grandparents today *anticipate* the deterioration aspects of aging before such deterioration has a chance to happen. Information from the Human Genome Project predicts that life expectancy is increasing rapidly. And recent medical advances now assure elders a healthy existence until very late in life. The ranks of healthy and vital centenarians is growing rapidly, you might join them one day.

Now there is one more thing to consider. It is hard enough to deal with inside changes; but you are going to have to deal with the way in which the world outside has changed too.

The Changing Times

During your lifetime, you have witnessed and perhaps taken an active part in radical changes in the prevailing American social order that changed the nature of the American family. These were brought about by feminism, high rates of divorce and remarriage, and the gay-rights movement, to name just a few. Perhaps your own mother, who most likely was an obedient and compliant daughter, wife, and mother, became liberated and reentered the workforce. Whatever your personal experience, now that you are a grandmother it's important to take the time to reflect on how these changes have affected your attitudes and behavior over the years. My experience shows that grandparents who have adapted to these changes have grown spiritually and emotionally. Those who cling to old-fashioned ways miss the excitement of fresh challenges and experiences and find themselves relegated to the fringes of society. One of the consequences of this scenario is that these women can have difficulty in relating to their grandchildren.

Consider the way you balance life's demands. If you work, you may be puzzled about how much time to divide between self, work, and family. Many grandmothers today had to work to help support their families. As a result, they relinquished some of the emotional influence they wielded in their family. In the old days, this power and influence was traditionally the territory of grandmothers. To reclaim this territory, today's working grandmothers must redefine their roles and balance their personal goals with their work life and the roles they must play within their families.

You Are Better Than Ever!

The good news is that older women are much better off than they were several decades ago. Just ask your children! As you have aged and matured, you have expanded your capacity for patience and tolerance. You are a better listener, smarter, more experienced, more circumspect, more generous, stronger, and more self-determined. It is possible that you are even more physically active than ever before. Certainly, you handle your emotions better than when you were young. Along with your increased wisdom and life experience, these are the qualities of grandparent power. They are yours to use to enhance the lives of your grandchildren and family.

Take a moment to contemplate the changes you have experienced during your lifetime. Review where you have been, where you are today, and where you are going. Think about the obstacles you are encountering in your quest to be the best grandmother possible. Never forget that you are a needed and powerful presence in your grandchildren's lives. The old adage "You've come a long way baby," is an apt slogan for today's grandmothers.

GUIDELINES

Here are some guidelines to help you feel good about where you have been and where you have arrived now that you are a grandmother.

- Take some time to reflect upon your life experience. How have your attitudes toward aging changed since you were young? How do you want to live your life in the future? How does being a grandmother fit into these plans? What thoughts get in the way of you being optimistic and enthusiastic about being a grandmother?

- Consider how work or retirement affects your life. At this stage in your life, do you celebrate the emotional and spiritual dimensions of existence on a daily basis or, more simply put, do you stop and smell the roses with your grandchild?

- Celebrate your grandmotherhood at home and in the community. Be proud to be a grandmother. Devote yourself to carrying out your roles as a grandmother.

- Establish your grandparent identity by unhooking it from any ageist ideas you may still be harboring. When you find yourself thinking negative thoughts about being old, stop!

- Work hard to remain healthy. Your family needs you around.

- Be emotionally available to your family, especially when a new grandchild comes along or when a troubled teen is involved (see Chapters 24, "Birth of a Grandchild," and 22, "Adolescence").

- Be a force in your community. Grandparents' presence is sorely needed in schools and community institutions. Mentor a child. Start a Grandparent's Day at your local school or in your community center or religious organization (see Chapter 48, "Grandparents and the Community").

- Look forward to being a great-grandmother too.

CONCLUSION

As a grandmother, you have honed your parenting skills over time and gained a great deal of experience by virtue of your age alone. Now you are there to support your children and enjoy your relationship with your grandchildren. Because your generation is living longer and healthier than any generation before you, grandparenting and even great-grandparenting will become a larger part of your life. Gain a sense of personal pride and self-respect by using your wisdom and experience to benefit your family and community. Teach the world why grandmothers are so very important.

CHAPTER 20

Grandfathers

G randfatherhood is a unique time in a man's life. It's a time to change gears; to grow spiritually, intellectually, and emotionally; and to relate to children better than ever before. Those who are able to accept this opportunity can find new meaning and joy in the heart and spirit of a grandchild. As a grandfather, a man is more suited than ever before to enhance the lives of his loved ones. However, often this cannot be achieved without a great deal of soul-searching, understanding, and attitude adjustment.

You Have Changed

Are you aware that you are not the same person you were several decades ago? If you want to find out more about how you have changed, just ask your children. Chances are they will say you are more tolerant and easygoing, a better listener, more circumspect and generous, and most of all, more patient and attentive. These qualities not only supply the emotional and spiritual foundation of grandfatherhood, but they also can help you to be a better father. This has proven true for older men who have remarried and had a second batch of children. Almost all will attest that they are better fathers than they were with their first families.

I can't emphasize too strongly how these changes can help you be a more kind, considerate, tolerant person if you allow yourself to savor them. Although grandmotherhood involves a relatively smooth psychological transition from motherhood, the transition from fatherhood to grandfatherhood can involve deep psychological, physical, and even temperamental changes. To illustrate, take a moment, as a grandfather, to reflect upon the qualities that make up your masculine self-image and your self-esteem. Some of these may include professional success, sexual prowess, physical appearance, strength, and success as a husband and father. How have issues such as power, control, money, aggression, and material and social achievement affected your self-image and your purpose in life? Have these qualities changed in importance or priority over the years?

Chances are your attitudes toward some of these factors have changed as you have matured. Whether you recognize it or not, as a grandfather, your emotional and spiritual strength is already much greater than it was when you were younger. The aging process—or "mellowing" as I prefer to call it—increases your capacity for compassion, contemplativeness, wonder, tolerance, unconditional love, and forgiveness with each passing day. All of these factors are ideal qualities for relating to children. These newfound qualities have enhanced your nurturing abilities and made you eminently more qualified (no matter how wonderful you were as a father) for duties that perhaps, in the past, you relegated to your spouse.

In addition to these personal changes you have experienced, there are social considerations. You belong to a new breed of grandfather—a generation of modern grandfathers who are, on the whole, more educated, healthier, financially better off, and more vital than any before. This makes you a pioneer with a future yet to be written.

If you are a bit confused about all this, you are not alone. To become the most effective grandfather you can be in these times, you will have to do some hard thinking. You'll have to understand how these changes and events affect you personally. You have to gather a great deal of information to make the right choices.

There are some key emotional, social, and psychological attitudes and events that have affected your thoughts and attitudes over the years and affect your grandfatherhood today. Understanding these factors will help enhance your grandfatherhood. As you read on, assess your own experience in the light of what I describe. You might be surprised at how far you have already come in your own life. I hope you will discuss the contents of this section of the book with your family and peers.

Program for Aging

Because you were raised in an ageist society, you probably have outmoded views on aging that have to be discarded. The idea of being old you learned as you were growing up was associated with social uselessness and a steady loss of vitality including physical, occupational, and sexual decline. According to what you were taught, being old, as one grandfather told me, "is a bummer." But, as many people will attest, today's grandfathers do not fit this stereotype. They are vital, physically and mentally active individuals (Viagra notwithstanding) with much to contribute to their families and to society. In other words, what you *are* does not really fit with what society told you would be at this time in life.

Nevertheless, many men have developed a fear of aging to the point where every life event is seen in terms of age. The classic excuse of "I'm getting old" is automatically linked to each and every ailment or memory lapse that granddad experiences, whether it lasts a minute, an hour, or a day. When a grandfather absorbs ageist ideas and pejorative value judgments, it leads to a decrease in self-esteem and self-image. There is such a prevailing fear of being labeled old that some men ask their grandchildren not to call them grandfather. As Reggie, seventy-three will tell you, "I'm divorced, Viagra-ed, and on the prowl, so the last thing I want is someone calling me grandpa."

Considering the recent increase in human longevity and the improved level of health you probably enjoy, it is time to jettison your ideas about aging and get up to date. Linking the concept of old to grandfatherhood is no longer valid in a world where grandfathers lead active, involved lives. *Older*, in reality, is now better in many ways.

The Women's Movement

Since the days when you were a father there have been major changes in family roles and relationships as well as social structure and attitudes. You have had to consider these changes and adapt to them to keep up with the times. As a result you and your peers have made (or were forced to make) major changes in your identities, values, attitudes, roles, and self-perception to adapt to social trends. Difficult as it may be for some, women have made men question the "macho" values and principles, as well as such issues as power, control, and sexuality.

One of the greatest changes you have experienced in your lifetime, and hopefully shared firsthand through your spouse or daughter, is the women's liberation movement. This movement forced many men to rethink the male chauvinist dictums they had been taught by the society of their youth. Consequently, their traditional attitudes and beliefs about women and family life were soundly shaken. Ralph, a sixty-seven-year-old grandfather, says, "I can't believe the changes I have seen in my lifetime. I used to put the women in my family on a pedestal and now they are at my side. This is good and bad. When they were on a pedestal, I always knew how to act, but I felt that I had all of the responsibility. As partners, it is more confusing, but, at the same time, I feel less pressured. The sexual revolution—well, that is something else. The bad news is that I missed out on it."

Like Ralph, you may have had a stay-at-home mom. You also lived through the period when women started to migrate beyond the confines of their homes and out into the world to work. You witnessed how women, because of this change, were forced to relinquish some of their power and authority in the home, and you may remember that many men experienced that absence as abandonment. This shook the foundation of many marriages. There was a lot of confusion in terms of roles and authority issues between spouses. Some men adapted by taking up some of the slack left by their wives by sharing in some of the traditionally female chores and tasks of housekeeping.

Indeed, not only are househusbands increasingly common today, some grandfathers have even become "housegrandfathers" by helping a single child raise their grandchildren. Luke, seventy-one and a widower, moved in with his daughter and four grandchildren after his son-in-law died. "I was kind of a macho guy when I was younger," Luke said. "I never thought I would end up part mother, part father, and part grandmother, doing a lot of what I always thought was women's work. I had to do a lot of thinking and change a lot of my attitudes, but I'm getting through it and getting a hell of an education."

Reflect upon how all of these changes have affected you. Evaluate what you were taught about women's roles, wants, and needs. Do any of your beliefs or opinions seem outmoded? What can you do to get in step with the times? Especially remember that when it comes to treating the opposite sex with respect, you are a role model for daughters and granddaughters. In fact, this is a wonderful topic to discuss with them.

Work and Retirement

In the past, men were trained to work to put food on the table and help the family survive. The family was the first priority, and the fruits of a man's toil supported a wife who maintained the family. As a result, many men labored long and hard at occupations they didn't particularly like. Such men understandably looked forward to retirement as liberation from occupational servitude.

The dream of retirement was born of these circumstances. The dream stated that, like the workhorse put out to pasture, a man's hard work would be rewarded with a well-earned rest. Supported by society, pensions, and savings, he would work no longer. Instead, he could move to sunny climes and, free of former constraints, play to his heart's content. That was perhaps fine for men who labored hard physically and were sick and in need of rest. But it does not work for today's grandfathers who find that instead of feeling tired and decrepit when society wants to put them out to pasture, they feel strong, active, and vital. Instead of saying "It's over," they are now saying, "What's next?"

As a result, many soon become bored with full-time leisure and begin to miss their children and grandchildren. Some, while perhaps still residing in a retirement community, begin to drift back into the workforce, open new businesses, or work from home as consultants. Others, having had their fill of the retirement life entirely, move to rejoin the families they left behind and to start anew. Yet others look around at their communities, identify problems, and do something about them. Jack McConnell, a retired physician, with the help of other volunteer retired doctors and nurses, started the Volunteers in Medicine organizations that currently serve the poor with free medical care in thirty-one clinics around the nation.

Today, as people consider the idea of "serial" occupations, the idea of retirement is being reexamined, and hopefully discarded. *Change* is perhaps a better word to describe this period of life. Our society needs new ways of looking at the concept of work, ways that involve living and working for others. Grandparenting is the culmination of serial occupations. The emotional and spiritual work of old age involves ensuring the health, education, and safety of children and grandchildren. This work is paid for in spiritual currency, a currency that includes a feeling of goodness, usefulness, selflessness, and service—in other words, grandparent power. Grandparent power means applying wisdom, experience, and the long view of life to better yourself, your family, your community, and society.

There Is Work to Do

Now that you have achieved the status of grandfather, take some time out to examine how far you have come and where you are going. Your life may well be very different from what you anticipated when you were younger. You may be divorced, single, or remarried. You may have stepchildren, stepgrandchildren, adopted children, or adopted grandchildren. You may be a long-distance grandfather, working or retired. As a grandfather, your importance to your grandchildren cannot be underestimated. Grandfatherhood holds the promise of a bright and meaningful future for you. But you will have to work hard to make it come true.

GUIDELINES

Here are some guidelines to help you be the best grandfather possible and to ensure your natural place in the family and society.

- Reflect upon your life experience and how it affects your grandfatherhood. How have your attitudes changed over the years?
- Plan ahead. How would you like to live your life in the future? How does being a grandfather affect these hopes, dreams, and plans? Make time for grandfatherhood.
- Consider how work or retirement affects your life. Do you now include more emotional and spiritual dimensions in your daily life?
- How do you balance your roles as son, father, grandfather, spouse, and worker?
- Make sure to unhook your grandparent identity from outdated ageist stereotypes. Catch yourself if you find yourself thinking old. Be a vital grandfather. Get involved in a program to keep you physically healthy.
- Enjoy fulfilling your roles as grandfather.
- Make yourself available to your family, especially your teenage grandchildren.
- Try to be on hand when a new grandchild comes along.
- Get involved in your community. Mentor a child. Start a Grandparent's Day in your grandchild's school.

CONCLUSION

The role of grandfather is powerful. It gives every grandfather the opportunity to light up a grandchild's life and contribute to his family and society in a meaningful way. Those who have held on to old attitudes and values have stunted their growth and development and watched the world grow away from them. Those who have embraced recent societal changes have experienced emotional and spiritual growth as well as a sense of empowerment. In a time when strong role models are lacking, grandfathers are more important than ever before.

CHAPTER 21

Effective Grandparenting

verything in this book is meant to help you become the best and most effective grandparent possible. But what exactly is an "effective" grandparent? I define an effective grandparent as one who

- rejoices in playing the roles and fulfilling the functions that grandparenting requires
- has taken on the challenges of modern grandparenting
- has succeeded in overcoming obstacles to fulfilling the role
- has grown and changed in the process
- as a result of these efforts produces a happy grandchild, and a respectful and satisfied parent (and child)

The motivation for categorizing grandparenting as effective is not to make people feel inadequate or that they are not doing the right thing. It is simply about using what we have learned over the years to do the best job possible under the circumstances. Of course, we do the best we can. The idea of being an effective grandparent helps to present grandparents with a clear set of goals. Success is measured by personal satisfaction and validation by parents and children. Having clear criteria to strive for helps us recognize where we fall short. Then we can do something about it.

My experience shows that effective grandparents have many qualities in common. The most important is that simply being a grandparent gives great satisfaction and is an important part of their lives. Although they represent a wide variety of personality types, they all share strong identities as grandparents. They have a strong sense of family, value family attachments, and spend considerable time engaged in grandparent activity. As people, they are altruistic, tolerant, understanding, patient, vital, and spiritually energetic. They make time to be available to their grandchildren. They are flexible and strive for personal growth. They make a point to deal directly with challenges that impede their grandparenting, such as distance or family problems.

Grandparents are not effective in a vacuum. Their children and grandchildren must always agree and have final say about whether or not grandparents are meeting their needs. After all, it is the grandchild who is the measure of the effectiveness of the grandparents.

Characteristics of Effective Grandparents

Grandparents can function "effectively" in many ways for their grandchildren. Some grandparents might function more effectively in one role than another. They may be better at one time or another—in a family crisis, for example. One grandfather, Milt, who confesses that he "doesn't take to kids," finally found a way to relate to his grandchildren by teaching them how to play golf. He started out by relating to them as a crony and teacher and, from that platform, became closer to his grandchildren. Although he is not effective in a broad spectrum of roles, he is, in the words of his two grandchildren, a "fun" grandfather. The children's parents agree. Their mother said, "My dad is not the most involved grandfather. He tries. But I know we can count on him in an emergency. When my son was hit by a car my dad was there and made sure that he got the best doctors." As Milt says, "I do the best I can." And that is fine.

Clarice, a grandmother, lives in the same town as her six grandchildren. She is broadly effective because she is involved in their lives on a daily basis and plays multiple grandparent roles. Her grandchildren (and their parents) feel she is a powerful grandmother and is physically, intellectually and spiritually available to them. As Clarice sums it up, "My family is my life."

According to grandchildren, ethnicity, age, and sex have no bearing on a grandparent's effectiveness. However, there are some other distinguishing characteristics of broadly effective grandparents. These include the ability to find joy in life, an optimistic outlook, the quest for continuing personal growth, openness to change, a sense of humor, and involvement with grandchildren and other family members. These characteristics will help you measure your own effectiveness. They represent a model to strive for to broaden that effectiveness. Here are some of the main characteristics of broadly effective grandparents as described by their children and grandchildren.

Altruism

The most defining characteristic is an altruistic orientation toward other people. The word *altruism* is derived from the Latin word *alter*, meaning "other," and the French word *autrui*, meaning "other persons." Someone who is altruistic is someone who selflessly devotes himself or herself to fulfilling the needs of others. Some people seem to be born altruistic. They are kind, caring, and compassionate. These people not only make effective grandparents, but great parents and friends as well! Interestingly, child-development studies have demonstrated the existence of altruism in some infants.

It is not unusual to find altruistic people working as health professionals, teachers, and social workers or volunteering in their community. Altruistic grandparents display responsiveness and empathy, excellent qualities for relating to children. Alois, a seventy-five-year-old grandfather says, "Before I do something, I always ask myself how my actions will affect other people."

Altruistic individuals are also "value-centered," finding direction and inner strength from a strong set of values that often puts them at odds with widely held social values. They act according to their own personal principles and often are religious or self-transcendent, and they display character traits of compassion and concern for others that are often associated with a deep spirituality (Cloninger, Svaric, Prybeck, 1993). Altruism, as a personality characteristic, is linked to empathy for a grandchild and forms the biological underpinnings of a grandparent's nurturing, protective, and supportive roles. Maintaining an altruistic view of life ensures that family relationships will be based on positive emotional priorities. In other words, altruistic people create and support well-functioning families. Alice, ten, says, "My grandpa is building shelters for the homeless on the weekends." Jake, sixteen, says, "I'm really proud of my grandmother because she's always knitting booties for AIDS babies." Altruism is an important motivator for grandparents who put aside many of their own desires in order to help raise their grandchildren (see Chapter 41, "Raising Grandchildren").

Temperament

Temperament may be described as an inborn psychological tendency to react to the environment in a certain way. Temperamental differences in infants are recognizable at birth. Effective grandparents possess temperamental qualities that are conducive to interpersonal relationships. Grandchildren who are close to their grandparents describe them as patient and understanding and easy to talk to and confide in (see Chapter 15, "Temperament and Personality").

Personality

Although I have discussed how personality affects grandparenting in earlier chapters, it is worthy of another mention here. Personality can be described as the characteristic and, to some extent, predictable behavior-response patterns that each person evolves, both consciously and unconsciously, as a way of being. Personality type determines cognition, emotion, and behavior; in other words, it is a predictor of how a person will think, feel, and act. Diverse personality traits have been described: introvert, extrovert, emotional, compulsive, passive, and dependent. Personality disorders have been clinically categorized too: hysterical, obsessive-compulsive, narcissistic, and so forth. Thus an outgoing extroverted grandparent might be seen as a fun person, a great playmate for a grandchild. Personality is sometimes not a reliable outward indicator for judging the effectiveness of a grandparent, however. A grandparent who may appear quiet and reserved in a social setting might be a bundle of fun when alone with a grandchild.

Vitality

Vitality refers not only to a grandparent's physical state, but also to his or her emotional, spiritual, and intellectual state (see Chapter 9, "Spiritual Guide"). Effective grandparents are vital people who bring excitement and wonder into their grandchildren's lives. It is interesting to note that effective grandparents and their grandchildren describe sharing a reverberating bio-psycho-social-spiritual feedback loop with their grandchild that is psychologically, spiritually, and physically vitalizing (Kornhaber 1989). Vitality affects attitude. Thus, effective grandparents tend to classify themselves as optimistic people. Vitality is a thing of the spirit and is not necessarily related to physical health. Just as a physically fit grandparent may not be a vital grandparent, so a physically debilitated grandparent can be perceived as extremely vital by his or her grandchildren. John, twenty-eight, says, "When I went away to college for the first time, I was really homesick. My grandmother, even though she was confined to a wheelchair, called me every day and talked me through it. It was like she was with me. She had more life in her when she was sitting in a wheelchair than some guys I knew on the football team."

A Priority of Availability

Effective grandparents make an effort to prioritize their lives in such a way that they can be temporally and emotionally available to their grandchildren. Because being near their families is so important to them, they are quite creative about finding ways to be with them or to stay in touch. Some grandparents have even gone so far as to seek employment in a new city so they can live near their children and grandchildren. Others start family businesses and employ their children and in-laws. Grandparents who are not fortunate enough to live close to their children and grandchildren, go out of their way to visit or to maintain regular contact.

Personal Experience and Philosophy

Many effective grandparents describe themselves as family people. They are devoted parents and grandparents. Some have learned how to be effective grandparents from having strong role models, others say it just comes naturally. Many were grandchildren who loved and respected their grandparents. Others were raised in stressed families where grandparents had a significant positive role and were valued and occupied a position of respect in the family system. Still others learned to grandparent by observing their own parents grandparent their children.

Samantha, fifty-four, said, "The most important thing I learned from my own grandfather is that children need protection, guidance, and discipline. He treated each of his grandchildren as a sacred trust."

Readiness

The majority of effective grandparents are emotionally and spiritually ready to become grandparents. Ideally, people become grandparents when they are ready, after a period of respite from raising their own children and after they are afforded an opportunity to fulfill some of their own needs and dreams. Then they are ready to take up the challenge of finding mental and temporal space in their lives for grandparenting. The degree of unreadiness a grandparent may find in the new role depends on how overburdened he or she already feels.

The readiness factor may be particularly pertinent for men. As men age, nature changes them "from warriors to wise men" (Kornhaber 1986). Emotionally, men settle down, becoming more reflective and contemplative. These are valuable qualities to bring to a relationship with a child. Young girls are especially attracted to relaxed and mellow grandfathers who can give them love and attention, something for which many fathers do not find enough time (Cath 1985).

Coping

In these complicated times, it may sometimes seem that life conspires against us and prevents us from being the grandparents we want to be. There are some grandparents whose hearts are with their grandchildren, but their grandparenting *activity* is impaired by unfavorable circumstances. Although they too possess a strong grandparent identity and place a priority on family life, their ability to act on it is restricted by factors such as geographic distance, family structure, or lack of time due to work or other obligations (for example, having an elderly parent to care for). Only advanced coping skills can begin to help with some of these almost insurmountable problems.

Effective grandparents demonstrate such abilities. Despite obstacles, they manage to fulfill some of their grandparenting roles consistently (family ancestor and historian, wizard, hero, mentor, role model), but others only inconsistently (nurturer, crony). Although their physical presence may be sporadic, they communicate well with their grandchildren (sometimes even on a daily basis), achieve an alliance of understanding with them, and are active partners in finding ways to be together. These grandparents manage to be effective grandparents even in dire circumstances.

Grandchildren of effective grandparents know that their grandparents adore them and love being with them. Astrid, nine, says, "My grandpa lives in the next state so I only see him once a month. But when he comes and stays at my house he gets up every morning at six o'clock and drives me to school just because he wants to be with me." Like Astrid's grandfather, the "long-distance grandparents" who attend our Foundation for Grandparenting's Grandparent-Grandchild Summer Camp in the Adirondack Mountains are good examples of grandparents who work to maintain emotional attachment with their grandchildren despite the fact that they are separated by geographical distance. Once a year these grandparents make it a priority to spend a week at camp with their grandchild where they can be maximally effective. For grandparents with limited financial resources, communication can be maintained by telephone, mail, fax, or E-mail (see Chapter 43, "Long-Distance Grandparenting").

Parent-Grandparent Relationships

Effective grandparents make an effort to get along well with their families. They have solid coping skills when it comes to the usual adversities of family life. Most effective grandparents seem to be involved and loving parents who experience few major problems with their own children. When problems do arise, they work to resolve them quickly. When their children marry, they welcome the new member into the family, communicate openly with their new in-law, refrain from destructive and unnecessary criticism, and respect family boundaries. By their example, they make clear that they view family as a mutually supportive and synergistic system. When their children have problems, they are available to intervene in a helpful way as mediators or healers.

GUIDELINES

Being as effective a grandparent as possible requires a great deal of time and attention, as well as feedback from parents and children. Here are some guidelines to help you increase your effectiveness as a grandparent.

- Review the characteristics of effective grandparenting you have learned about in this chapter. Relate these characteristics to your own standards for being an effective grandparent. If you identify any room for improvement go for it!
- Review the roles in Chapters 1 through 12. How much of each role can you perform, and at what level of effectiveness? If you can do more, do it!
- Take your role as living ancestor and family historian seriously. Set the emotional tone for your family: one of concern, caring, involvement, and emotional availability.
- Apply your natural altruism. For example, welcome new in-laws into the family and work at maintaining good relations with all family members.
- Be mature, nonjudgmental, and loving.

- When problems arise, address them directly and work toward a quick resolution. Try to see all sides of the issues.
- Keep up with the times. Share your children and grandchildren's world.
- No one's perfect. However, as a grandparent, it is worthwhile to make an effort to try to push that envelope a bit!

CONCLUSION

Being an effective grandparent is well worth the effort. Of course, no one is perfect. However, by striving to be the best you can be, you will experience growth on a personal level while fostering strong, long-lasting bonds with your grandchildren and other family members. And remember to ask your grandchildren and their parents how they think you are doing.

PART 3

The Grandparent-Grandchild Bond

The grandparent–grandchild bond is a unique human relationship, different from the parent-child bond. Keeping it vibrant and healthy poses a daily challenge. Even in the best of circumstances the relationship changes just because the child is growing. It is profoundly affected by personal, familial, and social circumstances too. It is especially important to understand, and respect, the role of parents as the linchpin of this attachment. In the following chapters, I will discuss many of the circumstances that profoundly affect your relationship with your grandchild for better or worse.

Adolescence

S omeday your grandchild will be a teenager. As you may remember from your own past, teenagers are often on an emotional roller coaster. And you are along for the ride. Your teenage grandchild can be exciting and challenging, interesting and fun, exasperating and lovable, all within the same day (or hour). Along with a teenager's growing pains comes a great deal of confusion. This is especially true today, when she can be bombarded with daily phenomena such as schoolwork, peer acceptance, raging hormones, and bodily changes—not to mention the stress of living in a consumer society such as ours that places great importance on physical and material conformity.

Along with internal changes, teenagers may be dealing with external stresses. These might include family problems such as divorce, parental remarriages, mental illness, family financial instability, drug abuse, and so on. Some teenagers handle these life changes more smoothly, while others may need to be guided and supported through this time. Ideally, a support team composed of healthy, loving, available parents and stable, understanding grandparents supplies emotional ballast for a stressed-out teenager.

So, whether you live near or far, you have an important role to play for your teenage grandchild. Naturally, if you live near your grandchild, you are more physically available. If you live far away, you will have to make regular communication with your family a priority. If necessary you may have to find a way to be mobile and available during these potentially troublesome years.

Parents of teenagers need lots of support and understanding too. As you already know from parenting a teenager, it is not an easy job. Acting as a referee between these two generations is one of the classic roles of a grandparent. This can be especially beneficial if there is an adopted grandchild in the family, because the identity issues that arise during adolescence are often more complicated for adopted children (see Chapter 35, "Adoption"). You have to be part teacher and part mediator. If the family agrees, you may even serve as a kind of volunteer family therapist. In this context you may be called upon to help put out family fires. To serve in all of these capacities for your teenage grandchild you have to educate yourself fully about what she is experiencing at this time in her life.

Understanding Your Teenage Grandchild

It is normal for teenagers to be in conflict with their parents as part of their psychological and emotional growth. Young children strive to imitate their parents; teenagers struggle to be as different from their parents as possible. They seek to discover their own identity and establish an independent self by separating psychologically and emotionally from their parents. (To learn about this process in more detail, see the excellent publication mentioned in the resources at the end of this chapter). Because of the changes in the child's attitudes and actions, grandparenting a teenager is very different from grandparenting a younger child. The little grandchild who once followed you around with adoring eyes has metamorphosed into a rapidly changing young adult. Physically awkward, often grouchy, and seemingly out of step with the rest of the world, your maturing grandchild is now obsessed with her peer group: What do they think of her? Do they accept her? Does she fit in? Is she "cool enough"?

Your teenage grandchild is also finding that the luster has somewhat worn off her relationship with her parents. Now dethroned, Mom and Dad are no longer the ultimate authority. As a result, be prepared to lend an ear to a litany of complaints from your grandchild about his parents. Sometimes your grandchild may see them as malevolent oppressors. As fourteen-year-old Solange, puts it, "My parents act like the police."

Your grandchild will tell you her parents "just don't understand." They are "too strict" and "uncool." They "never listen." Here is where your role as historian can be used to let your grandchild know about her parent's adolescence. A selective bit of history may help your grandchild gain some perspective on his own plight. If your grandchild asks, accept the role of mediating any disagreements she has with her parents. But if you feel that you are getting in over your head or that your family's conflicts or problems are serious, suggest seeking professional guidance from an outside party. Discretion is the better part of valor!

You May Not Be Spared

You may not be spared from your grandchild's adolescence either. There is the chance that even you, the sacred grandparent, may be nudged aside in your grandchild's battle for independence. After all, he is now in a steady transition from childhood to an adulthood, and thus his needs have changed. If he does not run toward you with open arms as in the days of yore, don't despair. This is part of his normal development. Don't feel rejected if he does not come to you with all of his problems, now that he has friends to talk with. However, if you think that it is time for a good discussion, take the initiative and approach him. You might have to knock on the door of his room for access, or call on the telephone and ask to speak specifically with him. If he tells you he wants to be alone, or isn't in the mood to talk, respect his need for his own space, but press on at another time. Be flexible, respectful of any boundaries your grandchild may set, yet available if he does feel the need to talk. As you weather the tantrums and rude behavior, keep reminding yourself this is a passing phase. Above all, don't retaliate for temporary rudeness. Your grandchild will eventually apologize. Guilt works!

External Pressures

Adolescents accommodate their internal changes best when they have a stable external environment (Baranowski 1982). When both of their internal and external worlds change at the same time things can get very difficult. Although temporary moments of catastrophe and emotional upset are to be expected, be sure to monitor the amount of pressure your teenage grandchild is experiencing. He might need rescuing—or at least some respite. Especially be alert to any severe emotional or behavioral changes that may be an indication of something more serious: a drop in school grades, blatant drug use (see Chapter 28, "Substance Abuse"), depression, or eating disorders. If your grandchild does abuse drugs or become chemically dependent, the parents (or you alone, if the parents are unable or unwilling) should contact a treatment center for help—the earlier the better. Unless your grandchild is in a crisis situation and his parents are negligent about seeking appropriate help, work *with* his parents when resolving problems of this nature.

You Supply a Natural Sanctuary

Nature has placed you smack in the middle of the no-man's land of the emotional conflict that teenagers create with their parents. The wonderful news is that same psychological dynamic involved in "emotional separation" between parent and child does not come into play between you and your teenage grandchild. That is because he is not as psychologically entwined with you as he is with his parents. Because he doesn't see you as the ultimate authority (indeed he may see you as a fellow victim) he won't feud much with you. It is easier for him to follow your rules and comply with your wishes. Of course, if you are also the primary caregiver for your grandchild, these dynamics are very different and too complex to be explored here (see Chapter 41, "Raising Grandchildren").

For the most part, you can rest assured that your relationship with your grandchild is devoid of the turmoil that plagues the parent-teenager relationship. Your teenage grandchild sees you as a source of stability, an emotional sanctuary. You are someone he can trust and rely on during this difficult life transition. If this sounds like a big responsibility, don't worry. Time and experience have already prepared you for this job. Most grandparents have a natural feel for interacting with the young: what to do, how to do it, and when to seek outside counsel.

You Are Your Grandchild's Secret Weapon

Teenagers know that you are their parent's parent. In their eyes, that gives you some major clout. Sam, sixteen, asked his grandmother to help him convince his parents to allow him to go abroad with a church mission after he graduated from high school. His parents were against it; they still felt Sam was too young to go so far away. But as Sam reports, "After my grandmother gave them a talking-to and told them they were being overprotective," Sam's parents decided to let him go.

You may also think of yourself as your grandchild's secret weapon to be deployed against parents in time of need. But this power over parents that teenagers accord you is to be used with discretion. Never go against your own good judgment or that of the parents. Your grandchild may ask you to intervene on important issues such as household responsibilities, curfews, choice of friends, diet, finances, and more, but it is wiser to feign helplessness than to support his desire to do something you don't believe is good for him. William, seventy-two, tells about the time his grandson Luke, fifteen, wanted him to persuade Luke's parents to extend his curfew until one o'clock on Saturday nights. "I thought one o'clock was too late for a boy of fifteen," said William. "I took the easy way out and told him that I just couldn't get his parents to extend the curfew. Actually, I never even mentioned it to his parents 'cause I agree with them. 'Course, I didn't tell Luke that," he chuckles.

When it comes to serious issues such as education, safe driving, behavior issues, alcohol, or drugs, it is important that you support the parents' position. Where such important matters are concerned, the more your grandchild is exposed to a consistent family policy, upheld by both parents and grandparents, the more he will take the policy seriously.

Your Payoff

Being available to your grandchild during this turbulent time can yield a big payoff for you as well. Teenagers can be a lot of fun. Especially if you have been feeling a little out of it lately. There is no one better than a teenage grandchild to be your guide to what is happening in the modern world, and to keep you up-to-date on the latest fashions, hairstyles, music, art, film, fads, trends, and people.

You learn from each other. While she is filling you in on emerging trends, you can share with her how it was in the old days. If your granddaughter is sporting spiked purple hair and a tattoo, you can tell her how racy it was when you bobbed your hair back in the 1930s, how your parents reacted when you showed up in a zoot suit in the 1940s, or what it was like being a hippie in the 1960s.

Your teenage grandchild has many questions about sex and romance. Make sure you are clear on how her parents wish to handle these discussions (although most children today seemed to be fully versed on the topic early on). Undoubtedly, your grandchild will be talking about sex with her peers. She will want to hear from you too. Especially when it concerns romance! However, your personal stories about how you met your spouse and what your first date was like are not just lessons to learn from. This is the family history she will one day pass on to her own grandchildren—your great-great-grandchildren. The personal stories you share will help her gain some perspective on her situation. She will realize that people have been struggling with these same issues since the beginning of time.

By involving yourself in the world of your teenage grandchild, you can obtain, in her eyes, the exalted state of being (in today's vernacular) totally cool. You will really know you have made it when she brings her friends to visit and show you off. This is your golden opportunity to get to know these youngsters, learn their ways, what they talk and think about, and most of all, serve as a positive role model for them. This alone will keep you up to date, and perhaps you can do some good for the youngsters as well.

Cecile, seventy-one, is fortunate to live very close to her granddaughter, Claire, and has a weekly get-together with her and her friends. "The girls are all around sixteen. They like to hear about the old days, what it was like when I was courting. 'Old-fashioned sex,' as they call it. To tell the truth I have learned a thing or two myself. Sometimes I hear things that make my ears red! They are exposed to so much so early. All that sex. And the drugs! Why, back then we didn't even know that stuff existed. The sad thing is one of their friends became pregnant at the age of fifteen. She dropped out of school and then gave the baby up for adoption. She's back in school now, but that sure scared the rest of the girls. I just try to keep an open mind and not judge, that's all."

Cecile continues, "They seem to learn a lot from me. And the surprising thing for me is the way they just drink up what I tell them. I've even taught a few of them how to knit. Now they call their weekly visit to my house their 'tea party.'" Cecile and Claire have grown closer because of Cecile's openness to her friends. "I am proud of my grandma," Claire smiles. "She doesn't look down on us, and she's interested in what we are doing. I can talk to her about lots of stuff, like this boy I like at school. I could never talk to my mom or dad about that. My friends are all jealous of me because I have a such a cool grandma." Claire's smile broadens. "What can I say? I'm just lucky, I guess."

If you are not geographically close to your grandchild, you can still apply these principles when you are together and share your experiences and worlds via E-mail, family teleconferencing, and, of course, the telephone (see Chapter 36, "Cybergrandparenting" and Chapter 43, "Long-Distance Grandparenting"). If you are a stepgrandparent your role can be especially important during times of strife because a teenager will see you as having more objectivity about what is happening in the family and want you as an advocate (see Chapter 46, "Stepgrandparenting").

Rescuing Parents

Having once been the parent of a teenager yourself, you know that teenage antics can be very stressful, particularly for working single parents. Be alert to how parents and teenagers are handling this. You may need to come to the rescue! You can make yourself available to listen when parent-child communication breaks down. You can take over when everyone needs a rest. After all, helping a child in turmoil is a family affair. Even if the turmoil stems from a natural part of life such as adolescence. Your support may be needed in times of crisis or in a "preventive" mode, improving the quality of your family's life and relationships. Bring some levity to the situation.

If your teenage grandchild has sisters or brothers, be alert to how they are handling things too. This is especially true if the teenager is the eldest grandchild; some teenagers can be downright cruel to younger siblings. You will have to tend to the younger ones too. They might need time alone with you for a moment of peace or to blow off steam about their adolescent sibling.

Reassure parents who are appalled by the sanitary condition of their teenager's room by reminding them that they were no strangers to dirty socks and dust bunnies at that age either. When serious issues such as divorce arise, you can help by keeping the children for a while, until the emotionally taxed parents can resume parenting. If you don't live near your grandchild, you might consider visiting more often, or even, if possible, moving closer during this crisis so that you can be there to fully support your family. I personally know many people who have done this. They responded to the family's need by moving back to the family from a retirement home or community or by arranging to rent a place nearby for the duration of the crisis.

You can offer the parents respite in many ways. Consider taking a vacation together—just you and your grandchild. Periodic weekend getaways will be a boon to the parents and a great opportunity for you to bond with your grandchild. Take walks, hike, bike, and dine out in restaurants—just the two of you. Be sure to sympathize with parents who may wonder if their adolescent child still loves them. Put things in perspective for them. There will be much arguing from your grandchild, but this is all part of the process of his individuation from his parents and should be taken with a grain of salt. Working with the parents supports everyone in the family, not just your grandchild.

GUIDELINES

Adolescence is not an easy time for your teenage grandchild and the rest of the family. As a grandparent, you are sorely needed to help everyone involved until this time passes. Here are some guidelines to help.

With Your Teenage Grandchild

- Go out of your way to keep in close contact with your teenage grandchild.
- Be available on his terms. Respect his need for space. Spend as much time alone with him as possible. If you do not live nearby, make it a priority to spend as much time together as possible. If you are a "long-distance" grandparent, keep in touch via phone, letters, or E-mail. If your grandchild cannot come to you, go to your grandchild. A vacation together with your grandchild is a wonderful experience.
- Listen to her. Learn about her interests and her world.
- Share your own coming of age with her.
- Allow your grandchild to help *you* grow by being open to new ideas.
- Get to know your grandchild's friends.
- Keep an open mind when listening to your teenager's concerns about subjects such as sex or drugs, but never go against your own or the parents' good judgment.
- When problems occur, assure the parents that this too shall pass.
- Have fun with your grandchild.
- Express your unconditional love and acceptance often.

With the Parents

- Ask the parents how you can help them raise their teenager.
- Be available to your family during crises. Be objective; do not take sides.
- Monitor how the parents and teenager are getting along. If appropriate, get involved in a helpful, loving, and compassionate way.
- Offer respite to all.
- If you don't live nearby, make sure to talk with the parents about a way to pool financial resources so you and your grandchild can be together as much as possible.

With Siblings

- Although a squeaky wheel gets the most oil, in this case your teenage grandchild, don't let his antics divert your attention from your other grandchildren.
- Lend an ear to siblings who complain about the teenager. Listen attentively until they have blown off plenty of steam and reassure them that this too shall pass.
- Give each grandchild plenty of private time and respite from the family turmoil that accompanies the teenage years.

CONCLUSION

Having a close bond with a teenager can be tremendously stimulating and fun. Spending time with your teenage grandchild will help keep you vital, active, and in step with the times. Because teenagers are growing into adults, they are hungry to know about your history, attitudes, philosophies, successes, failures, skills, family recipes, stories, family gossip, and more. Your history provides them with a road map for their own lives. If family problems arise, you offer a safe place for your grandchild to be nurtured and to regain composure. Parents will be comforted to know that you are involved and supportive. Care for your other grandchildren too.

This is a special time in your lives, so fasten your seatbelts, hang on tight, and enjoy your teenage grandchild to the fullest!

RESOURCES

Your Adolescent: Emotional, Behavioral and Cognitive Development from Early Adolescence through the Teen Years. The American Academy of Child and Adolescent Psychiatry. HarperCollins. Order at www.parentshandbooks.com or call (800) 242-7737.

CHAPTER 23

Attention

G iving your grandchild your undivided attention is the single most important thing you can do to ensure a close and loving attachment with her. Research shows that the degree of closeness of a grandparent–grandchild bond is proportional to the amount of undivided attention a grandparent and grandchild share (Kornhaber 1982). Conversely, the less attention a grandparent gives to the grandchild, the more superficial the relationship tends to be.

When you focus on just being together, or as one grandchild put it, "hanging out," with your grandchild, you are nurturing the emotional and spiritual aspects of your relationship (see Chapter 9, "Spiritual Guide"). With time and attention you are encouraging intimacy and displaying your unconditional love for her. This isn't always easy. Many grandparents find that providing this special one-on-one attention may be hard to do on a regular basis because of distance, time constraints, or family conflicts. Nevertheless, however formidable the challenge, the efforts you make to spend time alone with your grandchild will reap significant rewards. Modern technology can help. Phone or E-mail has its own benefits. Whether you live near or far, just knowing the importance of time and undivided attention in your relationship with your grandchild will help you to do your best.

The Gift of Time

If you give your grandchild the gift of your time, you go deep into one another and jointly reap the benefits of the wonder and pleasure that spring from your discovery of each other. Sit back and enjoy how good it feels to be with your grandchild, whether you are reading a story to a two-year-old or walking in the woods with a teenager. There are no judgments and no issues of power or control. You and your grandchild are simply and gloriously free to revel in the unconditional love you have for each other.

Your grandchild needs your time. Although he may not be able to convey how he feels, being the focus of your undivided attention makes him feel special and gives him time to absorb your being. Grandchildren cherish these moments. "When we are alone in my grandfather's workshop," says ten-year-old Art, "he teaches me lots of stuff, like how to plane a board, or use a lathe. I feel really happy because I know he is only thinking about me. Then when we take a bunch of wood and make something, like the birdhouse we did together, it's great. Sometimes on the weekends we go fishing, just him and me. We can sit for hours and not say anything, but I know Grandpa is happy he's with me."

Jack, a mature fifteen-year-old, understands the importance of what he calls this "special" time with his grandmother. "I see my grandmother when we're all together as a family, but it's way better when I have her all to myself." Since Jack was a little boy, he and his grandmother have had a weekly, now twice monthly, date. Part of their special time includes the tradition of eating ice cream cones together. "We spend at least one afternoon a week together. We used to go to the zoo or the museum, now we go to the movies. I don't care where we go or what we do and neither does she. If the weather is bad we watch videos at her apartment. Except she's gotta buy me an ice cream cone. That's the only rule. I feel like I know her real well. I've learned a lot about her life and some of the tough times she's been through. She really loves her family and me and I admire her for that. If I hadn't spent this much time with her, I wouldn't have been able to learn all that cool stuff about her."

Memory Making

Your undivided attention to your grandchild supplies the emotional and spiritual soil in which memories are planted and thrive. Jack's grandmother, Clarice, seventy-two, feels that her time alone with Jack has helped them to be very close and given them the chance to "make lots of memories together. When all of the family is together it's bedlam. It's hard to really talk to anyone when you're in a group situation. It's nice to see everyone, of course, but it's different from being alone with a child." Now Clarice is beginning to spend special time with her two other grandchildren, who are much younger than Jack. Soon it'll become a habit, just like with Jack. "They don't want ice cream cones, though," she says with a smile. "One likes licorice and the other always gets a book because she loves to read."

Clarice is aware of the long-lasting effects of her efforts. "I remember the times alone with my grandmother and how meaningful they were to me. I'll never forget them and I realize that every time we're together, I'm making these kinds of memories with my grandchildren. Next year, when Jack turns sixteen, I'm taking him to New York for a week. We'll stay in a hotel and go see some shows, just the two of us."

Shared activities such as story-telling, reading to each other, drawing, cooking from family recipes, car rides, playing games, music-making, dancing, and, yes, even watching television together can bring you closer to each other in the present, as well as create memories that last a lifetime and beyond if passed down from generation to generation.

Supplementing Parent's Attention

Unfortunately, many parents rarely have the luxury of giving much regular undivided attention to their children. Not only are parents caught up in the rush of the world, but also after working all day and enforcing the household's rules and regulations there just isn't much time left over. That is why the attention a grandparent gives a grandchild is so special and why most parents appreciate it.

Jack's mother, Ellen, approves of her son's special time with his grand-mother. "When it comes to his grandmother, well, he thinks she walks on water. They never miss their weekly get-together. It's wonderful the way she makes time to spend with Jack. I would have appreciated having a grandmother like that. She's such a stable force in his life. She's always there for him."

The Challenge of Paying Attention

It is all well and good if you know the importance of giving your grandchild undivided attention. But, let's face it; special time may be hard to come by. Consistently making time to spend with a grandchild can be difficult for a busy grandparent who lives far away. Even those who live close to each other don't always have the time or attention to spare. Time together is more difficult to come by because so many of us are separated from our families by distance.

Michiko, fifty-five, lives in California and visits her former home in Tokyo twice a year. She visits during school vacations so she can spend time alone with each of her three grandchildren. She takes each of them alone on a small trip for two days. "When I am with them" she says, "I try not to think about anything else but them. I know it's not the same as living next door, and it breaks my heart that I don't but a little attention can go a long way. And thank God for E-mail."

Being in the Moment

Even with the best of intentions, grandparents may sometimes find it hard to pay undivided attention to a grandchild. There can be times when a grandparent may find it very hard to quiet his worrying, planning, and daydreaming. Even the most easygoing, patient grandparent may find it a strain to listen on the telephone to a grandchild's half-hour dissertation on the toy she just got for her birthday. Yet grandchildren know when a grandparent is in the moment with them or not.

Ronnie, ten, says of visiting his grandfather Al, seventy-three, "When I'm at Grampa's he's always watching the stock market on TV and the phone rings every five minutes. I tell him don't answer the phone, especially when we're play-ing a game, but he answers it anyway 'cause he says it's important. I get so bored waiting for him to get off the phone, so then I don't want to play the game anymore. Then he gets off the phone and wants to keep playing, but I don't want to and then he gets annoyed at me. I guess I'm not as important as the stock market or his phone calls." Al was surprised to learn how Ronnie felt. "I never knew that giving undivided attention to Ronnie was so important," he says. "Now, whenever Ronnie visits, I get out of the house with him. We go for walks, whatever. That way I'm never tempted to answer the phone. Ronnie seems much happier now."

Dealing with a distracted or distractible youngster can offer a different kind of challenge to a grandparent trying to provide undivided attention. Seventy-two-year-old grandfather Ben, says, "My granddaughter, Lisa, is five and she's the apple of my eye. I love spending time with her, but she bounces around from activity to activity. First she likes to play with her dolls and wants me to join her. Then she wants to have a tea party, and then play horsey. When I lose interest she gets disappointed. Fortunately we both enjoy drawing and she can concentrate when she is drawing. So when I'm at the end of my rope I get out our pads and pencils and we sit at the table in the dining room and draw. While we draw, we talk about all kinds of things. She listens better to my stories when she is drawing, and she tells me about school and her friends. I know about things in her life that even her parents don't know. I just bought her a dollhouse. I like building things, so I think it will be fun putting it together with Lisa. We'll see about the tea parties."

GUIDELINES

Your undivided time and attention are the greatest gifts you can give your grandchild—and they cost nothing. Here are some guidelines to help you give your grandchild undivided attention and maximize the benefits of your special time together.

- Communicate to your family that you would like to spend time alone with your grandchild. Let them know how much you value this special time so that they respect it.

- If you live near your grandchild, establish a regular and appropriate time to be alone together so you can both look forward to it. Make sure to coordinate this time with the parents first.
- Agree on a prolonged special time during the year as well. If you do not live nearby, take your grandchild on a vacation or have her come for an extended visit to your home.
- Everything does not always have to be prearranged. Spontaneity can be fun. Go with the moment.
- Be creative in surmounting obstacles to your special time. If your grandchild cannot come to you, go to your grandchild (pick your grandchild up after school, for example).
- If you live far away from your grandchild, pay attention via E-mail, phone calls, letters, and visits.

CONCLUSION

The more undivided attention you give your grandchild, the stronger your relationship will be. Your grandchild will carry the memories you created together in her mind, heart, and spirit and immortalize them for the generations to come. Whatever your circumstances devote yourself to spending time together, in person or in other ways. This will ensure you a place in your grandchild's heart forever—and vice versa.

CHAPTER 24

Birth of a Grandchild

E|very time a new grandchild is born, you are reborn as a grandparent. This is a life-changing event. That is why it is so important to try to be present for it. I can assure you that being there to greet your new grandchild when he or she enters the world can be one of the greatest experiences of your life—a special moment of supreme joy and spiritual fulfillment for you as well as for the new parents.

A Family Affair

Difficult as it may be to do, being present at your grandchild's birth is worth every bit of the often considerable effort it takes. Every grandparent I have met over the past three decades who attended the birth of their grandchild—whether they were in the delivery room, right outside the delivery room, pacing the waiting room floor, rushing to get to the hospital, or even on the telephone during the process—found it a joyful, unforgettable, even magical experience.

Fifty-seven-year-old grandmother Ursula happily reports, "Being in the delivery room with my daughter was the most profound experience of my life. She gave birth to a beautiful baby boy on June 29, 1997, just before midnight.

Her husband and I had been with her since early afternoon helping her with her breathing and pushing. My husband was in the room as well, watching and taking pictures when appropriate. As midnight approached, she was exhausted, and then, with one more push, the baby's head began to appear. I could hardly contain my joy. I cried out, 'Oh, you can see his head coming.' She kept pushing and we kept counting and all of a sudden, he popped out, all slithery and pink and beautiful! The doctor tossed him up on my daughter's breast for his first cuddle with his mommy. The tears were flowing down everyone's cheeks and the excitement was almost unbearable. Our love and joy were boundless! It was the greatest celebration I've ever been to, that celebration of life. Of course I was overjoyed when my own babies were born. But this was different. In a sense it's hard to say but . . . it was more than me having a child; it was my *child* having a child. I heartily recommend that every grandparent who has the chance to participate in the birth of his or her grandchild do so. There is absolutely nothing on this earth like it. I sincerely hope I get another chance to do it."

Bringing Parents and Grandparents Closer

The birth of a child brings with it special moments for all involved. Of course, it is especially a sacred moment for the baby's parents. But what is often ignored is the profound mother-daughter moment that takes place. It is a unique emotional exchange between them. Ursula declares, "Being part of this birthing experience gave me the opportunity to see my little girl, my baby, turn into a beautiful, loving mother." Her daughter says, "I was a bit hesitant at first because I wasn't sure how I would be feeling when it came time to have the baby. But there was a moment when I was in labor and I looked over and saw my mom there. She looked so happy. It brought me closer to her because then I understood what she had gone through when I was born. . . . It was a perfect moment."

Another grandmother, forty-one-year-old Rosaria, said, "It was a sacred moment. The fact that my granddaughter was coming out of my daughter and my daughter had come out of me and perhaps one day a baby would come out of my granddaughter! I realized how connected we all were. There was a light that filled the room when my granddaughter came out. My daughter and I looked at each other and so much passed between us. It was pretty amazing."

Although most grandfathers may not relate in the same way to the labor and delivery process as most grandmothers can, the birth of a grandchild is an experience that is just as emotionally profound. While his wife and son were in the delivery room with his daughter-in-law and her mother, Simon, a fifty-nine-year-old grandfather held his two-year-old grandson, Allen, in his arms just outside. The nurse brought the newborn baby to the window for Simon and Allen. "It was a thrilling moment for me when the nurse showed us the baby—my new grandson and Allen's new brother. It brought me closer to my son and, strangely enough, to my daughter-in-law too. I had a personal feeling too, primitive, a strong feeling that I had created a family and was holding the next generation in my arms."

Of course this magic moment should be shared with the "other" grandparents too, who should also be invited into the delivery room. But when too many people are present medical discretion is always advised. As one obstetrician noted, "I believe in allowing family members to attend routine deliveries, but when a whole bunch of people arrive I give the two grandmothers first priority."

Why Is It Not a Common Practice?

Although historically it has been common for grandmothers to attend their grandchildren's birth (or even deliver the child), it is no longer common today. Many grandparents don't even consider asking to be present at their grandchild's birth. Why has this traditional practice been abandoned? Is it because people have lost touch with the joy this experience brings? Or perhaps they feel it is a private moment between the parents and not a family affair? Are grandparents afraid of interfering, thus depriving themselves of one of the greatest joys of life? Are they afraid of getting in the way of the couple, or the hospital, and so never even ask the future parents if they can attend the birth?

Of course, it's understandable that grandparents who live great distances away may not offer to come because they find it logistically impossible to get to the birth on the spur of the moment. Nevertheless, many people do not even consider that, with good planning, this is a surmountable obstacle.

Parents neglect to ask grandparents to attend their grandchild's birth for many of the same reasons. In a culture that emphasizes individuality and independence, many mothers-to-be view the birth as a private event between themselves and the fathers. For others, understandably, modesty about someone besides a mate being in the delivery room may pose a problem; the idea of a group of people peeking over her shoulder during the delivery can be off-putting to an already stressed-out expectant mother. And with the best of intentions some parents hesitate to burden their parents by asking them to attend the birth or stay to help out after the baby comes.

Being There Is Important

Whatever the reason, it is important that families think carefully about having grandparents attend the birth. Whatever the family decides, the wishes of the expectant parents should be respected. When differences arise however, things can be worked out to everyone's satisfaction. I recommend *presence*, not *intrusion*, on the part of grandparents. Grandma and Grandpa don't have to be looking over the doctor's shoulder at the moment of birth. They can be waiting outside the door, right there to hold their grandchild in those first few precious minutes of life, or they can be patched in by telephone or video. Being part of the celebration is what counts.

Sheila, sixty-two, was happy to wait outside of the delivery room as her daughter wished, but was asked to come in at the last moment. "I think respecting her wishes and not making her feel guilty about who she wanted with her was important. Grandparents should never force their way in, and certainly not with cameras, without being sure that it's what the mother wants. It was great to be there with her, but the waiting room would have been just fine, too."

Parents and grandparents can cooperate to include both sides of the family in making plans to help out before and after the birth. By coordinating duties and plans with the parents beforehand you can truly assist the parents and share in their joy.

Even when it is possible and practical, not all grandparents may be eager to attend a birth. For example, one grandfather said he didn't want to be in the hospital for "personal reasons." First, he hated hospitals; second, he was sure his daughter didn't want him to see her suffering. A grandmother said she didn't attend her grandchild's birth because "I didn't want to disturb my daughter-in-law. I just felt she would rather be with her own mother." Other grandparents are busy, don't live close enough, or don't consider the birth a priority. When Rosa, thirty-two, went into labor, she did not call her mother because she didn't want her mother to lose a whole day of work just to be by her side.

When grandparents do attend, there seems to be a protocol. For example, out of consideration, a new father may allow the mother's parents extra time with their daughter in labor until the baby arrives. Men will often defer to women's instincts and expertise in such matters allowing the future grandmothers to spend more time with the expectant mother during labor. As a nurse said, "when the grandparents are around during labor it's usually the grandmothers who are most involved—first the mother's mother, then the father's mother, then the men." On the other hand, Charlene, twenty-five, was happy to have her mother-in-law help her through her labor and delivery because her own mother was not available.

Logistical Problems

Even if everyone is in agreement, being there at the right time can pose a logistical problem if grandparents do not live close by, or aren't available when the baby decides to make its entrance into the world. Geographic distance can be an impediment to assisting at the birth of a grandchild. Roscoe, sixty-four, planned to attend his grandchild's birth. "I live in Boston and my daughter lives in Los Angeles. My wife and I planned to go out to my daughter the week before she was going to have a cesarean and look after my other two grandchildren. The date was set and we were ready to go. But she went into labor early. When she called we packed up and hopped on the first plane we could and raced to the hospital from the airport. She had just had the baby when we arrived so we missed the birth. But at least we could spend time with our daughter and the baby soon after."

If you live far away from your child, you will have to plan carefully to be around when the baby comes. Fortunately, many deliveries today are planned in advance.

Another impediment some grandparents sometimes run into is the attitude of hospital staff. In the past grandparents and even husbands were viewed as outsiders in the delivery room. Fortunately, there is a growing trend among obstetricians and midwives to invite family members to participate in all phases of the birth. Families are now discussing their wishes with hospital staff and making arrangements to attend labor and delivery.

Welcoming an Adopted Grandchild or Stepgrandchild

If you are not a biological grandparent, your role in welcoming the new baby is still very important. If you are a stepgrandparent, it is important that you become part of the welcoming committee for a new child as soon as possible. The more you are involved in the prenatal process the better (see Chapter 46, "Stepgrandparenting"). If you are expecting an adopted grandchild, attending the birth (or the first day an adopted child is received) can be a very meaningful experience too (see Chapter 35, "Adoption"). Whatever the situation, biology aside, the same joys and thrills are there.

Dora, sixty-three, was at the airport with her husband, and her daughter-in-law's parents to welcome their newly adopted twin grandchildren from Russia. "I couldn't wait to hold those darlings. We were all so excited. I started to cry when my son gave me Derek to hold . . . and I really lost it when I passed Derek to my husband. I said 'Here Grandpa,' and he lost it too. I knew it was important for the kids [the new parents] to have all of us there."

GUIDELINES

Being there when a new grandchild comes along can be one of the most thrilling moments of your life. Sometimes this is easy; sometimes it's not. Here are some guidelines to help you be as active a participant in your grandchild's birth as you and your family choose.

- Plan the logistics of your involvement carefully.
- Respect the parents' authority and wishes in all matters.
- Offer your support to the parents-to-be during the prenatal process and ask how you can be involved.
- Discuss your wishes to attend the birth of your grandchild with the parents-to-be, and ask them to make your wishes known to the hospital staff.
- If it can be arranged, attend a childbirth-education class with the mother-to-be.
- If you live far away and plan to attend the birth, make provisions ahead of time to be away for as long as necessary. Have your plans ready to be put into motion on the spur of the moment. After all, you never know exactly when your grandchild will be born.
- Coordinate your wishes and actions with the other grandparents and family members.
- If possible, plan to make yourself available to the new parents, to use you as they see fit, for as long as they need you. If you're a long-distance grandparent, the longer you stay the better you will get to know your new grandchild. The same holds true when you are welcoming an adopted grandchild or a stepgrandchild.

CONCLUSION

Sharing in the joy and wonder of your grandchild's birth is one of life's greatest experiences. Communicating to the parents-to-be that you are there to support them will send a positive message to begin your grandparenthood. Make an effort to work toward the best arrangement possible.

CHAPTER 25

Baby-Sitting

A s a grandparent, you may often be called upon to care for your grandchild. This privilege or duty (depending on the circumstances) is commonly known as baby-sitting. If you are fortunate enough to live near your grandchild, baby-sitting allows you to spend one-on-one time with him, thus strengthening the bond between you (see Chapter 23, "Attention"). When this arrangement works, everyone benefits because you help the parents by giving them some free time or supplying sorely needed child care.

Although single parents usually are more in need of an occasional respite from child-care duties, married couples are often desperate for relief as well (see Chapter 41, "Raising Grandchildren"). Unfortunately, some grandparents do not enjoy baby-sitting, and some parents take grandparents' baby-sitting efforts for granted. In these cases, baby-sitting can become a source of conflict.

Choice or Obligation?

Sy, sixty-two, made a conscious choice to baby-sit his two-year-old granddaughter every Tuesday. He also has a full-time job at a family-friendly home-improvement store, but luckily for him, his employers allow him to work Saturdays in exchange for his Tuesdays off. "It gives me time alone with my granddaughter and gives my daughter a day off to shop and do whatever she has to do. My wife works full-time, too, but her job doesn't allow her flexible hours like I have. I know it's something I don't have to do; it's something I want to do. My granddaughter and I are pretty close now."

Other grandparents say they do not feel that they have a choice when it comes to baby-sitting their grandchildren; they feel it's just an annoying obligation that comes with being a grandparent. Others even express feelings of being exploited by their children (although these sentiments are rare).

Frances, sixty-two and a single grandmother, is unhappy because her daughter and son-in-law want her to baby-sit their two children almost every weekend. Frances said, "My daughter told me that she and her husband needed time off from parenting to pay attention to each other, but I feel like they are putting their parental responsibilities on my back. One weekend I wasn't able to baby-sit and they got really angry. My daughter even began questioning me. She asked me if I truly enjoyed being a grandmother! Of course I enjoy being with my grandchildren, but I'm also feeling exploited. And I'm scared my grandchildren will think I don't want to be with them."

Clearing the Air

When such a situation exists, it is important to deal with it directly and thereby clear the air of resentment. "I believe there are two ways of looking at things, and I had to work it out," says Ricardo, sixty-five. "In one way I resented that my daughter always wanted me to watch her children. She acted like she didn't know that I have a life of my own. On the other hand, I love playing with my grandchildren. I just love to be with them. We are very close. I was in a curious place, enjoying something I wanted to do, but resenting it because I felt exploited." Ricardo decided to confront his daughter directly. "I sat down with my daughter and I told her how I felt. Would you believe that she had no idea at all that I would not jump at the chance to watch the kids! She even said she thought she was making the kids and me happy by leaving us alone! Talk about misunderstandings. When I told her she said she understood completely and thanked me profusely for everything. She said that I was such a good father and grandfather that she took me for granted. I guess that's what it was all about, being taken for granted. Anyway, now I am doing the same amount of baby-sitting as I ever did but the resentment is gone. It paid off to air my feelings."

When a grandparent feels exploited, open and direct communication is the answer. Grandparents and parents must sit down, discuss their feelings, and listen to each other and find a solution that all parties can live with (see Chapters 33, "Between Parents and Grandparents," and 44, "Mediation"). Parents frequently are not aware of grandparents' feelings simply because the grandparents never took the time to express them—or vice versa. Open communication and mutual respect between parents, children, and grandparents makes for the best baby-sitting climate.

How Grandchildren Feel

Unless a grandparent is openly resentful about having to baby-sit, most grandchildren prefer grandparents over paid sitters. Like their parents, grandparents are permanent. Grandparents are good for safety and support, and they're fun. Grandchildren find their grandparents usually let up a bit on rules and regulations and often are open to some spontaneous antics. One humorous exception to this rule is Bert, twelve, who had a crush on the eighteen-year-old high school cheerleader who was the baby-sitter. "I have fun when my grandparents baby-sit of course," Bert says, "but I like Patty to baby-sit me and my little sisters because she is *gorgeous*."

GUIDELINES

Baby-sitting can be a wonderful opportunity for grandparents and grandchildren to bond. However, it has to be done with an open heart and appreciated by all. Here are some guidelines to help to make the experience a positive one.

- Sort out your own feelings about baby-sitting. Don't do anything you resent.
- Sit down with the parents to discuss mutual needs.
- Schedule baby-sitting to coincide with your availability and the most necessary times for parents. For example, if a parent has a regular weekly appointment, make yourself available at that time.
- Remain flexible. Sometimes parents need an extra helping hand.
- If you believe the parents' demand for baby-sitting services is inappropriate, get supplementary help. For example, suggest the parents employ a baby-sitter or bring the grandchildren to daycare.
- If parents do choose to put the grandchildren in daycare, offer to drive them or pick them up at the end of the day.
- From time to time people's needs change. Discuss and review the family baby-sitting plan on a regular basis. Make sure it works for everyone.
- Keep the child's joy at having you baby-sit for her in the forefront.

CONCLUSION

Children usually love to have their grandparents baby-sit for them. When grandparents begin to feel that baby-sitting is more an obligation than a joy, it's important to communicate such feelings to the parents and try and reach a compromise. After all, baby-sitting a grandchild is a precious opportunity to solidify relationships and create new memories, as well as give parents a much needed helping hand.

CHAPTER 26

Favoritism

If you are conflicted about having a favorite grandchild, do not fret. You are not alone. Thirty years of research and casual conversations with grandparents have taught me that many grandparents have a natural tendency to play favorites. Even when a grandparent does not *want* to pick a favorite grandchild, the feelings are present and have to be acknowledged. As Sam, a sixty-six-year-old grandfather, put it, "Let's face it, don't we all like some people better than others? It's going to be the same with grandchildren, isn't it?"

Having feelings of favoritism toward a grandchild is understandable; it is how you deal with those feelings that counts. In fact, most grandparents do pretty well. They make a conscious effort to keep their feelings to themselves because they are aware that overtly choosing a favorite grandchild can be hurtful to the other grandchildren—and to the parents too.

Why Grandparents Want to Play Favorites

Why do some grandparents have stronger feelings of love, bonding, and companionship toward one grandchild over another? And how do the parents and grandchildren feel when they do?

In most instances, a grandparent favors a certain grandchild because the two of them share a common quality—for example, being the same gender, being a youngest or eldest child, and having similar personality traits, temperaments, physical characteristics, or talents. A grandparent may be attracted to a certain quality that one grandchild possesses (intelligence, musicality, athletic ability). Many grandparents who single out a grandchild for extra attention say that the two of them "fit" well in some way or another (see Chapter 15, "Temperament and Personality").

This feeling of being a good fit along with overt feelings of love and enthusiasm are the relevant factors many grandparents describe when speaking of their favorite grandchild. Listen to Jan, fifty-four, describing her granddaughter, Anna: "Joy—pure joy. I get such a kick out of Anna as a person. She is so sweet and good and so interested in everything I do. She just makes me so happy. When I come to visit, there is Anna on the stairs waiting for me. Her older brothers, whom I adore too, used to wait for me on the stairs, too, but that only lasted until they were three. But Anna, now five, still brings out the brass band whenever I visit. Of course, I do the same for her, too. We go so well together."

The Irresistible Attraction

I queried more than two hundred grandparents about having a favorite grandchild; all of them agreed that their first grandchild was special, just because it was the first. Studies show that the first grandchild makes a grandparent feel like a "valued elder" and supplies a feeling of well-being (Kornhaber 1982, Spruytte 1999). Otherwise, the reasons they gave for an irresistible attraction toward one grandchild over another were highly personal and diverse. Goodness, talent, and intelligence were high on the list. "She is a little angel," said one grandmother about her five-year-old granddaughter. "It's such a pleasure to be around her because she's so sweet." Another grandmother said her nine-year-old grandson was her favorite because he was a "genius." "My granddaughter, Lilia, is so beautiful. What a knockout!" said one grandfather.

Another grandfather, Reggie, seventy-two, was a former minor league baseball player. He now has seven grandchildren, but he named Darryl, now nine, as his favorite because "that kid has the best throwing arm I've ever seen. He's going to the majors."

Some grandparents described their attraction as a hard-to-explain, but exceptionally strong feeling. "I'll admit it," said Peg, sixty-three and a grandmother of six. "I'm extra-special crazy about Megan, my six-year-old granddaughter. I don't know what it is. It's an irresistible attraction that I can't quite explain. She does have my nose, but other than that we're not really alike. She likes to be the center of attention and I'm more the wallflower-type. But whenever I look at her she makes me smile. It's not that I love Megan more; in fact, I love all my other grandchildren just as much. Maybe it's just that I like her more as a person so I like being with her more. Wow, it makes me feel really guilty to say that. But that's the truth. I would never say that to my other grandchildren or their parents."

Not a Tenured Position

The position of favored grandchild is not necessarily a permanent one. That's because some of the factors that cause a grandparent to favor one child over another can change. Age is one such factor. As one grandparent said, "I treat them all special when they are babies. It's different when they grow up. Although I still love them, of course, they're not as cute or vulnerable anymore."

Other factors come into play too—accomplishments, for example. When Richard, twenty-one, announced to his attorney grandfather that he wanted to become an attorney too, his grandfather was overwhelmed with joy. "I immediately became his favorite grandchild," says Richard. "Before that I was just one of the bunch." His grandfather sort of agrees. "I wouldn't go so far as to say Richard became my favorite grandchild, but now we have so much more in common because we are going to have so much more to commiserate about. He'll get more attention, that's for sure."

The Problems of Favoritism

Having a favorite grandchild can be a wonderful thing if it is an only grandchild. When there are other grandchildren having a preference for one grandchild over another are feelings best experienced *covertly*. Sam, sixty-six, says of his thirteen-year-old grandson, "I love Adam a lot. There is something special between Adam and me. In my heart I favor him, but I don't show it because I don't want to hurt my other grandkids."

When a grandparent's favoritism is expressed *overtly* problems can occur. It's important to emphasize that if grandparents have a favorite grandchild, they cannot change what they *feel*. But they do have control over how they handle their feelings and how they *act*.

Handling Your Feelings of Favoritism

Phil, a sixty-five-year-old self-professed politically correct grandfather is adamant about not choosing between grandchildren. "I wouldn't even let myself think about playing favorites. How would you like it if your grandfather liked your brother or sister better than you?"

Not everyone of course, can be as evenhanded as Phil. If you have a favorite grandchild, you've no reason to feel guilty or ashamed. Acknowledge your feelings to yourself then learn how to manage them. You will be faced with two options: the first is to keep your feelings to yourself and/or only share your feelings with certain people when appropriate.

Your second option is to act on your feelings and blatantly display your favoritism. When grandparents behave in this manner, the parents and the other grandchildren can feel hurt and resentful.

Connie, fifty-six, said she adored her only grandson, seven-year-old Harold. Harold's parents were upset about how Connie favored Harold over all her other grandchildren. Connie's son, Walter, said, "It's pathetic. It makes the girls feel awful and I think it makes Harold feel funny, too, because it puts him in an uncomfortable position with his sisters. The girls resent Harold and their grandmother. My wife and I have talked to my mother about this issue numerous times, but she is so stubborn. She just doesn't get it."

Connie felt that her family took her fondness for Harold too seriously. "Harold is the only boy. He will carry on the family name. He's the only grandson I have. In my mind, he deserves special attention." Although Connie never changed her behavior, the situation eventually improved when Harold and his sisters grew up. Once Harold was more in charge of his own life, he could clearly express his feelings to his grandmother and the way her behavior made him feel.

What Grandchildren Feel

No matter how hard a grandparent may work at being discreet for fear of offending their other grandchildren or their grandchild's parents, children always know when they are their grandparent's favorite. They also know when they are not.

It is no fun when you are not number one. Carol, eleven, is the third oldest of five sisters and one brother. Carol said, "My older brother Tom is Grandpa's favorite. Maybe it's because he's a boy. Grandpa looks at him differently. When Grandpa says 'Who wants to go to the store with me?' he always looks at Tom. I wish I was a favorite, but I have too many sisters. It's hard to be special." Fortunately Carol complained enough that her grandmother made an extra effort to spend time with her by becoming a "soccer grandma" for Carol's team.

When there are only two grandchildren and one is chosen over the other, it can be very painful to the runner-up—and to the favorite as well! Jan, fifty-four, says, "I know I was my grandmother's favorite. And my brother knew it, too. It really hurt him and he took it out on me. My parents kept telling him that Grandma didn't have a favorite, but my brother knew she favored me. Kids aren't stupid."

Jan, Anna's grandmother, offers this advice: "Keep your feelings to yourself, act equally towards all the children. The less said the better. When Anna and I are alone we know we are each other's favorites."

What Parents Feel

Keep in mind that parents want you to adore all their children and can be hurt if they see you favoring one grandchild over another. This situation can arise within a family with several children, or between the families of siblings. When other problems are present in the family, choosing a favorite grandchild can fan the flames of a family conflagration.

Gwen, thirty-five and a mother of two, at one time would not allow her mother to see her children. "My mother and I don't get along in the first place. Then, because she's angry with me, she favors my sister's children," Gwen says. "Whenever we were together my mother would fuss over the other grandkids, but not mine. My kids felt really rejected. So one day, I called my mom and told her how I felt. I told her that was the last straw; she couldn't see my kids anymore. I would not have them treated that way. My mother was very shocked, denied everything, blah, blah, blah. But I stuck to my guns for three months and she finally got it that I was totally serious and would not tolerate her behavior. So one day she called me and we talked a really long time. I told her I thought she was acting that way toward my kids as a way of getting back at me. She said she missed my kids and would try to change. So I let her see my kids again and I must say I can tell she's making an effort. I can see her trying to be nicer and I know it's not an easy thing for her to do. I think it's just not in her nature. We're still working on it."

Being the Favorite Grandparent

It is very normal to want to be your grandchild's favorite grandparent as well. But beware! This is a dangerous path. Do not try to compete for this prize; you risk alienating family members. Being yourself is enough. (For more information, see Chapter 34, "Between Grandparents.")

GUIDELINES

Being a favorite grandparent or having a favorite grandchild is fine if you are the only grandparent with one grandchild. In any other case, you will have to curb your enthusiasm so others will not feel hurt. Here are some guidelines to help.

- Acknowledge and accept your feelings of having a favorite grandchild. It is very common and there is no reason to feel guilty or ashamed.

- Keep your feelings of preference to yourself. You can give your feelings free rein when you are alone with your favorite grandchild. Show how you feel, but do not say it. Your grandchild will know how you feel. Kids are kids. I have seen instances where a favorite grandchild used a grandparent's personal words of love, preference, and praise to hurt other grandchildren—and their parents.
- Be sensitive to how the parents feel about your relationship with their child.
- Be an equal opportunity grandparent. Treat all of your grandchildren equally so that no one in the family feels rejected, hurt, or ignored.
- Constantly reassess your relationship with each grandchild. Children grow and change. A grandchild with whom you did not have a good fit last year might have changed a lot for the better.

CONCLUSION

If you have a favorite grandchild, enjoy. Whatever the reason behind your special relationship (your grandchild may have a similar temperament, interests, skills, values, or whatever), enjoy the good feelings for as long as they last. They might last a lifetime, or they might be transferred to your next grandchild. Above all, enjoy what's in your heart. However, if you have other grandchildren, do be careful about how you act toward them. You wouldn't want your other grandchildren or their parents to feel rejected or ignored.

Keep your secret, and enjoy it.

Spoiling Grandchildren

D|o not be surprised if you have a natural inclination to overindulge your grandchildren. Most grandparents do. And most of the time parents will not mind, especially if their own grandparents indulged them. For the most part, parents are understanding and have few problems with normal indulgence. Indeed, they often delight in the pleasure their child gets from a grandparent's gift of attention or time. Sometimes, though, as the parents see it, grandparents can go too far.

Why Grandparents Spoil Their Grandchildren

A grandparent's natural instinct to spoil a grandchild is rooted in the unique nature of the relationship, which is quite different from the parent-child bond. Although a parent loves his or her child, out of necessity the relationship tends to be more conditional than a grandparent's relationship with the child. Parents have a duty to teach and train their child; therefore the child perceives that a portion of parental love will be given or withdrawn according to his behavior. Approval and rejection, praise and punishment are built-in conditions of a child's relationship with his parents. As six-year-old Selma puts it, "Mommy loves me when I am a good girl and gets mad when I do bad things."

To a child, part of the magic of grandparental love is that it is *unconditional*. In the best of circumstances, grandparents, exempt from the parental burden of constant disciplinary vigilance, can give their love and attention freely. Grandparents can reward their grandchild for just being. John, seven, says, "My grandmother never thinks I'm bad. She is happy when I eat and go to the bathroom." When we factor in the extra free time and financial resources many of today's grandparents enjoy, the stage is set for spoiling.

Making Up for the Past

Spoiling is often linked to a grandparent's past deprivation. For grandparents who were raised in tough times, spoiling is a reflection of their need to give their grandchildren a better life. Hedda is a seventy-eight-year-old grandmother who fled Nazi Germany and immigrated to America. As a parent, she and her husband worked hard to give her daughter the bare necessities that they'd never had at that age: enough to eat, physical safety, religious freedom, a good education, and more. Hedda's eight-year-old grandson, Lewis, has all his basic needs met by his parents, which leaves Hedda free to delight in buying him games and toys or taking him to the theater. Making her grandson happy gives Hedda a deep sense of satisfaction. "When I was young, I never thought I would ever live to have a child, but I did. I was blessed with my beautiful daughter. My grandson is my daughter *plus*, an extra blessing. Now that I have more time and money than when I was young, I can give more." Hedda's daughter Sophie is fine with her mother's behavior. "Mom might be a little overgenerous at times, but my son adores her. My husband and I have no problem with it."

The Boundaries of Spoiling

Understand that what may look like "spoiling" to someone on the outside, may not *feel* that way to a grandparent and grandchild. Jane, sixty-eight, says, "My son accused me of spoiling my granddaughter and namesake, Jane. I must say I honestly had no idea what he was talking about. Jane and I always have a great time together."

There is a fine line here that you need to know about. Spoiling is something that most grandparents do (see Chapter 31, "Spending for Your Grandchild"). If you enjoy a good relationship with your family and shower your grandchild with attention, gifts, food, or fun, there probably will be no complaints from the parents. You are happy, your grandchild is happy, and the parents are happy. Because the average parent is removed from the loop, the unbridled joy and pleasure they see their parents and children enjoying with one another can be perceived as wonderful and natural or, on the opposite side of the spectrum, inappropriate and disrespectful.

When a grandparent is insensitive to the parents' wishes, financial circumstances, or competitive nature, and continues spoiling their grandchild, it can result in family friction. So before you run out and buy that puppy for your grandson's birthday, ask his parents how they feel about their son receiving such a gift. It could be that the last thing they want in the house is a puppy or perhaps they believe their son is not ready for the responsibility of a pet. Whatever the case, discuss with the parents their policy on gift giving and respect their wishes.

Constructive Spoiling

Jean, a forty-three-year-old mother, related a wonderful story that demonstrates "constructive spoiling." Jean was hard pressed to meet her twelve-year-old son Bobby's demands for a guitar. "He had been asking for a guitar for so long. But he was not doing well at school and he's not very disciplined. He often starts things without finishing them and I do not have the money to be indulging his every whim. Frankly, I didn't think he deserved a guitar." When Jean told her parents about Bobby's constant demands for a guitar, they were more than eager to pay for the guitar as well as guitar lessons. But Jean was hesitant to accept their offer. "Bobby's grandparents give him almost everything he wants and sometimes I think it is just too much," said Jean. Jean wanted her son to be happy, but she thought it would be in his best interest if he could do something to earn his grandparent's gift. Finally, Jean and her parents decided that Bobby could have the guitar and the lessons, but only if he brought his grades up. "He worked really hard at school and actually improved his grades considerably. I was really very impressed. It showed me he really did want to play the guitar. He practices all the time. He is a lucky kid to have grandparents like that. And I'm lucky to have parents who will listen to me and work with me."

The Parents' Perspective

Parents are left out of the spoiling fun. Therefore, you must carefully monitor their responses to what you are doing. Always be aware of the boundary that separates normal spoiling as a charming aspect of your relationship with your grandchildren from the type of spoiling that is harmful. Be careful not to participate in behavior that undermines a parent's authority, thus hurting the parent and placing your grandchild in an awkward position.

Lily, a single mother of three, "enjoys watching my mom and my kids together. My mom is a very kind and generous person and the kids have a lot of fun with her. But one time we all went to Disneyland and my youngest, Sarah, kept asking me to buy her this doll. I told her no, because I had already bought toys for everyone that day. That night I found the doll she had asked me for lying on her bed. She told me grandma had bought it for her—I guess when I was not looking. For a minute, I got really mad, then I talked to my mom about it and we agreed that in the future we would work together when something like that came up. I want the kids to have fun with their grandma, but I don't want them disobeying or losing respect for me either. And I don't want them to think they are entitled to get whatever they want. Mom shouldn't have gotten Sarah that doll in the first place."

One of Lily's concerns is that her children are raised with a sense of fiscal responsibility. She has shared this concern with her mother so that her mother can support her in achieving the goal. "Now my mom makes sure my kids know that she is not a bottomless pit of money, and they have learned not to expect that grandma is going to buy them anything they want. I like it, though, that she buys them those little extras that I can't afford. It's a treat for them and it makes my mom happy, too." By communicating with her mother, Lily is able to maintain family harmony and set a good example for her children. "When we don't see eye-to-eye about the kids," Lily says, "we sit down, tell each other what's on our minds and try and work it out or at least find a compromise we can live with. We're two different people. Plus, I'm the mom and she's the grandma and the kids have to deal with that. She does indulge them a lot, but after all, she's the grandma. Isn't that what grandmas do?"

How parents handle overindulgent grandparents depends for the most part on the closeness, respect, and understanding among family members. If serious rancor or pathology is present and the parent-grandparent relationship is severely impaired, some parents may even go so far as to deny grandparents any time with their grandchildren at all (see Chapter 42, "Legal Issues"). You will be more clued in to the spoiling boundary if you understand and respect the parents' rules and the standards by which their children are being raised. With this knowledge, you can optimally manage your natural urge to spoil your grandchild and express it appropriately so that *everyone* is happy.

Parent-Grandparent Conflicts

The issue of spoiling can become especially sensitive in situations when parents see substantial changes in the way their own parents behave (in a more generous and kindly way) as grandparents than they did as parents. Old resentments are sometimes easily rekindled. Many grandparents, mellowing with age, are aware of the severity they displayed as parents and are eager to make up for it. Their grandchildren are the natural recipients of this benevolence. This change in attitude and behavior on the part of grandparents can sometimes bewilder and even wound parents, who may have felt deprived as children. The parent may feel envious and hurt, especially if the grandparent seems exclusively focused on enjoying the grandchild and does not seem interested in having fun with the parent. To the parent, this is like rubbing salt in a deep emotional wound.

Anna, six, says, "Every day Grandpa comes over and takes me to the park. We play together and he pushes me on the swing." Anna's mom, Sheila is a bit incredulous about these daily excursions. "Dad never took me to the park, much less pushed me on the swing or sat in the sandbox with me. Maybe Dad's spoiling

Anna." Peter, Sheila's father, says, "I am certainly not spoiling my granddaughter Anna. Not at all. We only have fun. I never had free time when I was a father and now I do. There is nothing I like to do better than to spend it with my grandchildren."

At the extreme, when a parent feels deprived of a grandparent's love and attention, or even rejected by the grandparent, the parent might actually feel a sense of rivalry with her own child for the grandparent's affections. Bernice is angry with her mother-in-law, Candy. Bernice says, "In the first place, she never accepted the fact that I married her son. And she spoils my daughter. Candy spends money on my daughter like it's going out of style. She has a lot more money than we do. They have a great time and when they come home so happy, I really feel resentful! I hate to say this, but it is the truth. I feel jealous that my daughter likes her grandma so much. Why can't Candy accept me, and treat me even a little like she treats my daughter?" As a grandmother who is older and allegedly wiser, Candy should make the effort to reach out to Bernice.

Overworked, overextended parents saddled with trying to make ends meet while being the best possible parents may feel pangs of envy about the carefree fun their children are having with their grandparents. If this scenario is taking place in your family, try lightening the parents' load as much as possible and add some fun to their lives. Li, seventy-one, was hearing complaints from her overworked physician daughter Tia, a single mother. "The harder Tia worked, the more she complained I was spoiling my granddaughter Mai," Li said. "So I thought about it. I think she just needed some pampering herself." Li decided to pay for Tia to go to a health spa for a weekend, while she babysat Mai. "That made Tia feel spoiled," smiled Li. "I swear she looked five years younger when she came back from the spa."

Considerate Spoiling

As a wise and sensitive grandparent, be alert to the parents' needs and wishes, and respect their position on the giving of gifts and relaxation of discipline. I call this considerate spoiling.

If parents have strict rules about bedtime, sweets, or television, respect these rules and do nothing to undermine them. Listen to the parents' feelings. Try to remember what it felt like when *you* were a parent. I can't emphasize enough that although spoiling may be viewed in a lighthearted way between family members who get along well, it can balloon into a serious issue when a family is experiencing problems.

GUIDELINES

Spoiling can be a lot of fun for you and your grandchild. But it requires being alert to any negative side effects that may be troubling other family members. If you spoil considerately, you will avoid problems. Here are some guidelines to help.

- Follow your heart when spoiling your grandchild.
- Make sure no one in the family feels left out.
- Treat your child as well as you treat your grandchild.
- Praise your child for being a good parent. Tell your child how proud you are of him or her.
- Tell the parent you love your grandchild.
- Respect the parents' rational rules (as much as possible) regarding discipline and gift giving.
- If parents believe you have gone too far with your spoiling, sit down and talk about it. Give everyone involved the chance to fully express his or her thoughts and feelings. Establish a family policy that respects personal differences and shares a common ethical and moral base.

CONCLUSION

Spoiling your grandchild can be a golden opportunity for you to give your generosity free rein and abandon yourself to the spirit of play with your grandchild.

You now have your grandchild's parents there to take responsibility for raising their child, allowing you the freedom to give your grandchild what perhaps you had to deny your children when they were growing up. Make sure to monitor the boundaries of your spoiling so it does not become a problem for the rest of the family or have a negative effect on your grandchild. Treat your children as well as you treat your grandchildren.

CHAPTER 28

Substance Abuse

W| e live in a time of widespread chemical plagues that are decimating the mental and physical health of our grandchildren. Children's addiction to cigarettes poses a serious public health problem. Despite many anti-smoking campaigns, more than three million teenagers are still smoking today. Three thousand more start smoking each day. Alcohol and substance abuse are additional plagues that continue to spread as increasingly potent substances become available. The average age of first-time drug use among teens is thirteen, although some children start earlier. About 15 percent of American children between nine and twelve are offered drugs—usually these offers come from their peers.

Although grandparents are often called upon to help when a child in the family is afflicted, it is imperative that grandparents be educated in these matters so they may take a more informed, active role. As a grandparent cooperating with your grandchild and her parents, your roles are both preventative and curative.

It is beyond the scope of this book to deal with the particulars of each substance. However, this chapter will provide you with some general information about commonly abused substances and resources that you can use to become more informed about them.

Tobacco

In spite of a major educational campaign, many children are still using tobacco. Chances are your grandchild will at least experiment with smoking. Be especially alert if your grandchild's parents or friends smoke because this increases the chances that he will try tobacco.

Try to combat the habit before it begins. It's never too early to begin your personal antismoking campaign. Educate yourself and your grandchild against the dangers of smoking, which include diseases such as cancer and emphysema, birth defects in future children, and so on. Emphasize that smoking may be a precursor to using other drugs (see the resources at the end of this chapter). Band together with parents to set a good example. If parents are not setting a good example, urge them to do so for the love of their child.

Alcohol and Substance Abuse

Most adolescents will experiment with alcohol and drugs at one time or another. Fifty percent of teenagers report that they have tried marijuana in high school. Usually they start with nicotine and alcohol before moving on to recreational marijuana and then proceeding to harder drugs such as cocaine, crystal methamphetamine, and even heroin. Many continue with these substances—especially if there is a family history of substance abuse, psychological and social problems, or depression. Continued substance abuse can lead to school failure. It also can play a leading role in some of the more disastrous social consequences such as addiction, traffic accidents, sexual problems, exposure to AIDS and other diseases, pregnancy, violence, incarceration, and death.

Signs and Symptoms

Be alert to the signs that your grandchild might be abusing drugs. Here are some of the most common signs to watch for:

- Physical symptoms: poor appearance, illness, glazed eyes, fatigue, and weight loss

- Emotional and psychological symptoms: personality changes, mood changes, irritability, depression, lack of interest, and sluggishness
- Family relationship problems: anger, violent outbursts, withdrawal, stealing, breaking rules, and lying
- School problems: decreased interest, falling grades, negative attitude, and truancy
- Social problems: change in friends to groups that are less interested in school activities, on the fringes of society, or frankly criminal

Huffing

Huffing, or sniffing inhalants, is a form of drug abuse that is on the rise. Children huff chemical products, such as nail polish remover, hair spray, gasoline, and other toxic substances, to get high. Unfortunately, these products contain toxic gasses like toluene and butane, which wreak havoc on the liver and kidneys, depress the bone marrow and destroy brain tissue, which can lead to permanent brain damage. Huffing begins at a very young age. Experts say that inhalants are the third most abused substances behind tobacco and alcohol. Inhalants are also habituating; this means that each use requires a larger dose to attain the desired effect. In addition to symptoms associated with other forms of drug abuse, the most common signs of huffing are illness, mouth sores, low appetite, breath odor, slurred speech, bleary eyes, general slovenliness, and stains on clothing or fingers from substances such as correction fluid or felt markers.

What Grandparents Can Do

Many grandparents today are unaware of the extent of the drug problem until it strikes their own families. It is important to educate yourself in-depth about substance abuse. Doing so will increase your awareness of the drug problem in your community. Read all you can, of course, but getting to know the issue *first-hand* is the best teacher. Volunteering in a local drug treatment program or treatment facility or program will give you a quick education on the subject.

Once educated, you will have the knowledge to help others—especially family members. Many parents of children with drug problems prefer to look the other way at first especially if the parents themselves are smoking or using alcohol or recreational drugs. When parents are late in their attempts to intervene, the healing process is just that much more difficult. That is why it is important to help parents to supply a good role model for their child.

GUIDELINES

- Let everyone know you are aware of the drug problem and active in doing something about it.
- Don't just talk about it; do something about it. For example, some grandparents have started community grandparent watchdog groups and hot lines to make sure the problem is recognized and dealt with.
- If your grandchild exhibits any signs of drug abuse, consider it an emergency. Intervene immediately. Remember that this is a serious disease. You have the right and the duty to respond in the same way you would if you discovered that your grandchild had diabetes, epilepsy, or any other life-threatening illness.
- If you suspect a problem, discuss it with your grandchild's parents, call a family meeting, get together with your grandchild, confront the child with the problem in a loving way, and decide together on a treatment plan.
- Then be fully involved in his treatment until he is better. If this requires going to a treatment center or attending meetings with him, so be it. Ask to serve as a clinical ally or, if your grandchild cannot go home for one reason or another, offer your own home as a halfway house.

CONCLUSION

Substance abuse is treatable. Early intervention and treatment is the first step toward healing. Your interest and involvement will not only benefit your grandchild physically, but he will know that you care. To learn more about this subject contact the following resources.

RESOURCES

Teen Help. 800-266-1437. This is a service that offers help and advice to teens and families about substance abuse and related issues.

American Academy of Child and Adolescent Psychiatry. www.AACAP .ORG. The Facts for Families series contains valuable information. The articles can be downloaded at no cost.

Partnership for a Drug-Free America. www.drugfreeamerica.org. 212-922-1560. This organization supplies information and advocacy services.

CHAPTER 29

Grandchildren with Special Needs

A new grandchild embodies a family's hopes and dreams: a child to carry on the family culture, to surpass one's own achievements, perhaps to make the world a better place. When a new baby arrives, parents and grandparents expect to greet a healthy child who will bring joy and happiness to the family. Unfortunately, that does not always happen. And it is a devastating moment when family members learn that their wonderful and innocent new child has a mental or physical malfunction, or is developmentally challenged. Joy becomes mixed with concern, disappointment, and confusion when family members find out that their new baby will need special care.

A Family Matter

Sometimes a child's problem is so serious that it requires intense and ongoing care. In such a case, fulfilling all the child's needs for special care is often more than the two parents can bear alone. That's where grandparents come in; they can offer help, both directly to the child and indirectly to the parents. For this to take place, the grandparents must form a coalition with the parents—a family team. Parents must allow grandparents to help. This can be initially difficult because they are understandably shocked, confused, and hurt when they first learn their child has a problem. They may feel embarrassed or defensive about their child's condition.

Fortunately, by working together, parents and grandparents can help one another to accept the reality of having a challenged child and grandchild and to handle it in a positive way. With thorough education, understanding, compassion, and the appropriate sharing of tasks, they can ensure that the child's spirit flourishes. They can achieve the best medical outcome for the youngster and the family. So if you have a grandchild with special needs it is important to understand what an important role you have to play.

Grandparents Are Indispensable

You are more than important; you are indispensable. Parents can't do it alone, no matter how wonderful and caring they may be. As a physician with more than forty years of clinical practice, I have come to count on grandparents of chronically ill or developmentally challenged children for help. Most of the time they are assisting the parents, but sometimes grandparents are put in the position of having to go it alone (see Chapter 41, "Raising Grandchildren").

Everyone involved with the child's care—from doctors to parents—needs to understand how to access the helping and healing power of grandparents. No matter what the problem is, the normal, healthy part of any child with special needs wants to love and be loved, to grow, to learn, to have freedom, and to have fun. Although parents have the primary responsibility for following medical regimens and giving direct care, grandparents can supplement their efforts.

This is not often as easy as it sounds. First, the grandparent must sort through his or her thoughts, feelings, and actions concerning a grandchild with special needs. Is there disappointment, grieving, anger, or despair? The grandparent must come to terms with the situation, to reach some form of acceptance in his or her own mind and heart before beginning to help others. This is especially important when it comes to supporting parents.

It is beyond the scope of this book to discuss all the mental and physical conditions that can affect children. If you have a grandchild with special needs, you will have to educate yourself about his or her specific condition. What follows applies in general to whatever affliction a grandchild may have. Although you may be called upon to help in a specific manner with a particular clinical problem, the way you support your grandchild and the parents is the same in just about any condition.

How You Can Help

Many grandparents have grandchildren with a clinical syndrome named Attention Deficit Disorder (ADD). This condition afflicts approximately one out of twelve children. It is five times more common in boys than in girls. It can exist with or without hyperactivity. It is a confusing malady because, most often, the child looks fine and healthy but behaves in an impulsive way, often erratically, under various circumstances. For example, a child with ADD visiting a zoo, or watching a favorite television program might seem to behave as any other child. But should you ask the child to pay attention to something that requires concentration in a subject in which he is not interested, symptoms begin to appear.

Although the ADD child is usually quite intelligent, he has trouble concentrating, paying attention, and controlling his behavior. This bewilders not only the confused youngster (who does not want to act in such a manner), but also everyone else, most of all parents and grandparents. (Additional problems may stem from grandparents who may think the beleaguered parents are exacerbating, if not causing, the child's problems.) It is common for a child with ADD to cause conflicts between both parents and between parents and grandparents. Left untreated, ADD can seriously impair the child and create a great deal of marital and family turmoil.

For grandparents with an ADD grandchild, a great deal of maturity and compassion is necessary. To nurture parents and help grandchildren cope with problems requires shedding old attitudes and behaviors and a major learning effort. It can be a painfully slow process of education and understanding.

Growing and Changing

Following is an example of how some grandparents have grown and changed with an ADD grandchild. Their experience serves as a model of compassion, understanding, and self-examination. Here is an edited version of a letter they wrote to the parents explaining their journey of experience. I have included some parenthetical comments in italics in the body of the letter.

Dear Kids (you are still kids to us):

This letter is not easy to write but here goes. A lot has happened since our grandchild was born. We remember the worry and nervousness that go along with any birth, the fear of the birth defects, the unknown . . . then the burst of joy when everything seemed to be OK. Our expectations and hopes soared with you, as our grandchild appeared to be free of problems and ready to thrive in this world. We remember starting to watch you raise your child and we gave our advice generously basing it on the wisdom we had gained from raising you. You turned out fine, which proves that we are experts! Then, as your child grew and started to present problems that you could not solve, despite our ever-so-helpful advice, we thought to ourselves that *you* must have been doing something wrong. *[They were becoming judgmental.]* Both you, and we, his grandparents, were caught unprepared for the scenario that began to unfold before our eyes.

Behavioral patterns seen only in "other families" became a very real tragedy for you, and this situation was completely misunderstood by us. We muttered in the background, "If only they would. . . . Whose genes? Not mine, that's for sure! Why do they indulge him? Nothing is wrong when he is with us! . . . A good old-fashioned spanking!" *[This expresses a vast array of emotions that a child's problem can elicit in adults— anger, frustration, social embarrassment, and more.]*

As our advice developed an edge, we were unknowingly joining the chorus that accompanied you as you moved through your daily routines with your child. *[Here they are moving away from, and being critical of, a parent trying to do her best and needing their support.]* You felt blamed from all directions. People in stores glared at you as you tried, over and over, to get your child to behave. You were constantly embarrassed by being "obviously" bad at parenting, unable to put our infallible advice to use.

The next bitter pill came when you let it be known that you were seeking professional help, not only for your child but also for yourselves. To us, who had based our philosophies of life upon self-reliance and religious principles, you may as well have signed up with a witch doctor! We felt you were rejecting our tried-and-true ways, and were about to be exploited by false experts, who spouted mysterious labels such as "oppositional," "ADD," "ADHD," "LD," "fine and gross motor delay," and other mumbo-jumbo, who would take advantage of your gullibility, take your money—and do no good. We let you know of our misgivings, but we had gotten used to your weary voices and eyes telling us, in response to our objections, what your so-called experts were telling you.

Thank God there was enough love in our family to weather those awful times when we actually added to your burden. And thank God you listened to the experts! Finally, after years of heartbreak, all that mumbo-jumbo started to make sense. *[Now the education starts and they are moving toward the parents.]* Gradually, we began to see that our grandchild was not just a spoiled brat. We began to recognize patterns in his behavior, which were at last understandable to us, based upon principles promoted by your experts. We became more familiar with the jargon, as we tentatively entered what was, for us, foreign and uncharted territory. We, who thought we were educated, experienced, and tough, are babes in the woods compared to you, you *kids*, who are now able to teach us. Now we can listen to you and *hear* you. *[Here they are reestablishing the family team.]*

Although we have felt all along that we are in the same boat, now all of our oars are pulling in the same direction. It is still a rugged journey, but we hope it is a little easier now that we aren't sniping at you. So kids, please forgive us. We hope we can heal the hurt brought about by our misunderstanding of your struggle. Our hearts are filled with love and the best of intentions for you and our grandchild. We are your flesh and blood. We want so much to help that we pray that our clumsy efforts can provide some measure of comfort and support for you all! Thanks for hanging in there until you could reach us and teach us. One thing we have learned: you are *good* parents for our grandchild, the best. He needs you.

And now let us preach a little. We are lucky. We are bonded together by love, strengthened by the trials that could have fractured a less fortunate family. Thanks to that love, we have a unified family-support group that will not waver, essential if our grandchild is to have a solid foundation upon which to build his life. We will always be here for you, if you should ever need an ear, a shoulder, or, God forbid, advice! That is what grandparents are for!

*Love, Mom and Dad**

Stages of Grandparents' Experience

The letter clearly illustrates the unfolding process of what grandparents experience with a grandchild that has special needs.

■ Shock, denial, and disbelief. There is pain upon discovery that the grandchild has a problem. The hurt is made all the more powerful because of the joy of having a grandchild in the first place.

---

*This letter was adapted and edited with permission from CHADDER, the magazine of the parents organization for children with attention disorders. It was first printed in the 1990 fall/winter edition. If you would like more information about attention deficit disorder or CHADD, write to CHADD, 499 Northwest 70th Ave., Suite 308, Plantation, Florida 33317; or call (305)-587-3700.

- Blame and disappointment. Often even if grandparents are supportive, parents will feel guilty, defensive, and even ashamed about their child's condition.
- Sadness, depression, hopelessness, and despair. Many parents hit bottom at this point and need maximum support.
- Acceptance. When this occurs the initial pain and disappointment begins to wane.
- Reality sets in. What can be done about the child's condition?
- Action. Now is the time to take positive steps to do the best for the child. The family works together to develop and implement the necessary remedial plan.

This last phase is tailored to the form and location of family members. Although long-distance grandparents may only be periodically available, they can help a lot financially or by keeping up to date with the latest information concerning the child's condition. Planning for parent respite is very important. Grandparents can help by taking the child in their home for a while or baby-sitting while the parents get away for some needed rest.

The Education Process

Many grandparents of children with special needs say they have learned a great deal and grown because of their grandchild's condition. Yosh, fifty-five and the grandmother of a child with Down's syndrome said that she had never experienced such powerful love and attachment as she does from her granddaughter. Her husband baby-sits two days a week for his grandchild too. When the child was four months old, the grandfather learned to do tube feedings and administer medicine to the child. "This allowed her parents to put in some time at work," he said. Yosh is very close to her granddaughter, who is now five years old and can care for her own basic needs. "She has intellectual impairment," says Yosh, "but she is good company, so sweet and loving. Her spirit lights up the room. She is a pure soul. I don't see her disability anymore."

That says it all.

GUIDELINES

If you have a grandchild with special needs, here are some helpful guidelines to use or to share.

- Understand your own feelings about your grandchild's condition.
- Whenever necessary, talk to your spouse, a friend, or a confidante about what is going on with your grandchild and your children. After all, you need support too.
- Establish a policy in your own mind for how you want to help.
- Become highly educated about your grandchild's condition. Visit his doctor; learn about the affliction and the treatment process.
- Discuss the situation with the child's parents and formulate a cooperative family policy on helping. For example, many grandparents help financially. Others are involved in the child's daily treatment routine, which might include such tasks as doing exercises with a physically handicapped grandchild on a daily basis or helping out with a remedial learning program.
- Tune in carefully to the parents' distress and be available to give them respite. If any differences of opinion arise—and they will—iron them out sooner rather than later.
- Be vigilant about the state of the family's mental and physical health.
- It is unfortunate but true that when people are faced with difficult external stresses there is often a tendency to turn on one another, to become judgmental, critical, and angry. This adds to the hurt everyone is feeling. Do not let that happen.
- Don't get so wrapped up in everyone else's well-being that you neglect to take care of yourself.

CONCLUSION

Having a grandchild with special needs is a family problem. As a grandparent, you are the bedrock upon which the family stands. In such difficult circumstances, you are indispensable to your grandchild and to your children. Your emotional leadership and physical involvement will help you grow and learn, bring your family closer, and set a positive example for future generations of grandparents in your family.

RESOURCES

The Special Kids' Network, (800) 986-4550—a free statewide service for families of children who have special needs

CHADD (305) 587-3700—for families of children with Attention Deficit Disorder

For specific conditions—learning disabilities, epilepsy, etc.—we recommend doing an Internet search for organizations that address the condition you want to learn about. For example, to find out more about diabetes, go to www.diabetes station.com, which caters to grandparents, for support and networking.

CHAPTER 30

Traveling with Your Grandchild

T raveling with your grandchild allows you to see other places and people. The greatest value in traveling together, however, is that it allows you to spend time together with little distraction or interruption (see Chapter 23, "Attention"). Sharing an exciting new adventure together not only brings you closer, but also creates memories that will last a lifetime. And, of course, let's not forget the benefit to your grandchild's parents.

On the Road

There is no limit to where you can go with your grandchild, how you get there, or where you stay once you arrive. You can take in the local zoo for a weekend, while staying at a local motel, or travel far away and see things you have never seen before. Sylvie, seventy-two, says, "I saved my money for twenty years and then had enough to treat my three grandchildren to an African safari."

You can travel for almost any reason. Some grandparents use vacations with their grandchildren as an opportunity to teach them about their heritage. "I took my granddaughter to the little town in Italy where my parents came from," said Frank, seventy-one. "She loved it."

You do not have to spend a bundle to enjoy a vacation with your grandchild. If Africa or Europe is beyond your price range, stick closer to home. Every summer, Milt, sixty-eight, takes his grandson fishing to a lake that is only fifty miles away from home. They camp in the woods. Keep in mind that camping can be a peaceful, low-cost alternative to a hotel. Choose the accommodations and activities that work for you and your grandchild.

Planning Is Everything

Whether you stay at a castle or in a pup tent in the woods, you will want to plan ahead to make your trip as safe and hassle-free as possible. There are all kinds of variables that come into play depending on the age and interests of your grandchildren.

Age

Before you begin planning your vacation, consider your grandchild's age and level of maturity. For example, if you have a younger or active grandchild, it is not advisable to go on a trip that requires a great deal of passive listening and learning. Ask your grandchild's parents for their advice and input regarding your vacation. Include your grandchild in the planning process. Ask her what she is interested in doing or where she is interested in going. Make your plans well in advance so you can get excited and talk about the trip before you go. Anticipation is fun, so tell your grandchild exactly what you plan to do. Take your grandchild to the public library or go on-line together for information about your destination.

Activities

For youngsters, keep the more intellectual activities, such as museum visits, short and sweet. Hands-on activities such as those available at chldren's museums keep young ones entertained. If you visit a zoo, for example, choose one that has a petting section, where younger children can interact with the animals.

Duration

If your grandchild is *very* young, it is best to travel for only a few days, only for short distances, and to places that are able to support small children. The Foundation for Grandparenting's Grandparent/Grandchild Summer Camp has played host to children as young as three. Because the camp is in the woods and highly supervised, children and their grandparents can roam freely. If you are unsure about whether a child is ready for a night away from Mom and Dad, try a fun, quick overnight stay at a motel close to home.

Expectations

As part of the planning process, discuss your behavioral expectations with your grandchild before the trip. Whatever the activity level of your grandchild, emphasize that you are counting on him to be on his best behavior. Some issues may be of more importance to you than others—for example, table manners, hygiene, noise level, and so on. Keep in mind that teenagers love to sleep in, so, when traveling with one, expect to get a later start on the day. Avoid overplanning activities. The object of the trip with your grandchild is to spend time together and give each other your undivided attention.

Itinerary

Always share your complete itinerary with the parents in case of emergency. Ask them to inform you about any special rules or regulations regarding bedtime or diet. It is a good idea to obtain a medical authorization for your grandchild (more on this later in the chapter) as well and a temporary power of attorney (see Chapter 42, "Legal Issues") if you are traveling across borders.

During Your Trip

No matter how long or short the trip there are a few basic things to keep in mind while you're on the road with your grandchild.

Routine

Incorporate as much of your grandchild's regular routine into the trip as possible by maintaining normal naptimes, meal schedules, and bedtimes. Ask your grandchild to bring along a favorite toy, especially if the child is young. Bring favorite books, games, and other materials that you can dole out during the trip and thus avoid boredom. Allow older children to bring CD or cassette players with headphones (these devices are known to reduce bickering among siblings).

Unstructured Moments

Many good things happen during downtime, so make sure your trip includes plenty of unstructured moments. You can have as much fun reading a story together in bed on a rainy afternoon as riding the roller coaster at a theme park. One grandmother, who took two of her grandchildren on a two-week trip, woke up one morning and told her grandchildren that they were "staying in pajamas" all day. She ordered room service and they watched movies in bed until evening. "I ordered a rest," she said.

Physical Activity

Children have enormous amounts of energy and need to blow off steam. So, arrange time for swimming, bike riding, walking, and other physical activities. It is not necessary for you to participate. Kids love to be watched when they play. Alternate activities. Follow an active day with a restful one. Going to the movies is also fun.

Lodging

Most kids love staying in hotels. For them, it is an adventure. Stay at a place that welcomes children and, if possible, has swimming facilities. Pools are the perfect place for children to get rid of their excess energy. You can take a breather while you watch them, or you can join them. Your grandchild will get a kick out of it when you splash, or try to stand on your hands in the water, or attempt a back flip.

Safety

Rest assured the parents will be worrying a bit while you are gone with their child so be aware of the safety requirements for the activities you plan. Bring along the parents' notarized authorization for medical care as well as a power-of-attorney statement in case of an emergency and if you are crossing international borders. Don't forget your and your grandchild's passports if you are leaving the country. If you are traveling overseas, make sure to bring along vaccination certificates.

Pack a night-light and comfortable shoes. Bring along a travel first-aid kit. Make sure to include a painkiller (acetaminophen), cough and cold medicine, diphenhydramine or hydrocortisone cream for allergies or bug bites, and antibiotic ointment for wounds. Sunscreen and bug repellent are important as well. Consult with the child's pediatrician about specific medications for certain travel destinations.

When driving, stop at least every two hours for stretching and restroom breaks. Drink plenty of water, eat healthful snacks and meals, and pack moist towelettes for clean up.

Homesickness

Don't feel rejected or inadequate if your grandchild is a bit homesick for the first day or two of your trip. This is to be expected, especially with younger children or those who are concerned about something at home. I have found that in most cases it is best not to allow the homesick child to call home immediately because it tends to make things worse. If the distress is not too great, wait at least forty-eight hours to let the child call home. The acute phase usually disappears at this time.

During this initial period it is helpful to allow your grandchild to talk about her homesick feelings. Every year, at our Grandparent/Grandchild Summer Camp, we have one or two homesick children. Here is something that usually works for mild homesickness that involves the positive use of the child's powerful imaginative abilities. When the child goes to sleep at night, sit by the bedside. Ask the child to visualize the face(s) of the parent(s) they miss. Then tell the child to imagine talking to the parents about the day and wishing them good-night. You talk to them too. Tell them you both love them. You can take it from there. Use your own judgment about what you think the child needs to say. This usually helps.

Writing parents a postcard or sending them an E-mail also helps. Phone calls should be short because the child will usually pick up on the fact that the parents miss him or her, which can make things worse. If the child is exceptionally homesick, make a calendar counting the days until the trip is over. Very few grandparents I know have ever had to cut a trip short because a child was homesick. However, it can happen. If it does reassure the child that he or she was too young to go this year and that you will try again at another time.

GUIDELINES

Here are some more useful tips to help you enjoy traveling with your grand-child.

- Be excited and enthusiastic about the trip. Anticipate and plan. Educate your grandchild about your journey beforehand.
- When traveling together stay flexible. The best things happen when you and your grandchild are completely in the moment. Set a flexible routine. Children need limits, but don't be too rigid. Spontaneity can be fun.
- Tuck in your grandchild at bedtime and review the highlights of the day.
- Encourage your grandchild to make a record of your voyage by videotaping it, keeping a journal, or drawing pictures to share with others or to present at school for extra credit if appropriate.
- Make a permanent record of the trip. Take photos of your vacation. When you get home, make a special album devoted to your trip together. Sit down with your grandchild and relive your memories together.
- If you are gone more than a few days, keep parents up to date on where you are and what you're doing.

CONCLUSION

Vacations together create memories that last a lifetime. With the proper planning, you and your grandchild will have safe, happy, exciting times together that will strengthen your bond and reinforce your love for each other.

RESOURCES

For more information about traveling with your grandchildren, consult the following resources.

"Get Kids Involved in Getaway Plan" (article), www.aaa.com/news12 /Travel/travelnews/kidstravel.htm

Traveling with Your Grandchildren (brochure), American Association of Retired Persons (AARP), www.aarp.org

Have Grandchildren, Will Travel: The Hows and Wheres of a Glorious Vacation with Your Children's Children (book), by Virginia Spurlock (Pilot Books, 1997)

Grandparent-Grandchild Summer Camp, Sagamore Conference Center, Roquette Lake, N.Y., (315) 354-5311

Grandtravel, www.grandtravel.com or (800) 247-7651—upscale travel packages for grandparents and grandchildren

Elderhostel, www.elderhostel.org or (877) 426-8056—intergenerational programs for seniors fifty-five and over and their grandchildren

CHAPTER 31

Spending for Your Grandchild

The Grandparent Buying Bug

O ne of the more frivolous and enjoyable aspects of grandparenting I am happy to address here is the uncontrollable urge to "buy stuff" most grandparents experience when a grandchild comes along. A recent AARP survey estimates that 72% of grandparents buy their grandchild a gift monthly. Most grandparents spend a minimum of $500 a year on each grand-child. Not even individuals who previously prided themselves on their thrifti-ness, or those with limited means, are immune to the magic of this strange urge. Once under its grip, your symptoms will mutate and shift as the grandchild matures. I have identified this affliction as the grandparent buying bug, a syn-drome not yet acknowledged by most members of the medical or psychologi-cal professions.

Diagnosis

The buying bug afflicts grandmothers and grandfathers differently. When the bug appears in a family, it seems to hit grandmothers first. My research shows that grandmothers tend to leap in to "buy stuff for the new baby" before grand-fathers are willing to make the jump. This is partly because grandmother's purchases tend to be more appropriate for a new baby's needs, since women usually have more hands-on experience caring for babies. In fact, women who knit begin spending money on supplies as soon as a pregnancy is announced.

Although grandfathers usually will spring for a teddy bear or dollhouse or computer when the child is a bit older, many are confused by or uninformed about baby products and can well end up buying clothes and toys that are the wrong size or not age-appropriate. Jack, seventy-two, is one example. "When my granddaughter was born, I went to the baby store to get her something. I did not know anything about baby clothes, even though I'd had three children of my own. I ended up buying socks for a four-year-old child and my granddaughter was only three days old. No one in the family will ever let me live that one down."

This minor difference in the spending behavior of grandmothers and grandfathers ends after the first few years of the new grandchild's life. As it becomes easier to buy things for a grandchild, both grandparents become partners in a kind of equal opportunity spending.

Grandfathers have more opportunities of scoring with just the right gift as their grandchild ages. Scooters, bicycles, and skis make great gifts for growing girls and boys. Unlike some grandmothers who may hesitate at shelling out for something they feel might be dangerous, many grandfathers enjoy chipping in for a high-tech bicycle or even a grandchild's first car. When it comes to clothes or a vacation alone with their grandchild, the sky is the limit for grandmothers.

Big-Ticket Items and Investing in the Future

While buying big may be welcomed by the majority of parents, in some cases it can get grandparents into trouble with others. The more expensive the item, the more important it is that you consult with parents about your intended purchase, especially if there is an imbalance between your own purchasing power and theirs. In these situations, it is very important that grandparents and parents come up with a policy regarding the giving of high-priced items. Children should know that the big gifts come from both parents and grandparents, or even both sets of grandparents—and with the parents' blessing. This way no one is especially singled out as the source of unlimited goodies.

Giving on a More Serious Note

If you have the financial resources, you can help assure your grandchild's security and future in many ways. Here are some ideas; however, make sure to check with a tax professional before you do anything. Although these suggestions are appropriate at this writing, the IRS can change rules rapidly.

- Cash: You can give as much as $10,000 a year to each grandchild without owing any federal gift taxes.
- Helping with debt: If you pay your grandchild's *medical or educational bills* directly you can bypass gift taxes.
- Educational help: *State-sponsored savings plans* (called 529 plans) allow for a one-time contribution of $50,000 toward your grandchild's education. The IRS as of this writing considers this as five $10,000 gifts. If your grandchild does not use these funds, they may be allocated for another grandchild. If you give an educational gift to your grandchild, be sure that it does not compromise any financial aid. Make sure to talk with the parents first.
- *The Education IRA* allows you to contribute up to $2,000 per year for your grandchild's college.
- Giving Stock: If you have appreciated stock (held more than eighteen months) and are in a high tax bracket, you can give the stocks to a grandchild and save on capital gains taxes.
- Paying off loans: It is always greatly appreciated when a grandparent helps a grandchild pay off a student loan. The $10,000 cash gift can be applied in this manner.
- Make your grandchild your beneficiary: If you are afraid that you might not be able to give your grandchild a gift directly, there are many ways you can put money aside for him. It is best to see an attorney to work out the best possible terms for such an arrangement.

Treatment

The spending bug is not fatal, and although it cannot be eradicated, it can be controlled and channeled into productive pathways. For example, although slipping a bit if cash into the envelope containing your grandchild's birthday card is always a good idea, creating an education fund for your grandchild is even better. Begin early in the child's life by partnering with the parents and the other set of grandparents to create the fund. When the buying bug surges over you and you find yourself considering something a little frivolous, step back, take a deep breath, and contribute the money to the education fund instead. You will derive deep satisfaction from watching the balance grow and knowing your grandchild's future tuition is secured.

Ask Before You Give

Before your new grandchild arrives, no matter how strongly the buying bug has you in its grip, avoid major purchases for the baby. Instead, first consult with the parents and find out what would be most appreciated. Parents know exactly what carriages, cribs, high chairs, car seats, etc. they want and need for their baby. Don't be like the overenthusiastic but well-meaning grandmother who bought her granddaughter an extremely valuable antique chest of drawers only to find it wouldn't fit through the door of her granddaughter's parents' apartment.

A homemade gift is especially meaningful. A chair, a bookcase, and a crocheted blanket are useful gifts and carry the added benefit of sentimental value. Sarah, seventeen, treasures a sweater her grandmother knitted for her and plans to give it to one of her own children someday.

Twenty-year-old Greg, on the other hand, has had his fill of his grandmother's favorite gift. "My grandmother makes me these doilies all the time. What am I going to do with a doily? I just throw them in a box and kick it under my bed." Before spending hours on a handcrafted item, make sure it's something your grandchild will use or appreciate. Otherwise, do not be surprised if your hard work ends up in mothballs, exiled to the attic.

GUIDELINES

Let's face it: it's fun to buy stuff for a grandchild. A little bit of the bug does not do permanent damage. Here are some tips to help you spend wisely and manage your buying bug.

- Make a habit of consulting with parents before purchasing gifts for your grandchild, especially when it comes to more expensive items.
- Buy items that fit the baby or the baby's environment. Grandparents who are handy can give the gift of time to parents by contributing their skills and manual labor. For example, some grandparents may be especially talented at assembling cribs or wallpapering a room, tasks that are greatly appreciated by working moms and dads.
- Be sensitive to the fact that mom or dad may want to be the ones to buy their child their first bicycle or doll. Sensitive and caring grandparents should not interfere when a parent's sentimental purchase is involved.
- Buy some gifts that your grandchildren someday can pass on to their own grandchildren—for example, a family portrait, baby's first silver cup and spoon, a rocking horse, or a small rocking chair.
- As your grandchild gets older, you can consult with him directly about what gifts are most appreciated and/or appropriate.

CONCLUSION

Spending money on your grandchild is one of the benefits of being a grandparent and can be tremendously satisfying and fun. However, your buying bug should be tempered with respect for the parents' wishes and policies. Before opening your wallet, coordinate your expenditures with them. Keep in mind that parents, too, appreciate gifts as much as grandchildren.

Currently there are no twelve-step programs to help deal with the buying bug, so it's up to you to manage your impulses while savoring the special pleasure that buying gifts for your grandchild can bring.

CHAPTER 32

When Your Grandchild Visits

A grandchild's visit can be an exciting and love-filled adventure. But attention must be paid. For example, although many grandparents look forward to spending time with their grandchildren, some may have forgotten what it is like to have a small child around the house. Others may feel concerned about how to keep their grandchild entertained. Some worry about safety and disciplinary issues. And, of course, parents are going to be concerned that their precious progeny is being well taken care of.

That is why it is important to prepare for your grandchild's visit well in advance. Remember, whether you are alone with your grandchild or have another family member present, you are going to have to be part concierge, part doctor, part housekeeper, and part travel agent. But it is worth it. Carefully reading this chapter will give you ideas and suggestions that will considerably improve your chance of having a healthy and happy visit and a satisfied visitor.

Plan Ahead

The key to a successful visit with your grandchild is *plenty of planning and preparation*. The first thing is to generate excitement and enthusiasm well in advance.

If the parents are not coming on the visit, they can plan to spend time alone together. The optimum situation is to have one grandchild visit at a time. If that is not possible, keep in mind that the more grandchildren that visit at once, the more work and upheaval you can expect.

To plan correctly it is important to recruit the parents' input and advice. This includes information about your grandchild's medical, nutritional, or other needs during her stay with you. If your grandchild is visiting you without her parents, get a medical authorization form from the parents in case of any medical emergency (see Chapter 42, "Legal Issues"). If age-related special equipment is necessary (stroller, highchair, car seat, hula hoop, or skateboard), ask her parents if they will provide them, or if you should obtain them yourself. Some of these items are available for rental. Or perhaps someone you know may be able to lend you the items for the duration of the visit. As an aside, it is very helpful for people caring for children to take a course in CPR. You will be surprised how much you can do to help in an emergency! Knowing that you are certified in CPR can be comforting to worried parents too.

A Private Place

To make your grandchild feel both comfortable and special, make a private safe place for him in your home. This is a place that is his alone. Maria, seventy-eight, has a chest of drawers she has reserved just for her grandchildren. Each grandchild has a private drawer to use when they visit. "When I know one of my grandkids is coming to visit I usually put something special in their drawer as a 'Welcome home to Grandma's' gift. The first thing they do when they come in the house is run into the bedroom and open their drawer."

Learn the child's daily routine too, so you can emulate it as closely as possible. This will help your grandchild to feel more at home. During longer visits, plan to have a backup person to help out if you become ill or overtired or you just need a break or some time to run errands.

If you have not already done so, explain the rules of your house to your grandchild. These will depend on the child's age, but be sure to emphasize politeness, consideration, manners, privacy, chores, and cleanliness. Most often your grandchild will follow your lead.

Safety

With the passing of the years, it is easy for elders to forget what it is like having a child in their home. The younger the child, the more carefully you will have to keep watch, the more changes you will have to make in your home, and the more available you will have to be. Always remember that children will be children. Parents too want to be rest assured that your home is safe for their child.

If your grandchild is very young, it may be helpful to take a look at the rooms in your home at the eye level of your grandchild. (Yes, this means getting down on your knees.) You might notice a hazard you overlooked from a standing position. When your grandchild visits, stash the Dresden, houseplants, and other breakables far from the reach of small hands. A grandchild is unlikely to get into trouble if there is nothing around to destroy.

Keep in mind that, as horrible as it is to think about, toddlers are susceptible to burns, falls, drowning, suffocation, poisoning, strangulation, and electrical shock. Install gates at the top and bottom of stairways; remove items from low-lying areas that could break and cause cuts; lock cabinet doors that contain household cleaners, poisons, or medicines; put foam protectors on sharp edges of low tables, and whatever else you see. Be especially careful about securing loose wires and the cords of window blinds and shades. Also, make sure to seal all electrical outlets in your home. When running the bath for your grandchild, make sure to turn on the cold water first.

Activities

The best times grandparents have with their grandchildren are when they are just hanging out together. Nevertheless, grandparents often worry about filling up the time when a grandchild comes to visit. If this is your concern, make a list of possible activities and discuss them with your grandchild. She can pick and choose from the list at will. It is best to be spontaneous, though, and take things as they happen. There are some days when you and your grandchild may just want to stay in and watch movies. On other days your grandchild may be particularly active and in need of a physical outlet. It can be a lot of fun to get in the car and take a drive without plans. Above all, relax and go with the flow.

No matter what your grandchild's age, reading together is an important and bonding activity. Create a small library for her, and place her books next to your books. You may want to find out what your grandchild is reading in school or on her own, then read the same material and have fun discussing it with her. At night, you may want to fill your grandchild in on the family history with tales about family members' escapades, scandals, or heroism. These visits are also the perfect times to work on your "treasure chest" together (see Chapter 49, "Making Memories: Keeping a Memory Chest").

Listening to music together is another activity you can share. Actually listening to music is a good way to keep up with the times. One grandfather I know, a concert clarinetist, made a deal with his grandchildren who like him to listen to their music. He listens to their current favorite music, and in turn, they have to listen to grandfather's classical music. "That's one way to reel them in," he says, "but what a price I have to pay."

Try to have your grandchild's favorite foods available when she comes to visit. Make your grandchild's favorite dish, or, better yet, allow her to prepare it with you. This is a great time to pass on family recipes.

If you know your way around a computer, there are lots of interesting games and stories for all ages you can enjoy with your grandchild. Instructional and educational software is available for all age groups. "Lapware" games are meant to be used by an adult holding a young child in his lap. You can find out more about these programs at your local computer store.

Board games and card games are a lot of fun. Be sure you have plenty of age-appropriate games on hand, as well as drawing and painting supplies. Keep a jigsaw puzzle going in a corner of the house. If your grandchild has a favorite game, practice playing it so that when she comes to visit, you can play together. Share some down time. There is nothing better than curling up on the couch, munching on popcorn and watching a movie.

Allow your grandchild to help with your housekeeping routine. In most cases, children love to help with shopping and even simple chores around the house. Try to make it fun. When appropriate take your grandchild with you to visits friends, do errands, and more. This is a great opportunity to share your world with her, and for her to revel in the adoration of your friends and neighbors.

GUIDELINES

Having your grandchild all to yourself is a wonderful opportunity to share your particular skills and talents with him. Allow him to share his skills and talents with you as well. Here are some important guidelines to ensure your visit with your grandchild is the best it can be.

- Plan ahead. Get medical authorization from parents. Learn CPR.
- Talk about the visit well in advance with your grandchild to generate enthusiasm and excitement.
- Childproof your home according to your grandchild's age.
- Go with the flow. Although it's helpful to have a list of potential activities for you and your grandchild to do, spontaneity can be fun!
- During the visit, be sure to telephone or send E-mail or postcards to the parents with periodic updates.
- Take advantage of the visit to teach your grandchild new skills or activities. She will remember the visit for the rest of her life.
- When the visit is over plan for the next time.

CONCLUSION

Adequate preparation will ensure that your grandchild's visit goes smoothly and that maximum fun is had by all. The visit will give you a great opportunity to spend time with your grandchild and play out all of your grandparent roles. Enjoy!

PART 4

Understanding Family Relationships

Your bond with your grandchild is profoundly affected by the quality of your relationship with the grandchild's parents and others. Your relationship with your grandchild's other grandparents is important as well. In this section, I will help you understand some of the intricacies of these relationships, identify potential areas of conflict, and offer some guidelines for dealing with them effectively.

CHAPTER 33

Between Parents and Grandparents

Your grandchild's parents are the portals to your grandchild. That is why your relationship with them requires your close attention. If your relationship as a parent and an in-law is going well, all is well. You will have access to your grandchild. If the opposite is true, and there are serious problems between you, then your relationship with your grandchild might be jeopardized. If you are like most people, you have a basically good relationship that runs into inevitable conflicts and problems once in a while. Consequently you have to monitor any problems with care so they do not spread. When adults are having interpersonal problems children are well aware of what is going on; they intently observe what the adults are doing. That is why it is especially important that conflicts and problems be successfully worked through in a mature manner.

I cannot emphasize this too strongly. No matter how grandparents and parents feel about one another at a given time, *for the grandchild's sake* it is important that they resolve their differences. Conflicts and problems can either be alleviated or exacerbated by the people involved. Indeed, rarely is one person the cause of a conflict. Unfortunately, conflicts between family members can spread like a prairie fire consuming all that gets in the way. And it is always the children who suffer most.

Parent-Grandparent Conflicts and Problems

Before I get specific about parent-grandparent problems, it might help to point out how conflicts and problems tend to evolve over time. Whether they are temporary or long-standing, conflicts usually evolve through several stages. The trigger event initiates the conflict; someone says or does something that offends another. The reaction to the event follows. A positive outcome involves discussing the issue and working out a resolution. When this resolution does not take place, the bad feelings fester, which can result in hurt feelings, arguments, anger, or complete communication breakdown. The latter can lead to a permanent or temporary estrangement.

The conflicts and problems between parents and grandparents occur for many reasons. They can arise from a general disagreement over issues such as childrearing or religion (see Chapter 40, "Religious Differences"). Often conflicts are the result of plain old bad chemistry between people; for example, a son-in-law who dislikes his wife's father and thus wants no contact with him. Very often, the problems are due to old resentments and unresolved parent-child issues notched up into another generation. They can be due to acts of commission (doing something hurtful) or omission (failing to do something helpful).

Acts of Commission or Omission

A conflict may occur by an act of *commission*. An example might be a mother who does not want her children to visit her mother's house because grandma smokes cigarettes. In this case, the grandmother is doing something the mother finds dangerous for her child. A parent is justified being concerned about her child's health. Therefore, it is appropriate to expect grandma to alter her behavior if she wants her grandchildren to visit.

A conflict may also occur by an act of *omission*; in other words, it is something that someone *does not do* that creates conflict. Lack of communication is a prime culprit here. One grandfather deliberately stayed away from his daughter's home in an effort not to meddle in her life (he never asked her if she thought he was meddling). To his bewilderment, she became angry and accused him of never visiting his grandchildren. They worked it out with grandpa promising that he would never think for her again.

Natural Antipathy

Unfortunate but true, some people just object to aspects of one another's personality or outright do not like one another. When this type of antipathy occurs, especially between a grandparent and an in-law, it takes a great deal of maturity to control feelings, monitor actions, and hold one's tongue when necessary. *And it is up to the grandparent to do so.* "My son-in-law irritates the hell out of me," said Cecil, sixty-seven. "He never sits still, always on the go, never reads anything. Can't have a decent discussion with him unless it's about sports or cars. Loud too. Never can just sit still for a moment. He is nice enough to my daughter, and a good father, so I cannot fault him. It is just *him* that gets on my nerves. Of course, I never tell anyone how I feel. What's my daughter going to do if I tell her I can't stand her husband? That's why keeping my mouth shut is the best policy."

Communication Breakdown

The simple fact that parents and grandparents do not talk openly with one another can cause serious problems. People cannot change their behavior if they are unaware that what they are doing is hurtful to others. Mary, twenty-six, was upset by the way her own father roughhoused with her young daughter. Not wanting to hurt her father's feelings she made excuses to limit his contact with her child. Naturally, her father became concerned and felt rejected without knowing what he'd done. Fortunately, Mary's mother intervened and was able to let her husband know how Mary was feeling and that she was hesitant to confront him. Grandpa changed his behavior.

Priority Issues

The various priorities parents and grandparents may give to personal values, roles, and responsibilities can cause conflicts. For example, parents and grandparents may disagree on the amount of time a child spends in day care, how much time a grandparent should spend baby-sitting, or how much a grandparent is willing to help parents with their financial situation. Grandparents may not approve of the lifestyle of parents who choose to work and place their children in day care. Many grandparents are willing to baby-sit but lack the funds to cover transportation to and from their grandchild's home.

Some grandparents may have little interest in their grandchildren. This can generate a great deal of hurt, rejection, and resentment on the part of the parents. An overworked young mother, whose parents were uninterested in her children, wrote me that her parents were "more interested in their social life than being grandparents." After her efforts to involve her parents more had failed, I suggested that she find someone else to grandparent her children. She started an adopt-a-grandparent program in her church community and found an older couple that became involved with her family. "I thought that doing this would stir up my parents so they would want to get more involved," she wrote. "Make them jealous, you know. But although they don't like the idea of their grandchild having an adopted grandparent, they don't dislike it enough to do something about it. But at least my kids have Claude and Tricia who they're crazy about."

Family Favoritism

One of the most frequent issues of discord between parents and grandparents is favoritism. The majority of research shows that grandparents on the mother's side often are more involved as grandparents, and especially if a divorce occurs (Furstenburg 1991). When a grandparent has more than one child and shows favoritism toward one child's family over another there is often trouble. For some, it may be very natural to fuss more over a daughter's family than a son's whose wife already has her own mother who is willing and able to be an involved grandmother. It is also common for the mother's mother to be more involved, and for the father's mother to recognize this situation. Especially if she has her own daughters.

On the other hand, I know of many cases where the situation is reversed. Sometimes a woman who is feuding with her own mother becomes very close to her husband's mother. In fact, there are many cases where divorced parents maintained good relationships with the parents of their former spouses to the benefit of their grandchildren (see Chapter 37, "When Parents Divorce").

Although I cannot go into the infinite ramifications of this issue in this short space the implications for grandparents are clear. Although your son's wife may prefer her parents to be the number one grandparents, understand her feelings, discuss it openly, and continue to do what you do. Always treat *both* your grandchild's parents with love and respect, just as if you are the only parent they have.

Temporary or Permanent

Most problems between parents and grandparents are temporary when they arise from intergenerational differences about childrearing. For example, one young mother and her parents argued endlessly about the fact that she allowed her baby girl to sleep in bed with her and her husband at night. The grandparents just could not understand why they would do such a thing, especially when the three of them were cramped together in a relatively small bed. In fact, the parents hardly slept at all and constantly complained about being tired. The way the frustrated grandmother saw it was that here were two exhausted parents complaining about being tired but refusing to do anything to change the situation. The young mother felt that her parents were old-fashioned and not aware of the latest ideas about co-sleeping practices. Fortunately, when the little girl began to sleep in her own bed at two years of age, the family disagreement vanished.

On the other hand, problems that arise from differences in values, objectionable behavior, or even grandparental fear for the safety of grandchildren can remain permanent. Some even result in permanent alienation and estrangement, which ruptures the grandparent-grandchild bond. Such cases follow the traditional pattern described above.

Sophie, sixty-two, called social services because she believed her drug-addicted son-in-law was abusing her granddaughter (the "trigger" event) and her daughter did nothing about it. Sophie's daughter and son-in-law were furious about her mother calling in the authorities, and open warfare ensued. They banished Sophie from their home and forbade her to see her grandchildren. Sophie had no choice but to go to court to attempt to regain visitation. Her case is still pending, although she has little hope of succeeding because her daughter's marriage is intact; therefore the grandparent visitation laws do not apply.

Boundary Issues

New parents and grandparents are understandably a bit confused both about assuming their new roles and about defining the boundaries of those roles. One of the most frequent conflicts between parents and grandparents occurs when boundaries of authority and responsibility are usurped. When a grandchild is born, both parent and child are catapulted into new roles—parent and grandparent, respectively—which can result in many radical changes in roles and relationships. These changes can give rise to a variety of conflicts, most of which tend to resolve themselves over time as the parties mature and adapt. Common boundary areas where grandparents and parents clash involve

- differing methods of childrearing
- the amount of involvement the grandparent will have in their grandchild's life
- grandparents not respecting their own child's new role as a parent

Most problems can be resolved. However, it often takes a great deal of maturity and flexibility to do so. Lil, Pete, and their two youngsters used to live two floors below Pete's parents, Joan and Stan. Lil and Pete complained that the grandparents gave them no peace. "They rushed down the two flights of stairs at breakneck speed whenever they heard one of the kids cry. They were constantly checking up on us and popping in at all times of the day to play with the kids."

Paul was especially perturbed. "My kids had more fun with my parents than with me," he said. "I never had that much fun with my parents. I had very mixed feelings about the whole thing." In spite of the fact that these boundary issues needed to be addressed, Lil and Pete never shared their feelings with Joan and Stan because Lil felt that if she did, "it would just kill them." They felt that moving away was the best solution. To the grandchildren's disappointment, they moved a mile away.

Resolving Conflicts

When a disagreement occurs, it is usual for the parties to blame one another for the problem. This is a very human response. However, if the issue is never addressed, people become estranged from one another. We have all heard stories of relatives who have not spoken to each other for decades over a conflict the root cause of which has long been forgotten. Whatever the cause of the conflicts and problems between parents and grandparents, the method of solving them is the same.

Do not let bad feelings or an outright conflict go unresolved. When a conflict occurs, *take immediate action*. First figure out what is going on. Carefully assess the situation and ask yourself the following questions.

- What is the conflict about? (What was the "trigger" event?)
- How have you contributed to the conflict?
- How would you feel if you were the other person, or persons, involved in the conflict?
- What options do you have to improve the situation?
- What would happen if you exercised each option?
- What is the best option to use as a healing plan?
- Would objective feedback from other family members be beneficial? Will their input help to point out where you are at fault?
- What is the best way to discuss your plan with other family members?
- How can you monitor progress toward resolution and healing?

Here is an example of how one family dealt with a conflict that could have brought down the family house:

Marylin is a shy and formal thirty-nine-year-old mother of six who dreads the semiannual visits of her in-laws. Temperamentally she would be described as slow to warm up (see Chapter 15, "Temperament and Personality"). When her in-laws arrive, she always feels sad and resentful, not nearly as enthusiastic and pleased as her husband and children. Marylin feels guilty about the way she feels.

She keeps her feelings to herself wondering what is wrong with her that she is so irritable while everyone else always seems to be having a good time.

By judging her feelings and blaming herself for them, Marylin is blocking her healing process. Rather than expressing her feelings openly, and identifying what is making her feel bad in the first place, Marylin chooses to hold in her feelings, letting them fester inside of her. Her discomfort is evident but no one is talking about it. Marylin's children sense their mother's discomfort and act out by being unruly. Her in-laws are uncomfortable in her presence and tell her son Ricardo that they think that Marylin does not want them around. Ricardo is repeatedly caught in the middle between his wife's aloofness and his parents' discomfort. The atmosphere in the house becomes increasingly tense and, although Ricardo's parents love seeing their grandchildren, they are relieved when it is time to go home.

Instead of feeling guilty about her irritability, Marylin should recognize her feelings as a signal and say to herself, "Hmm. I wonder what is wrong. Why am I feeling like this?" If she took the time to explore her feelings, she might identify that the trigger of her discontent is the disorder and confusion the visit from her in-laws always brings into her home. Not only must Marylin change her children's sleeping arrangements to make room for the in-laws, but she must also rearrange her daily routine to cater to her in-laws' needs. Because Marylin had never communicated her real feelings to Ricardo, he is unable to support her.

Let us now revisit Marylin's example to figure out a better way for her to deal with her conflicts and problems. The following is a step-by-step analysis of Marylin's conflict during her in-laws' visits and how she could have handled the situation differently for a positive outcome.

- Marylin should have asked herself why she felt so unhappy during her in-laws' visits.
- What was making her so irritable and withdrawn? If she had evaluated her feelings in this manner, she would have discovered the trigger.
- Marylin then should have asked herself, "What am I doing to contribute to the situation?"

- Marylin should have communicated her feelings to Ricardo and his parents and allowed them to find ways to lessen her burden, thus leading to resolution of the problem.

In reality, Marylin did follow these steps and discovered that her in-laws were sympathetic to how she felt. They wanted to help. In response to her breaking her resentful silence and expressing her feelings they offered to reduce the duration of their visits at her home from one week to three days and to spend the rest of the visit in an inexpensive motel so Marylin's home life would not be disrupted. Marylin agreed that the family would eat out more often and allow others to cook to ease her cooking burden. She accepted her husband's offer to take care of the kids periodically and give her a little time alone. As a result of these positive changes, Marylin felt greatly relieved and no longer dreaded her in-laws' visits. Indeed, she began to enjoy them.

GUIDELINES

Conflicts and problems between you and your grandchild's parents are inevitable. They are a normal part of doing family business. When they occur, deal with them right away so that they don't grow out of proportion. In fact, if you do have a problem I urge you to act immediately. Here are some guidelines to help.

- When the conflict occurs, do not react. Assess the situation. What is happening and who is involved? What is the trigger event?
- What is the status of the problem? Is it a temporary disagreement that will soon blow over of its own accord? Is it ongoing? Does open warfare exist?
- Are the parties shunning each other or estranged?
- What are the stories and attitudes of the people involved in the problem? If you are directly involved in a conflict or problem, remember to assess your own feelings, thoughts, and behavior. Ask yourself if you are helping or hurting the situation. Might you be able to do better?

- Talk to other family members and listen to their side of the story. A good way of understanding the other party is to pretend you are their attorney defending their case.
- Analyze the components of the problem with the other party. Are differences in lifestyle, personality, or attitude the root of the problem?
- Define the common interests of the parties involved.
- Based on your common interests, discuss the best available options and formulate a plan.
- Discuss the plan and have all parties agree to honor it.
- If necessary, have periodic meetings with the involved parties to monitor, discuss, and improve the plan.
- Remember, children are watching and reacting to the actions of the adults.
- Working on conflicts before they become major catastrophes is the most effective way of maintaining family harmony. Even the stickiest problems can usually be resolved by means of early identification, direct communication, open discussion, and continuous monitoring.

CONCLUSION

Parent-grandparent conflicts are inevitable. When they occur, try to work them out immediately. Forgiveness is not only important but also essential to keeping a family together. Parents and grandparents owe it to the children involved to do whatever it takes to reconcile their difficulties. Family members must be open about their feelings and communicate freely with one another to accomplish this goal. Grandparents have a major responsibility in healing conflicts and problems. When directly involved in a conflict themselves, they must put themselves in the other person's shoes and attempt to look at the situation anew. Between grandparents and parents, direct communication and compromise lead to conflict resolution, which sets a wonderful example for the children involved as well.

CHAPTER 34

Between Grandparents

A grandmother who rarely saw her granddaughter took her out to lunch. After indulging her grandchild's every whim, the grandmother said, "So who's your favorite person in the whole world?" The child thought for a moment and replied, "My other grandmother."

As this amusing and somewhat harsh story points out, your grandchild is apt to have other grandparents besides you. And hopefully, unlike the little girl in the story, your grandchild believes in equal opportunity when it comes to spreading love around. On a more serious note, however, a competition to be the favorite grandparent is quite common—and the way maternal and paternal grandparents handle the situation and get along with one another can have a strong effect on the family.

Nature has been generous enough to supply every grandchild with four biological grandparents. However, it is unusual for a child to have a thriving relationship with all four. Some grandparents may no longer be alive. Others may not be physically or emotionally available for their grandchild. But no matter how many grandparents are available, the unique relationship between them must be considered. This relationship has its own characteristics, and like any other relationship it must be carefully tended lest problems arise.

Complicated Relationships

The way you relate to your cograndparents before your grandchild comes along will give you a hint of what is to come when you eventually become grandparents together. If you get along well, that's a good sign. The other grandparents may be more than happy to share your grandchild. You may even become good friends. If you do not get along well, or if outright conflicts exist, chances are that things will heat up when the first grandchild comes along. Competition may rear its ugly head. You may notice that one of your grandchild's other grandparents wants to be the number one grandparent; or you may notice these feelings in yourself. Day-to-day conflicts might be blown out of proportion. If your child, now a parent, is not getting along with the in-laws, the arrival of a grandchild will force him to deal with them; and you might well find yourself becoming enmeshed in these difficulties too.

Some of the most common problems grandparents encounter in relating to one another are due to the natural competition between them to be the number one grandparent. This can happen even when grandparents get along well with one another. Other conflicts can stem from a broad range of personal, psychological, and social differences. Such differences, often leading to conflicts are rather common. That is why it is important for you to understand what is involved in the grandparent-to-grandparent relationship, identify possible conflicts and problems, and deal with them immediately and successfully.

Natural Competition

The grandparents' desire to be top grandparent is natural and understandable. Such a desire should be expected and taken lightheartedly. But not all grandparents take these feelings lightly. Indeed such feelings can make them quite uncomfortable. When they experience such thoughts and feelings they try to hide them for fear of creating problems in the family. Others freely acknowledge their feelings and act on them. They mount a campaign to be top grandparent for the grandchild.

Why do so many well-adjusted, kind, generous grandparents have these feelings? Perhaps it stems from a primitive need to pass on a personal legacy to their grandchild without any competition (see Chapter 1, "Grandparent Roles"). Such a desire would naturally cause a grandparent to envy a close relationship that their grandchild might share with another grandparent. And for almost *any* grandparent, the idea that a grandchild prefers another grandparent is hurtful.

Factors Affecting Grandparent Competitiveness

For better or worse, competition among grandparents is affected by the number of available grandchildren and how close they are to a particular grandchild. The more grandchildren a grandparent has, the less threatened by other grandparents they feel. The more time they are able to spend with their grandchild, the less threatened they feel. For example, a grandparent who lives next door to a grandchild has the opportunity to be more involved than the grandparents who live far away. When the other grandparents come to visit, the local grandparent's feelings of competitiveness are insignificant because, in a way, there is no competition. He or she is number one.

Ralph, fifty-nine, sees his three grandchildren daily. They all live together on the family farm. When his grandchildren's other grandparents visit, Ralph and his wife welcome them with open hearts. "We are so lucky to have the kids and grandkids living on the farm. When our son-in-laws' parents come to visit, my wife and I just take off for a few days and give them the run of the house so they can have fun with the kids."

Parents are especially sensitive about how their own parents get along with each other. For example, Ralph's son admires his parents for allowing him time alone with his in-laws; he's grateful that they do not force him to choose between them. Ralph's daughter-in-law is grateful that Ralph and his wife respect her relationship with her own parents, and are generous enough to open their home to them. The children understand that they have two sets of grandparents who love them equally. These grandparents' secret is that they do not compete. Rather they share each other's love and respect.

Competition Versus Sharing

Even the most dedicated grandparent must understand that grandchildren are meant to be shared. Children abhor demands for loyalty and choosing one adult over another. Nature supplies newborns with two parents, four grandparents, and many other family members. It is quite normal to want to be special to a child. This is much more easily accomplished when there are many children in the family. But when there is only one child to go around, competition for the child's love and attention can heat up; grandparents must learn to share.

Many grandparents understand the dynamics of the situation and go out of their way to be equal opportunity grandparents. They are respectful of one another's needs and their roles in the family. Some recognize their natural competitiveness, but laugh about it. Celeste, seventy-four, has a "friendly competition" with her lifelong friend Clarice, who just happens to be her grandchild's other grandmother. "We always wanted our children to marry one another. Well, they did, and now we have grandchildren in common. We tease one another about who the children like best, but we really don't mean it," says Celeste.

In less amicable circumstances, the competition can quickly get out of hand. Freddie, forty-four, is upset with her parents and her in-laws because they are so competitive. "You won't believe how they try to outdo one another to be the favorite grandparents. My father gave the kids fishing rods as a present, and then the following week my husband's father bought them more expensive ones. My children know their grandfathers play games with each other like this and sometimes it seems like the kids take advantage of it. My son is already lobbying for a car. He told me that both his grandfathers promised him one. My husband and I have to constantly remind our fathers to quit it, but they never listen. It's very frustrating. It's getting to the point where we are going to forbid them to buy *any* gifts for the kids."

Parents have enough to deal with without having to straighten out problems between grandparents who should know better. When conflicts arise, grandparents should take the lead in resolving them. After all, grandparents are supposed to set a good example for the rest of the family.

Possessiveness

When a grandparent attempts to fill a grandchild's mind with propaganda about having a special or exclusionary relationship, it not only hurts the child, but it also alienates the other grandparents, and often the parents. At the extreme, such overpossessive grandparents may experience bad feelings toward the other grandparents simply because they exist! For example, Barbara, fifty-two, is concerned that her daughter-in-law's mother will monopolize her new granddaughter.

"I wish my granddaughter didn't have other grandparents. Then I'd have the cutie all to myself," Barbara says. "I'm close to my daughter-in-law now and I hope this continues. But she wanted her mother to care for her when she came home from the hospital, not me, and that made me feel like an outsider. I get the feeling that my daughter-in-law's mother does not want me around, that she wants to be the only grandmother. I went to see a therapist because this was bothering me so much. I'm working on how to handle the situation."

Problems with competitiveness and possessiveness can also arise between marriage partners who are grandparents. Seymour, seventy-six, and his wife, Becca, seventy-seven, are experiencing problems because of Seymour's attempts to monopolize their grandson's time and attention. Seymour says, "There are so many things I want to teach him. We don't see him that often, and because we have only limited time together I think I should be with him more than my wife. Boys need their grandfathers more than girls do. When we have a granddaughter, Becca can spend more time with her." Becca, disagrees. "Seymour is living in the Dark Ages. This is my grandchild, too. It doesn't matter if he's a boy or a girl. Seymour is trying to dominate our grandson, and I'm not putting up with it."

Conflict Between Grandparents

A frequent cause of conflicts and other problems between maternal and paternal grandparents can be attributed to intolerance and disrespect for one another's culture, religion, race, or socioeconomic status. This type of conflict is becoming increasingly frequent as society becomes more and more diverse. The chances that your grandchildren's other grandparents come from another culture, or embrace religious beliefs that differ from your own, are pretty high today.

Although experiencing family diversity can be enriching for a child, grandparents may initially feel that the boundaries of their own tolerance and understanding are being stretched. When grandparents handle diversity in a mature manner, everyone wins. Mishandling the situation can have serious consequences.

People with different backgrounds and experiences may have little in common on the surface and may hold divergent views and opinions on a wide variety of subjects. It is the way the differences are handled that determines a happy or sad outcome. Here are a few examples.

Ethnic-Cultural Differences

When grandparents have different cultural backgrounds, it can lead to a lack of personal understanding, identity confusion, and cultural competition. Often such grandparents will compete for one belief system or another to prevail. Paul, nine, has a set of Italian and a set of Swedish grandparents. "I've got to act one way with Omah and Opah, and another with Nonna and Poppa. Sometimes they tell me not to act the way the others want me to. Nonna does not like Omah. I tell my parents and they have a fight."

Paul's mother confronted both sets of grandparents and explained to them that learning about diversity is educational and culturally enriching for Paul. She explained that Paul was learning many interesting things from all the grandparents. She told them they were not to criticize each other anymore. Omah said, "I have learned to keep my tongue in my mouth. Now I worry about what *I* am doing with Paul, not what *they* are doing."

Socioeconomic Differences

When one set of grandparents has more economic resources than the other, it can give rise to misunderstanding, competition, and resentment. Bertha, fifty-seven, a single grandmother trying to make ends meet, said of her well-off counterparts, "My grandchildren's other grandparents are trying to buy the kids' love." Grandparents and parents in this situation must acknowledge the economic difference and set the financial guidelines for all to follow. Emma, Bertha's daughter-in-law and a mother of three, recognized that her in-laws were much better off financially than her own parents. She quickly made it clear to both sets of grandparents that she has an "equitable policy" about gift giving. She allows only three gifts per set of grandparents at Christmas. "I didn't want gift giving to get out of hand," she says. "I laid down some rules and now the children know what to expect." Bertha agreed. "Emma taught me something. I never buy my grandkids anything that makes their other grandparents feel poor." After all, money does not buy love.

Religious Differences

Grandparents who demonstrate respect for another grandparent's religious beliefs teach their grandchild tolerance, understanding, and acceptance. When it comes to maintaining good relations with grandparents of a different religion, it is essential to avoid forcing your religious beliefs onto your grandchild. Demonstrate your acceptance of other religions and your grandchild will learn to do the same (see Chapter 40, "Religious Differences").

Personal Attitudes and Opinions

Differences in personal values, politics, and lifestyles can raise strong passions that divide families. Lila, fourteen, says, "My mom's parents are vegetarians. My dad's parents are not and eat just about anything. My mom's parents tell me that meat is bad. My dad's parents tell me that I'll be anemic if I don't eat meat. My mom's parents get mad when my dad's parents take me to McDonald's for a hamburger. My parents told them both not to talk about food with me."

Dan, sixteen, says, "One of my grandfathers I love very much, but he's kind of a redneck, and sometimes he says things that are kind of racist. My other grandfather hates him, so we never invite them to the house together." Dan's father says, "My dad was a good father to me and he loves his grandchildren.

The problem is that he does say some stupid things. I've told him to keep his opinions to himself when he comes over, but then he has a couple of beers and he starts spouting off."

How does the family deal with such a grandfather? Dan's father now only invites Horace over alone and will not allow him to drink while visiting. Even though he does not approve of his views, Dan's other grandfather respects Horace's need to spend time with the grandchildren and makes himself scarce when Horace comes to visit.

Plain Old Personal Dislike: "Bad Chemistry"

For reasons that we may attribute to differences in personal chemistry, some grandparents just do not care for their grandchild's other grandparents. Roger, fifty-five, says, "I don't like my daughter-in-law's parents. They are loud, materialistic, and narrow-minded. Frankly, I would prefer that my granddaughter not be exposed to them or their ways. But there is not a damn thing I can do about it unless I want to start trouble in the family. I just have to live and let live. After all, my granddaughter is their granddaughter, too."

Grandparents United

When grandparents acknowledge issues and work together to solve them it sets a wonderful example for the whole family. Grandparents can be supportive of one another, especially if one set or other is having a conflict with the parents. When Elise was having a disagreement with her son Jeff and stopped coming to visit his family (and her grandchildren), it was her daughter-in-law Melie's parents, Edward and Ellie, who helped reconcile matters. Edward and Ellie listened supportively to Jeff's complaints about his mother. Melie was mature enough to listen to Jeff rather than to join in the criticism. Edward and Ellie suggested to Jeff that they take the children to see his mother at her house, for a short period of time. He refused. Rather than being self-serving and pleased that the "other" grandmother was out of the picture, both Edward and Ellie mentioned that the children were being deprived of their other grandmother. Jeff said he understood. So Edward and Ellie took the grandchildren to see Elise. This act brought them closer, and the closeness endures today—long after Jeff's feud with Elise has blown over.

Grandparents can spare their children and grandchildren's suffering by developing a personal relationship with one another. If conflicts exist, it is incumbent upon the grandparents (allegedly older and wiser) to work out the issues by themselves. Because they have so much in common, grandparents, can learn to enjoy one another if they communicate directly and work together to iron out any differences. Most of all, a successful fit among grandparents requires a commitment to a long-term *positive personal relationship*.

GUIDELINES

Your grandchild's other grandparents are a fact of life that you must deal with in a loving, respectful, and caring way. Here are some guidelines to help you enhance your relationship and manage conflicts that may arise.

- Take the lead and set the example in creating a harmonious extended family.
- Make a positive effort to get to know the other grandparents. Take them out to dinner and have fun. Make an effort to include them in family get-togethers and holiday celebrations. Establish relationships with other members of their family.
- Talk to your grandchild about the other grandparents in a positive way. Let your grandchildren know they don't have to pick a favorite grandparent.
- Talk to your son- or daughter-in-law about his or her parents. Express interest in what the other grandparents are doing.
- Be magnanimous! Share and coordinate family activities and holidays.
- Coordinate big gifts with the other grandparents. Giving the grandchild a special holiday gift from both sets of grandparents sends a wonderful message. This may mean helping the parents

get together the financial resources for such things as your
grandchild's educational expenses. Ask the parents what they need
from both sets of grandparents.

- If a problem arises with the other grandparents, deal with it
  directly and openly. At all costs, avoid putting the parents in the
  middle of the conflict. Keep the parents up to date on any
  progress you make toward resolving the problem.

CONCLUSION

Your grandchild's other grandparents are a reality of life that you must accept
and honor. It is every grandparent's responsibility to deal effectively with this
and spare parents and grandchildren any grandparent-induced turmoil. Making
an effort to cultivate a positive relationship with your grandchild's other grandparents will benefit not only yourself but also—most important—your grandchild. This statement from Marcia, eleven, says it all: "My grandparents are nice
to one another and never fight. I am happy when they are all together because
we have a good time. They are all different, but they are all nice to me. I love
them all because they make me feel safe."

PART 5

Modern Grandparenting
Issues Facing Grandparents Today

Today's grandparents face enormously complex issues arising from changes in family structure and society. Many of these issues put a great strain on the relationship between grandparents and grandchildren. When complex situations arise, grandparents have to acknowledge them and consider how to handle them in the best way possible to maintain a meaningful relationship.

CHAPTER 35

Adoption

Although the rewards are equal, grandparenting an adopted grandchild is a bit more complex and challenging than having a biological one. With an adopted grandchild, however, it takes a bit more effort and understanding to anticipate, address, and deal with the challenges that arise—especially if the child has special needs.

Grandparenting an adopted child is not unusual today. There are more than 120,000 reported adoptions in the United States each year, with experts stating that the actual number of adoptions is much greater. Most grandparents of adopted children report that the experience has brought them a great deal of personal happiness and a golden opportunity for personal growth. As I mentioned, it poses some unique challenges as well. "Having an adopted grandchild made me a better person," one grandfather said. "At first, though, before I could get close to my grandson, I really had to examine some of my feelings and beliefs about accepting him. I'm not going to say it was all fun and games, but once I faced up to some of my own old-fashioned thinking, loving him was easy. Now my love for him just keeps growing." A grandmother concurs: "It's been no big deal. I have three adopted grandchildren and there's never a dull moment, especially from the teenagers. Adopted or not, I don't know the difference anymore."

Grandparents' Tasks in Adoption

Like having a biological grandchild, grandparenting an adopted child is a dynamic and ever-changing experience. However, there are a few added twists relating to the adoption process itself that grandparents need to know about. As I will explain, the process and logistics of adoption can create very specific tensions in family relationships, especially between parents and grandparents. The child's own development can be challenging to deal with. When parents and grandparents handle difficult situations successfully, adopted children usually thrive.

Bumpy times are a normal part of the picture, however. During adolescence, for example, a child's normal strivings to cope with rapid internal growth and change, and to establish a sense of emotional independence, can be complicated by the adoption experience and put extra strain on the parent–child relationship. This is an excellent opportunity for grandparents to employ wisdom and experience to keep the family on an even keel.

Understand that your relationship with your adopted grandchild will be very different from the relationship of the parents to their adopted child. They will need a great deal of support, especially at first. I cannot emphasize enough how important it is to be supportive and sensitive to what the parents are experiencing. Try to keep in mind that this is a learning experience for everyone.

Over the years of interviewing many hundreds of grandparents on this topic, I have learned three basic things a grandparent can strive for to make grandparenting an adopted child more meaningful and satisfying for the parents, the grandchild, and themselves:

- Understand the parents. Be compassionate, helpful, and supportive.
- Understand yourself. Monitor and process your own feelings about issues concerning your adopted grandchild.

■ Understand your adopted grandchild. Be there for your grandchild and stay tuned in to his experience.

Understand the Parents

It is important for you to know the exact reason that parents are choosing to adopt. Some families adopt children because they are unable to produce a child of their own. This is often the case with infertile heterosexual couples who cannot conceive and with same-sex couples. For other individuals and families, adoption is a primary option; they adopt children without ever having wanted or tried to produce a biological child.

Providing Empathy and Support

For families adopting because of a biological inability to bear children, the decision to adopt is often arrived at painfully. Couples who are unable to conceive may have feelings of guilt, inadequacy, frustration, sadness, and anger. Furthermore, the process of attempting to conceive—with its interminable visits to the doctor, its medicalization of sexuality, and the attendant anxiety and disappointment around repeated attempts and failures to conceive—is highly stressful, emotionally and physically exhausting. As an elder with more life experience, you can be an enormous source of comfort for the parents. Your understanding, empathy, and support is needed and valued.

Before contemplating adoption, it is important that the infertile couple has the time to process the emotional and psychological loss and disappointment involved in not being able to conceive. After they have mourned their loss, they can examine the option to remain childless or to adopt. Your role at this juncture is to nurture, support, and comfort them. If their choice is adoption, celebrate their decision. Take the time to learn about the adoption process and understand what the parents are experiencing as they navigate through it. Perhaps you can offer to help them wade through the mountains of paperwork generated by the adoption process. Demonstrating your eagerness for the new arrival can be very reassuring to nervous parents.

Educate Yourself About Adoption

There are important aspects of the adoption process that parents have to consider and you need to know about. One such aspect is the background of the child. Is the child healthy or does it have special needs? Will the parents choose a closed adoption (birth parents unknown to the adoptive family), an open adoption (birth parents known), or adoption of a child from another country?

"When my daughter and her husband told us they were going to go with an open adoption, I had my reservations," one grandfather, Tony, says. "I had these visions of the real parents coming to visit their child and him wanting to go home with them instead of staying with our family. But I figured they had their reasons, and they were the parents. After all is said and done, it worked out pretty well for my grandson. I think our daughter and her husband did the right thing."

Educate yourself by visiting your public library and consulting the many books and magazines on the subject. Also, talk to other families who have adopted. There are numerous sites on the Internet that provide information about all aspects of adoption (see the resources at the end of this chapter). The support you offer to the parents will be much more effective if you are attuned to what they are going through. In the parents' eyes, your involvement in the process validates their choice to adopt.

Primary Adoptions

If adoption is a primary decision, the situation is less complicated. There are no feelings of parental guilt and no sense of failure involved. On the other hand, single or gay parents who decide to adopt may be under additional stress because of the lack of support or positive validation for their choice from their family or society. Although societal attitudes toward single-parent and alternative families are changing, there is still a long way to go before single-parent and alternative families achieve the same acceptance and legitimacy that the so-called "traditional" family now claims. Be careful not to inflict any of your own prejudices on your children regarding their families.

One grandmother, Sylvie, told me, "Because my daughter is gay I always figured grandchildren were out of the question. But when my daughter and her partner decided to adopt a child, well, what can I say? My husband and I were just overjoyed. And we sure love that baby."

Ideally, families who adopt children have taken the time to work through difficult or painful issues before they are ready to become parents (or grandparents).

Join the Fun! Awaiting the Arrival

Awaiting the birth of a grandchild is always an exciting and energizing process. There are some differences in the process of *expecting* a biological grandchild and *waiting for* an adopted one. The birth of a biological grandchild is preceded by the announcement that your own child or your child's partner or spouse is pregnant. The announcement heralds a happy occasion: celebrations are in order! Other family members may eagerly anticipate the arrival of the grandchild and share in the pregnancy with the expectant parents. Celebrations such as baby showers can heighten the anticipation. You and your family have the luxury of knowing approximately when the grandchild will arrive, and can therefore plan to be physically present at the time of birth. You know that with the advent of a new generation, your biological family and ancestral line will be perpetuated. This is an important issue to some grandparents, while for others it is a matter of little or no importance.

The process of awaiting the arrival of an adopted child can be somewhat different. Some parents want their family to be very involved with the adoption process; others prefer little or no family involvement. Nevertheless, once the decision to adopt is made, and the process begun, family members can also enter into the happy "expectant" phase, just as they would with a biological child. The only difference here is that the arrival date of an adopted child can be unpredictable, often dependent upon a last minute phone call or a frustratingly long wait. Another difference is the age of the child. The awaited child may not nec-essarily be a newborn. Indeed, adopted children come at all ages. Disappoint-ments can be encountered; sometimes a child is not delivered when promised, or birth parents can have second thoughts about giving up their child. If these glitches occur, grandparents can empathize with the parents' disappointment and lend encouragement while the wait continues.

In most instances, how the grandchild arrives will have little effect on how much the child is loved. Emma and George are grandparents to both biological and adopted grandchildren. They have gone through the experience of expect-ing a biological grandchild and expecting an adopted one. "With our oldest daughter's first child we went through the whole thing, getting excited about the pregnancy, the baby showers, buying all kinds of things for the baby, and we even knew the baby was a boy in advance. But it was different with our second daughter, Pauline. She had a bad pelvic infection when she was young, so she couldn't get pregnant and had to adopt," Emma told us. George added, "And that was hell. We suffered together with the pregnancy tests that were never pos-itive, and shed tears with Pauline when she accepted the fact that she would never have her own baby. And then there were the long discussions we had with Pauline and her husband about whether to adopt, and how we would feel with an adopted grandchild." "Our hearts went out to them," Emma sighed. "The fact that they couldn't get pregnant didn't do their marriage any good." George added, "Things did a complete turnaround when they decided to adopt."

Emma continues, "Yes, but there was no nine months to get ready. Then, hard as it is to say, but it is the truth, we were a little put-off when they told us they were going to adopt a two-year-old Russian boy named Michael. But they were so happy we did not question their decision. We helped them prepare the papers for the adoption and go through the whole rigmarole." Emma laughed. "Then two years later they adopted Michael's sister, Mimi. And they are both great kids. We never think about them being adopted. They are just ours."

Like Emma and George, you can get the adoption off on the right foot by letting the parents know that you would like to be involved in all steps of the adoption process. It can be very comforting for parents to know that you are on their side and emotionally available to them.

Understand Yourself

Your job as a grandparent begins before your adopted grandchild arrives—during your time as an expectant grandparent. It is very important that you take the time to evaluate your own feelings about having an adopted grandchild. Furthermore, get in touch with how the rest of your family is responding to the adoption. It is not necessary to share these feelings with anyone, just to be aware of them. However, if you feel it would be beneficial to do so, seek out an objective third party, such as a good friend, therapist, or member of the clergy. Be alert that unexpected situations may arise with an adopted grandchild. As one grandmother, Fiona, said, "I became very quickly attached to my grandson when my son and his wife adopted him. Then, when he was ten, his birth mother contacted him. That took me aback. I was overwhelmed with anxiety. I kept thinking the birth mother would change her mind and want him back. Fortunately my son and his wife handled it all well."

On a regular basis, monitor and process your feelings regarding these important factors: the state of the adoption, your level of involvement as a grandparent, and any differences in thoughts or feelings you might experience between adopted and biological grandchildren. As you support the parents in their decision process and await the arrival of the grandchild, it is quite normal that new and unexpected thoughts and feelings will surface inside you. You might reflect upon how the grandchild was adopted in the first place, where the grandchild came from, his prenatal experience, his future physical and mental health, and so on. If this happens just let your thoughts and feelings run their course. They will dissipate the moment you first see your new grandchild!

When the Grandchild Arrives

It is a magical time when the child arrives. And you can share in the excitement. Some grandparents reported feeling a bit strange with their adopted grandchild at first, but the more time they spent with the child, the closer they felt. Other grandparents immediately took to the child as if it were their own flesh and blood. One Caucasian grandmother, Francine, said the first time she took her adopted Asian granddaughter in her arms, she felt instantly connected to the child. "I knew this was meant to be," she said.

As so many grandparents know, the old aphorism that "every child brings its own love" is blissfully true. Be aware that parents will appreciate your expression of love and support for them and their adopted child, especially when legal problems or other issues complicate the adoption process. You will be looked upon as a source of strength for your children, and you will set the stage for developing your own vital connection to your beautiful new grandchild.

Heredity and Family History

One of the bigger issues that some grandparents wrestle with is heredity, the transmission of genes and, sometimes, inheritance, which includes the passing on of personal and material property. Since your adopted grandchild is not a biological descendant, he will not genetically inherit any of your inborn traits (although he may pick up some of your mannerisms or habits from imitating you). Your adopted grandchild may never have your Aunt Fanny's way with a paintbrush, for example, or your father's blue eyes, but she will most certainly have talents and traits of her own to be celebrated. Some grandparents have strong feelings regarding the flesh-and-blood issue; they would prefer a biological descendent to carry on the family name. Others place more of a priority on the quality of the actual relationship rather than genetic links. However important this issue is to you, it is a good idea to sort out your feelings and priorities before the adoption takes place. After the adoption, your love for the child will supersede any other factors. To fully love an adopted grandchild, a grandparent must give up the notion of flesh-and-blood attachment and quite simply love the child because it exists.

Max, seventy-one, says he was a bit sad when he realized that his adopted South American granddaughter "probably would not care about the accomplishments or history of our family over the centuries. I'm of European descent and my Leah is from Peru. But now I wouldn't trade her for anyone in the world. She's my little princess." And Leah knows it. She loves to hear her grandfather's stories about the "old country." She may not have his genes, but he's her grandfather all the same. Though you will not share a common biological family history with an adopted grandchild, as Max learned, you will be blessed with the opportunity to create your own family history together.

The beauty of it is that biology has little influence on some of the most important grandparenting roles you play for your grandchild: mentor, nurturer, spiritual guide, role model, crony, or hero. Clark, forty-one, adopted when he was an infant, shared the following with me: "I don't feel adopted. My family never treated me any different from the other kids. My grandfather was the best of all. I learned more from my grandfather than I learned from my father, and I learned a lot from my father. My grandfather was a pilot for forty years, and he even fought in World War I. He taught me how to fly. I was always his little grandson to him."

Special Situations

Ideally you will be in total agreement with the parents' decisions and behavior concerning the adoption, and the adoption process will be a happy and harmonious event for all. Sometimes, though, a grandparent's compassion and tolerance might be tested when there are clashes over parental choices and values. If you accept the fact that there will be moments of emotional strain, and you are willing to ride out the bumpy periods, you can make a highly constructive contribution to the experience. There are other unique and often complex circumstances that can affect grandparenting an adopted child. Here are a few to consider.

First Grandchild

Whether biological or adopted, there is nothing quite like a first grandchild. Similar to a first biological grandchild, a first adopted grandchild has the special privilege of creating a new generation of parents and grandparents. That makes the moment of the child's arrival a once-in-a-lifetime experience indelibly etched in everyone's hearts.

Karina, a fifty-year-old grandmother who was involved in the entire process leading up to her daughter's and her son-in-law's decision to adopt, explains:

"This was not only my first experience with adoption, but also my first time as a grandparent. My daughter and her husband were happy when all the final arrangements were made to bring the baby girl home. In my heart, I was apprehensive. This little girl was going to make me a grandmother, something entirely new for me. I knew that on some level my daughter was very concerned about how I would react to the baby because she could sense my nervousness. I had a lot of fears. My main fear was that I wouldn't bond with the baby because, being adopted, she wasn't really 'mine.' But as soon as they brought that baby home, something took over. I had feelings I can only describe as grandmotherly. Seeing my daughter in the role of a mother made me melt. When my daughter put little Claire in my arms, that child looked at me with such love and won my heart. Every day I love her more and more—and does she know it! I am also enjoying my daughter's happiness at the fact that all of us are so close. That's very important to me. No matter how many other grandchildren I have, adopted or not, Claire will always be special because she was the one who made me a grandmother."

An Adopted Grandchild Following a Biological Grandchild

If your first grandchild was biological and you subsequently became a grandparent to an adopted grandchild, you may not experience the same thoughts or feelings about your new adopted grandchild that you felt with your biological grandchild. Some grandparents report feeling an instant bond with their biological grandchild because they know the child is genetically part of them. Your biological grandchild may inherit aspects of your looks and temperament that can be very endearing. "My grandson looks a lot like my dad," one proud grandfather said. "It's really amazing."

For many expectant grandparents, the sight of their pregnant daughter swollen with their grandchild is enough to elicit a very powerful biological connection to the child. This does not happen in most adoptive situations unless there is a surrogate carrying the grandchild.

Keep in mind however that adopted children today are usually aware that they are adopted and have strong feelings about the situation. This is especially pronounced when the adopted grandchild's siblings are biological children. Extra care is needed in this situation to make sure that your adopted grandchild feels she belongs in the family just as much as the biological grandchildren do. Needless to say, it is very important to avoid playing favorites between a biological and adopted grandchild (see Chapter 26, "Favoritism").

A Biological Grandchild Following an Adopted Grandchild

It is not uncommon for couples that were initially unsuccessful in their attempts to have a biological child to conceive after adopting a child. If this happens, you can expect to experience some feelings of favoritism toward the biological grandchild. Velma, fifty-nine, was very aware of a change in attitude toward her first adopted grandchild when her daughter surprised the whole family by getting pregnant and subsequently giving birth to a little boy. "My granddaughter Laurie was adopted and now she has a new brother, Seth. I can't help my attraction to Seth; he actually looks a bit like me. He's my blood. Of course I love Laurie, too, and would never in a million years let her know how I feel. Inside of me, frankly, I feel terrible that I have an inclination to favor Seth, but I will never, ever let it show." The adopted grandchild always senses the difference. It is up to the adults to show both the adopted and biological grandchildren that they are equally loved.

Racial/Ethnic/Religious Diversity: A Grandchild "Not Like Me"

Another recent trend in society is an increase in the number of racially diverse adoptions. There are also an increased number of adoptions of brothers and sisters from the same family. This has come about through adoption agencies broadening their scope of operations, increased parental failure, as well as poverty and war in foreign lands. As a result, it is becoming more and more common for American grandparents to welcome into their families adopted grandchildren of different ethnicity, race, or religion. An elder may unexpectedly find himself the grandparent of a developmentally challenged child, a child with a disability, a child who is a war survivor, or even a child who has fallen victim to its environment (for example, a "crack" baby).

If your child adopts such a grandchild, you may have to deal with certain feelings and attitudes about grandparenting a child who is so different from yourself. The boundaries of your understanding and tolerance may be stretched. You might not respect yourself for experiencing these feelings. Maria, a sixty-eight-year-old Latina grandmother, says she did her best to relate to her adopted granddaughter, Li. The child had been brought home by Maria's son who served in Vietnam. "I wanted to love her, but we were so different. I just couldn't feel the same about her as I do about my own. I used to baby-sit her a lot when she was growing up and really had to crack the whip with her. For a long time we didn't get along at all, although she got along with my other grandkids. Now I see her from time to time. She and my son are close. He's her dad. She married a white boy and I have a white great-grandchild who calls me 'Grandma.' I did my best; perhaps I could have done better."

For others, like Valerie, the process is easy. Valerie is a Hungarian-born grandmother with a great sense of humor. She is delighted with her new adopted grandchildren. When her son Matt and his wife first decided to adopt three Chinese children at the same time, "I thought they were kidding," she laughs. "But now I am totally over my concerns." One of the requirements of their adoption agreement was that the adopted children must learn about their Chinese heritage. "So now, would you believe it? My grandchildren aren't becoming Hungarian— I'm becoming Chinese. I am the one who takes them to their Chinese classes and their Chinese playgroup. The parents are too busy to do it. I even made some really great friends there. And I am learning about the culture. And I do tai chi with the kids. Can you believe it? Surprise, surprise. I know the kids don't look like me on the outside, but that's where the difference ends. We are all the same."

Valerie has a few more words of wisdom to share. "If you feel funny about the whole thing at first, don't worry about it too much. The more time you spend with your grandkids, the more they'll feel just like any other grandkid. Plus, they're still kids and all they know is who loves them. What else matters?"

If you are having trouble with this issue, try not to blame yourself or feel guilty. Do, however, consult a trusted friend, counselor, or member of the clergy. Talk the issue through and try to resolve things in your mind. Above all, work toward preserving and nurturing your relationship to your new grandchild.

Understand Your Grandchild

Being adopted is not easy. Studies show that adopted children who are told early in their lives that they are adopted adjust better than children who learn about it later in their lives. Hopefully your family will discuss the adoption openly with your grandchild. As the child grows, she will have the same questions every adopted person has: Why was I given up for adoption? Was there something wrong with me? Are my birth parents alive? Do I have biological siblings? (For help discussing these issues with your adopted grandchild, see the resources listed at the end of this chapter.)

It is critical that grandparents recognize and understand the emotional dimensions of family life that the adopted grandchild is experiencing. Every adopted child, no matter how loving and caring his adoptive family might be, has questions and emotional issues to resolve. Adopted grandchildren question their origins, their place in their adopted family (especially if there are siblings who were *not* adopted), and most of all, the strength of their parents' love and commitment. Because they may feel insecure, adopted grandchildren will often go out of their way to test this level of commitment. It is helpful to make sure that everyone in the family knows that the child is aware she was adopted.

If your grandchild approaches you wanting to discuss any issues or vent feelings she may be grappling with, do your best to serve as a calming influence and an attentive sounding board. Your grandchild is most likely coming to you because she's concerned about her parents' reactions to these issues. She may want to protect them from the emotional turmoil that these issues might engender.

As a grandparent, you are special to your adopted grandchild not only when it comes to normal issues of growing up, but also in times of stress. Your grandchild will regard her relationship with you as a safe haven because it is not complicated by the emotional and psychological issues that she has with her parents. Many adopted grandchildren say that it sometimes is easier to talk to their grandparents than to their parents about adoption. Grandchildren feel secure and comfortable with grandparents, seeing them as confidantes apart from their parents and, at the same time, as a connection to their parents with whom they are experiencing conflict. Because the grandparents are also parents of one of the grandchild's parents, the grandchild sees them as having a position of power. Often a grandchild might want to invoke a grandparent's influence with his parents to support his cause to change a parent's behavior. That can result in a sticky situation to say the least!

Seeking Birth Parents

Whether they verbalize it or not, adopted children often feel a need to know about and even to meet their birth parents and/or other biological relatives. This is "normal" and should not be taken as a reflection on the quality of parenting and grandparenting the child has experienced. The process of connecting with birth parents is becoming easier these days as many birth records are now open— meaning that adopted individuals have free and unlimited access to them. When it is hard for a parent to deal with this emotionally, a loving grandparent can bring perspective to the situation. Zach, fourteen, first consulted his grandmother about his need to find his biological mother: "I asked Grandma to be there when I spoke to my parents about it. I couldn't have done it alone because I thought I would hurt their feelings, and I knew Grandma would help explain that I didn't want to hurt them." Vanessa, Zach's adoptive mother, was grateful that her mother helped Zach share his feelings. "I knew he must be wondering about his birth mother, but he never brought up the subject with me or my husband. I guess he thought he would hurt our feelings. He's such a nice kid. I am really glad, though, that my mother was there for him. Now we all talk openly about it, and he can see that we didn't fall apart. He knows it's not easy for us because we feel so close to him. We are his real parents in every sense of the word, but he knows we accept his decision on the matter. Grandma was great during the whole thing. She kind of acted like a mediator."

Some grandparents even help their grandchildren in the search by approaching it as a family adventure. With his children's permission, Joel, sixty-six, helped his grandson find his birth parents. "In the beginning, it wasn't something I was happy about doing, but Joey wanted me to help him. I knew how much it meant to him, so I did it. His parents and I discussed it and agreed to help him, but I must confess it wasn't easy. We were scared about what we would find, and wondered if Joey would still love us. I tell you, all of our fantasies were going wild. But with the new open-disclosure policy we were able to find his birth mother. Joey also found two sisters and a grandfather. It was pretty amazing. He was happy, we were happy, and it all worked out."

Joey was very pleased to have found his birth family. "I really appreciate how Mom and Dad and Grandpa helped me find my other family. Now I've got another grandfather, too. I know one part of them was really afraid to help me look, but I love them all the more for it. They helped me do something I needed to do for myself. They're the best."

Some adopted children, though, are not as fortunate as Joey. Once they locate their birth parents, some find themselves rebuffed, and this can be very hard to take. The image of a happy reunion in the adopted child's mind can also be shattered by the discovery of who the birth parents really are. There is always the possibility that the birth parents will be less than thrilled about being contacted by their long-lost child. If this happens to a child, his grandparent can be a loving, steadying presence to help soften the blow.

Although it is understandable for loving family members to feel threatened when an adopted child begins to search for birth parents, these worries are most often unfounded. It is unlikely that the child will ever leave his adopted family to live with his birth family. As Sophia, an eighty-two-year-old grandmother, says, "I'm adopted, too, so I understand my adopted granddaughter's doubts and fears. Especially when she went to meet her birth mother. I listened carefully to her confusion. She was able to tell me that she wanted to know her birth mother better, but she did not want to hurt her parents. I went through the same thing, although I never met my birth parents. I was able to help her parents let the child have free rein to follow her own feelings in the matter. She got to know her birth mother but never wanted to live with her or leave us. Like I told her, she has us all."

Stormy Times

When conflicts arise, biological children know they are stuck with their parents no matter what! Adopted children are not as secure, and neither are parents. That is why grandparents can be very helpful when a parent-child relationship becomes strained. Normally, parents and older children battle over many things: manners, grades, curfew, and so on. Sometimes children get mad at parents and threaten to run away from home. But most don't follow through with the threat because, as eleven-year-old Carl says, "They are my parents forever."

Things can be a bit different for an adopted child. As many an adoptive parent will attest, there are times in the heat of the fray when a rebellious teenager will blurt out the classic refrain: "You're not my *real* parents!" Such a comment can add an extra dimension of panic and insecurity to the conflict because it tears at the fabric of the relationship. Often, just as an adopted child may think or say, "You're not my real parents," a parent may think, "You're not my real child." Joan, a forty-year-old mother who was having difficulties with her adopted adolescent daughter, put it this way: "Sometimes I think, why did I ever adopt Sally? She doesn't listen to me at all, and she's caused us so much pain. But thank the Lord, Sally still gets along with my parents. At least *they* understand what I am going through. Just having someone understand is a relief, because sometimes I feel like the bad guy with my daughter. Right now I think I can say my parents are keeping us together as a family." (See also Chapter 22, "Adolescence.")

Aaron, sixty-four and the adoptive grandfather of sixteen-year-old Larry, describes how he defused one such explosive situation. "Larry comes to my house whenever it gets too hot for him at my daughter's. The other night they locked him out because he broke curfew. He came knocking at my door and I let him in. He was ranting and raving that they are not his real parents, and that he could do what he wanted to. I told him to take it easy, and that I was his real grandfather and he has to listen to me. He laughed and I know that made him feel good. Then we watched movies until three in the morning. He ate half an apple pie, too. I raised some hell myself when I was his age and I turned out all right. That's what I keep telling his parents. In fact, my daughter used to raise hell, too." Aaron's daughter added, "Well, at least I know Larry's safe when he's running off to Grandpa's. I don't know what his secret is with that kid. He said he'd tell me when I become a grandparent."

Setting an Example in the Family

Some family members may have negative attitudes and feelings about your adopted grandchild that you do not share. This is a golden opportunity for you as a grandparent and elder to set an example of love and acceptance. Show your family the way. Treating your adopted grandchild as one of your own sets the standard for the whole family. Marilyn, fifty-five, was confused when her gay son, Bob, and his partner, both Caucasian, adopted a crack baby of color. "I didn't exactly know how to react," Marilyn said. "First, it was two men with a baby, and two gay men at that. But my son is a wonderful father and he saved this sweet Petey's life. It was hard at first, but now I love the baby. Of course, I had to deal with my other children's feelings and the feelings of relatives, too. One of my daughters won't speak to Bob, so I had to make peace in the family. I told everyone, look at this beautiful child. How can this be a bad thing when the child is so beautiful and loving? That's what I told everyone. And now that time has passed and everyone knows Petey, it's OK."

GUIDELINES

If you have an adopted grandchild, you will face many challenges. But you will be rewarded with extra joy too. Imagine, for example, what would have happened to the child if he were not adopted? Savor the joy he has brought to all family members. Here are some useful guidelines to follow to help enjoy this sacred experience.

- Set a positive and enthusiastic tone in the family for welcoming the new child.
- Be supportive of the parents' decisions and choices regarding the adoption process.
- Be sensitive to the feelings of the parents and grandchild.
- Monitor and be aware of *your* feelings in adverse situations that arise. Then go to work to resolve any problems or conflicts before they become magnified and erode the quality of your family life.

- Get informed by educating yourself about the adoption process. Reflect upon what the experience means and feels like for you, the parents, and your adopted grandchild.
- Be supportive of and emotionally available to parents during good times and bad.
- Be available and involved as your grandchild grows.
- Understand your grandchild's experience and discuss it together when appropriate.
- Nurture your vital connection to your grandchild and have fun together!

CONCLUSION

Having an adopted grandchild may initially challenge many of your preconceived notions and attitudes. When you shed these preconceptions, then you will know what grandparent power is all about. All you need to do is open your heart to your grandchild; support and love the parents; and show compassion, understanding, and tolerance. Then you will be open to the magic of your vital connection to your grandchild.

RESOURCES

Helpful websites:

> http://www.adopting.com
> http://www.adoption.com
> http://www.ABCAdoptions.com
> http://www.adopting.org
> http://www.adoption.org
> http://adoption.about.com

Also check your local public library for books and magazines on adoption. Reading children's books is a wonderful way for parents to tell their child about being adopted. Here are some excellent choices of books to share with your child and grandchild:

The Day We Met You. Phoebe Koehler, Aladdin (ages 4–8)

I Love You Like Crazy Cakes. Jane Dyer, illustrated by Rose A. Lewis, Little Brown (ages 4–8)

The Little Green Goose. Adele Sansone, illustrated by Alan Marks, North South Books (ages 4–8)

Tell Me Again: About the Night I Was Born. Jamie Lee Curtis, illustrated by Laura Cornell, HarperCollins Children's Books (ages 4–8)

Tell Me a Real Adoption Story. Betty Jean Lifton, illustrated by Claire A. Nivola, Knopf (ages 4–8)

CHAPTER 36

Cybergrandparenting

I f you use the computer to communicate with your grandchild and your family, you are a certified cybergrandparent! If you do not use a computer, it is time to start. Thanks to technology, the reach of your influence as a grandparent is now extended beyond the constraints of physical proximity. Using the Internet allows you to learn, grow, and communicate with the wider world more fully than ever before. The latest advances in technology now allow you to maintain a "real-time" relationship with your grandchild through cyberspace. This is a revolutionary blessing if you live far away from your grandchild. (See Chapter 43, "Long-Distance Grandparenting").

With the Internet, you can keep up with your family as well as the rest of the world, including grandparenting news and education, on a daily basis. If you are not yet on-line because you are a bit intimidated by computers, don't be. Experts conservatively predict that 80 percent of American homes will be on-line by the year 2010. I believe being a cybergrandparent is not only necessary to keep up with the times, but it also allows you to be part of the everyday life of your grandchild no matter how far apart you live. That is why I am devoting a chapter in this book to this important topic.

The following information should help you overcome any fears or mental resistance that are preventing you from reaping the benefits and enjoyment of using the Internet so you can be a cybergrandparent.

Beyond the Three R's

Just as reading, writing, and arithmetic opened new and exciting vistas for you as a child; learning computer skills will do the same for you as an adult. Join the throng. More and more grandparents are becoming computer literate. According to a recent SeniorNet study, 30 percent of American adults between the ages of fifty-five and seventy-four own a computer, compared to only 21 percent in 1994. Of those users, 52 percent call their computer "extremely useful." The results of this study demonstrate that once people get the hang of using a computer, they love it!

I want to reemphasize the most important benefit to you as a grandparent. With a computer, millions of cybergrandparents are now able to be a daily part of their grandchildren's lives, regardless of where they are geographically located. Cybergrandparents converse with family members via E-mail, help their grandchildren with their homework, participate in family chat rooms, play games together, publish family newsletters, research and share their family history, and maintain contact with their peers all over the country. And if you purchase a special video camera that you plug into your computer, you can actually see the person on the other end.

Now that you are convinced, let's get started.

Learning to Be Computer Literate

Although many people feel intimidated by computers, they find that once they get started it is a lot easier to use than they thought. Look at it this way: if it were really that difficult, there wouldn't be so many people using the computer! The following section contains a few basic guidelines to help get you started.

Obtain Access to a Computer

Ideally, it is best to purchase your own computer. Fortunately, computers are getting less and less expensive. If you can't afford a new or used computer, you might be able to partner with someone in your family and buy one together, or ask for a computer as a gift. Make a wish list, noting all the different components you will need—keyboard, mouse, monitor, etc.—and send it to family members. When your birthday, Christmas, or other gift-giving holidays roll around, you might just get what you need!

If you are unable to afford a computer, many public libraries have a few available for use by the general public at no cost. If you are unable to leave your home for some reason, there are many computer catalogs out there with toll-free numbers. The salespeople are usually patient and will answer any questions you may have regarding your purchase. Of course, in the beginning you can practice on a friend or relative's computer—or even your grandchild's. By displaying your interest in learning new things, you are setting a great example for your grandchild.

Taking classes can help. Many grandparents have become computer literate by visiting the school nearest them and asking the principal if they might join the computer class. The children enjoy having a grandparent around. And if you bring a batch of cookies for the kids, you might well turn out to be the class star!

Learn How the Computer Works

Learning how to operate a computer is quite easy. Although you may feel overwhelmed by all the new information at first, all you need do is relax and take it one step at a time. No one comes into the world knowing how to use a computer. Visit a computer store and ask a salesperson to let you look inside a computer and explain how it works. When you are able to visualize how simply computers are made, it will demystify them and help you feel much more at ease.

Computers are made up of *hardware* and *software*. Hardware is the body of your computer; software is its intelligence. The mechanical parts of the computer are also part of the hardware. Here are some examples of hardware.

- The *box* or *housing* contains the *central processing unit (CPU)* and is equipped with switches that allow you to turn the computer on and off.
- The *hard drive* is inside the housing of the computer and is where the vital information necessary to run programs is stored.
- The *mother board* connects electronic circuits and is contained inside the housing.
- A *modem* enables your computer to connect to your telephone line, which then allows you to access the Internet and send E-mail.
- A *keyboard* and a *mouse* allow you to run software programs. The keyboard is used mainly for word processing, although you can also use key commands to tell the computer what you want it to do. You use the mouse for a wide variety of "point and click" commands.
- The *monitor* (or screen) is the television-like screen that allows you to see what you are working on.
- The *printer* prints hard copies of what you create on the computer screen.
- A *scanner* enables you to move copies of photos and documents into your computer's storage bank. You can then send these items to others via E-mail.
- A *videocam* allows you to see another person and to chat with your grandchildren in real time provided that they too are equipped with a videocam.
- A *digital camera* lets you take pictures, download them to your computer, and send them to family members.

The hardware of a computer is no more complicated to deal with than the TV, dishwasher, or microwave you use every day. *Software* is what makes the hardware do what you want your computer to do. An *operating system* is a software program that runs the computer; the same way that you, the operator, drive your car. Great advances have been made in this area, and software is

getting easier and easier to use. Most computers already have built-in help programs that will teach you as you go along. When you turn the computer on,
it "boots up." This means your operating system is working. Once your computer is booted up, you then click your mouse on whatever program you would
like to use.

One of the computer programs you will use, a *browser*, connects you to the
Internet. The browser is a tool that helps you get around the Internet quickly
and efficiently.

E-mail is another program that allows you to communicate with others,
including your family and friends, colleagues, and so on. If you are a fan of
antique cars, for example, you can make friends with others all over the world
that share your passion. You can talk to them from your desk, your kitchen table,
or even in bed while you sip a glass of wine. No matter where you are or whatever the state of your health, the Internet is always there for you to use.

That is all there is to it. Once you become familiar with the workings of
the computer you can use it to create a family newsletter, do your accounting,
buy and sell stocks, research information, and most important of all, have a cyber
relationship with your grandchild! One of the most ingenious uses of the Internet involves on-line photo services like www.shutterfly.com. This service allows
you to put photos you take with a digital camera on the Internet and E-mail
them to family members in an instant. Arthur, sixty-four, amazed his family
members scattered around the country on Thanksgiving. First, he took digital
photos of the Thanksgiving turkey and the family members who were present.
Then he "uploaded" the photos into his computer and (using the website) sent
them out to his far-flung relatives. He called his relatives one hour later, after
they had received the photos. His grandson, Bobbie, eight years old, said
"Grandpa sent me his Thanksgiving pictures and called me right after he
E-mailed them to me. I could not smell Grandpa's turkey but I felt pretty good
that everyone was having a good time. It was the next best thing to being there."

To keep up to date with new developments, log on to websites such as
www.grandparenting.org to learn about the latest grandparenting news and ideas.
This site also offers program ideas and suggestions to enhance your cyber relationship with your grandchild.

Joining the Revolution

By using your computer, you can become the communication center of your family, no matter where you live. You will be able to keep up with current events and trends no matter where you are or how physically active you are. The stimulation you will receive from being in touch will enhance your mental and physical health as well as your self-esteem.

Bear in mind that having access to such a rich world of information will supply you with plenty of material for discussion with friends and colleagues—and especially family members. One grandmother I know serves as a self-appointed research assistant surfing the Web to help her granddaughter with her college term papers. Family members who are interested in computers find they communicate with one another more frequently than other families do. Because children today grow up using computers, this is a wonderful way for you to participate in your grandchild's world. Discussing new and exciting computer programs is a great way for family members to share.

GUIDELINES

Here are some specific things you can do with a computer.

- Practice the computer games your grandchildren like to play. Then surprise them by giving them a run for their money.
- With young children, purchase learning programs "lapware" that you can use together.
- Host a family website and have regular family chats.
- Subscribe to a computer magazine and keep up to date on the latest hardware and software developments.
- Consider giving computer programs as gifts to family members, such as children's stories, games, educational programs, encyclopedias, etc.
- Keep in daily touch with your loved ones, and especially your grandchildren via E-mail.

- Get access to a video camera so you can have real-time conversations with "long-distance" grandchildren.
- Get a digital camera too so you can send photos to your family no matter where they live.

CONCLUSION

If you want to be a more effective grandparent, it is essential that you become computer literate—a cybergrandparent. Even though it may seem overwhelming at first, do not be discouraged. Everyone you see using a computer was once in your shoes; they all learned, and you will too. Ask your grandchild to teach you computer skills. It is a great way of spending time together and also demonstrates to your grandchild that elders are capable of learning and evolving.

RESOURCES

www.grandparenting.org—to keep abreast of grandparenting issues

www.Seniornet.Com—a website for seniors with information and events

www.familyedge.com—for the latest in learning and fun games you can play with your grandchild

CHAPTER 37

When Parents Divorce

T|he national divorce rate is approximately 60 percent. Statistics show that 50 percent of children experience a divorce in the family before their eighteenth year; and 40 percent of all second marriages in the United States end in divorce. Given this information, it is likely that divorce has touched your life in some way. If you are divorced yourself (see Chapter 38, "When Grandparents Divorce") or if you have a divorced child, you are already familiar with the pain and conflict divorce creates within a family. You also have probably learned that the manner in which you and the parents handle a divorce can be critical to the children's health and well-being. That is why it is so important to monitor and understand what your grandchild experiences as a child of divorce.

Understanding Your Grandchild

Divorce generates a storm of feelings in children. Without someone to share their feelings, children can suffer through their parent's divorce alone, standing as a silent witness to the emotional chaos of their elders. A child is further affected by the family changes that can occur after divorce—for example, if the divorced parents begin new relationships or remarry (see Chapter 46, "Stepgrandparent-ing"). To a confused and suffering child in a divorce situation, the love and sup-port of a grandparent can be enormously reassuring. It provides a sense of security and continuity at a time when the child's world seems to be crumbling. Although children are the most vulnerable during a divorce, parents too can greatly benefit from a grandparent's positive intervention.

In a parental divorce situation, the grandparents' primary role is to help their grandchild deal with the drastic changes occurring in his life. We will now explore a small sampling of children with regard to the emotional aspects of the divorce experience—and we'll learn what their grandparents' support means to them.

Grief

Luke, ten, mourns his parent's divorce. "I feel so sad. I tell myself that my par-ents will always love me no matter what, but it is so sad when parents get divorced, especially for children. It's like my family died. I was happy before they started fighting. I had a normal life with a mom and dad at home, doing things together. That's over now. I still love my parents, but my parents don't love each other anymore. Since I come from both of them, what does that mean I am? But my grandparents are forever. I want them to listen to me."

Fear

Kathy, eleven, feels frightened and insecure. "My parents don't want to be together. If my sister and I were not alive they probably would not have to talk to each other. Don't kids need *two* parents to take care of them? I feel scared. I am also mad at my parents for getting divorced so I make trouble sometimes. But it's different with my grandparents. They are together and I love them and am important to them. So I am good for them. They are older and I don't want to hurt them, so I never make trouble for them. I know they care for my parents and me. I feel safe when I am with them and know I can always live with them if something happens."

Guilt

Children may feel personally responsible when parents divorce. They need to be reassured that the divorce is not their fault and that everybody loves them. Ira, twelve, feels, as so many other children do, an irrational sense of responsibility for his parents divorce. "I know they fought over me sometimes. My mother would protect me when my father was angry. Then sometimes my father would get mad at my mother when she was after me for making a mess. Maybe if I was better they wouldn't have fought so much. Sometimes I think that maybe if it weren't for me, they'd still be together. I've told my grandparents how I feel, but they said I shouldn't worry about it because it's a normal feeling. I know my mother feels guilty about the divorce, too. Like she let us down. But my grandparents don't blame anyone. 'These things happen,' my Grandma said."

Anxiety and Depression

All of the above emotions are often accompanied by anxiety and depression. In children, anxiety typically manifests as nervousness, feelings of panic and a sense of impending doom; some have difficulty breathing. Sometimes a child will experience brief yet intense panic attacks. In other instances, a child may experience low-level anxiety. The longer the anxiety continues, the more a child will become depressed.

The signs of depression are rather easy to identify. The child's functioning is affected. She may exhibit a lack of attention, lethargy, negative attitude, and irritability. She may also express feelings of helplessness, hopelessness, and worthlessness. On the other hand, the child may begin to act up and develop behavioral problems. With more severe depression, the child's sleep and eating patterns become chaotic and he may even have suicidal thoughts or exhibit self-destructive behavior. If you notice any of these symptoms, seek professional help for your grandchild.

Twelve-year-old Misty is the oldest of four children. When her parents told her they were getting a divorce Misty blamed them both, but was especially angry with her father because he was the one who wanted the divorce and had moved out of their house. Misty took to her bed, sobbing and angry. She refused to go to school or to talk to her friends. Both sets of grandparents visited Misty daily, but could not get through to her. On the fifth day, her father returned to the house and took her to the emergency room. On the way to the hospital, Misty begged her father to return. In a gentle way, he said that he couldn't do that, but that he would still be her dad and would see her often. Misty attacked him in a rage. Arriving at the hospital, she was sedated and kept overnight for observation. The next day both sets of grandparents came to see her. Misty was diagnosed with a reactive depression and the doctor agreed to send her to stay with her paternal grandparents as an outpatient under the care of a child psychiatrist. Misty's mother was also seeing a psychiatrist and was too distraught at that time to help Misty.

A week later, Misty returned home. Eventually, with the help of her psychiatrist and several joint therapy sessions with her mother, Misty accepted the divorce and was able to work through the trauma. Both sets of grandparents wanted to help in any way they could. They chipped in to help pay Misty's medical bills.

What Your Grandchild Needs from You

If your grandchild is suffering from a parental divorce, you can do a lot to help. Here is what most grandchildren need.

Comfort and Support

Larry, fourteen, is aware that he needs a loving and supportive person with whom to share his feelings. "I am very upset about my parents' divorce. Especially since it happened so suddenly. One day my Dad just did not come home. I get very emotional about the divorce and I cannot talk to my mom because she gets too upset and we end up in a fight. So it's very important for me to be able to talk with my grandparents about my feelings and about the future. After all, they have known me since I was born and have always been there for me. When my parents divorced, I became frightened. My grandparents reassured me that the whole world was not falling apart and that I would survive. I feel they are sad, too. We share our sadness."

Spare the Grandchild from Adult Conflicts

Sal, twelve, is pleased that his grandparents do not put him in the middle of family conflicts. "If my grandparents criticize my parent who is their own child, it's OK. But they shouldn't criticize my other parent, especially to me, because it makes me upset. I would rather not hear about the differences the grownups have. My grandparents criticized my parents and it made me more upset. Grandparents should help parents instead of criticizing them. What good does criticizing do?"

Coping with a Parent's Dating and Remarriage

Twelve-year-old Lillet was upset when her mother started dating again. She told me what she expects of her grandparents. "One thing grandparents can do is give advice. Parents don't realize that children are frightened when their parents get divorced and then start dating other people. That new person might turn into the new stepparent and that can scare a kid, especially if they don't like the person. And then they have to pretend they like the person or their parent will get upset. I can complain to my grandparents about who my mother goes out with and they listen to me. Sometimes they talk to my mom about it, too. I like it when they help my mom." Grandparents can especially help a grandchild adjust when a parent remarries, and give the parent some time to adjust too. Some grandparents I know took their grandchildren into their home to allow the newlyweds some private time together.

Security and Protection

Barbara, fourteen, summed up how available and involved grandparents can help children feel more secure. "My grandparents will always love, protect, and encourage me. I wish my parents would be together, but sometimes things can't happen the way I want, so I have to make the best of it. Being close to my grandparents is part of making the best of it. I can always stay at their house. They have been married for a long time and I don't think they are going to get divorced and that makes me happy. I hope my parents can find someone else to make them happy. Since my grandparents are happy together, I know it's possible."

Help in Dealing with Parents

Because children know their grandparents are their parents' parents, they naturally ascribe a great degree of power and influence to their grandparents over their parents. Therefore, when a family problem exists, it is natural for a child to turn to a grandparent for help. If the grandparent is not directly involved in the problem, the child can feel safe expressing confidential feelings and opinions about his or her own parent. Some grandchildren simply need their grandparent to listen to them talk. In other cases, a grandchild may ask the grandparent to intervene and help a parent change a behavior that frightens the grandchild. There are also extreme cases, of course, such as those involving parental abuse, etc. (see Chapters 41, "Raising Grandchildren," and 42, "Legal Issues").

Before the Divorce

In stressful times, parents need a bit of help as well. Grandparents can provide it by taking on some of the caretaking of their grandchildren. Keep in mind that the problems leading up to a divorce have percolated for a long time, which has most likely had an adverse effect on the grandchild. Chances are also good that the child has been keeping many of her feelings to herself.

Be on the lookout for a decrease in your grandchild's functioning or any behavioral problems. Also be aware of the state of the parents' marriage and any tensions that may be affecting the parents and the grandchild. If you spot any problems ask to help in a loving and noninvasive way. Being a stable, loving figure in your grandchild's life will serve all of you well should there be a divorce in the family's future.

Think Before You Act

When parents divorce, it is almost impossible for a grandparent to remain objective about the situation. It is perfectly natural to have strong feelings about certain issues and, as a parental reflex, to want to take your child's side in the fray, rather than your in-law's. It is also natural for you to tend to blame your child's spouse for the divorce. Your feelings of sadness, disappointment, anger, or loss about the divorce can be quite strong, but it is essential to your future relationship with your grandchildren that you handle these feelings in a constructive way. You can benefit all family members by putting your own feelings and judgments aside and instead focus on the pain and suffering of the divorced parties and the welfare of your grandchild.

Do not suppress your feelings. Express them appropriately with a friend, counselor, or member of the clergy. Avoid sharing them with the divorced couple and your grandchildren. They have enough to deal with and do not need the added burden of seeing to your emotional needs. If you do choose to vent your emotions to family members, chances are that the divorced couple, already overloaded by their own feelings, might shun you in the future or even prevent you from seeing your grandchild. I cannot emphasize too strongly that the divorced couple will not have emotional space to listen to you. They are primarily concerned with their own pain and confusion. They want you to be strong, confident, and nurturing. *You need to be part of the solution, not part of the problem!*

Your first priority is to help your child (and his or her spouse) who are experiencing a rough time and need your support. If you support your children well, they will in turn, be more emotionally available to your grandchildren. In addition, your grandchild needs their parents to be as calm as possible during the divorce.

Wendy, sixty-two, was very upset when her daughter Paula divorced her alcoholic husband because he would not seek treatment and was abusive to her and her children. Instead of supporting her daughter's decision, Wendy believed Paula should have tried to make the best of it—that divorce should have been absolutely the last option. In retribution for the divorce, Wendy cut off all contact with Paula for several months. She shut herself off from her daughter and her grandchildren, each of whom needed her desperately at the time. "Why did she get mad at us?" asked seven-year-old granddaughter Alice. "We didn't do anything." In time Wendy's anger subsided and she came to her senses. She called Paula and asked her forgiveness for not being understanding and supportive.

Make an Effort to Maintain Emotional Ties

If you have a close relationship with your ex-son-in-law or ex-daughter-in-law, there is no reason why you should surrender that relationship just because of the divorce. Your grandchild must deal with both divorced parents on a permanent basis. Studies show that the relationship between grandparents and grandchildren can be adversely affected after a divorce (Drew 1999). So be alert to the health of your relationship.

To be as helpful as possible to your grandchild and family, don't express your opinions about the parents. If you harbor negative feelings toward your ex-in-law, keep them to yourself. Your *child* needs to vent feelings about an ex-spouse to you, and your *grandchild* needs you to listen about a parent. Listen quietly. If you add your two cents' worth, you will find that you will create a corking effect—the more you vent your own feelings, the less venting the other person will do, and the more you might get into trouble.

So be an observer. Stop and listen. Above all, do not participate in the emotional storm between your child and ex-spouse. It is perilous to give unsolicited opinions or advice. One parent might use what you say as ammunition against the other.

This happened to Monique, a sixty-five-year-old grandmother. Bill, Monique's ex-son-in-law, was furious; he'd heard from his ex-wife that Monique had said she thought he was a "loser." The worst part was that Monique had said this in front of her grandchild, Bill's son. Because of this, Bill denied Monique any visitation with her grandson. It took Monique a year of constant entreaty to be able to meet with Bill and explain that she had never said such a thing in front of her grandchild. In fact, it was her daughter Carol, who, in a fit of rage, attributed her own comment to her mother. Monique was eventually able to convince

Bill that she was honestly concerned about the happiness of *both* her daughter and him.

Be an Agent of Healing

Understand that everyone involved in a divorce situation is suffering; therefore do not fan the flames of the family fire. Try to be emotionally available to everyone. To do this you may have to make radical changes in your own lifestyle. As a therapist, I have called grandparents back from retirement to help a parent involved in a divorce. Some grandparents have taken sabbaticals from their jobs to help divorcing parents. One widowed grandfather, Adam, seventy-three, had always looked forward to retiring to the sunbelt. But two years into his retirement, he returned home when his recently divorced daughter asked him to move in and help her with her six children. "It was the best thing I ever did in my life," Adam said. "All I did in Florida was relax all day. Now I am helping my daughter and my grandkids get back on their feet. I know I am being useful and helpful. The kids tell me that every day and that really makes me feel good."

If you can, try to understand and support your child's ex-spouse. Although you will most likely side with your child in the divorce, don't be overzealous in judging the other party. Remember that your child's ex-spouse is a parent of your grandchild and has control over your access. Never force your grandchild to choose between you and a parent.

When you are alone with your grandchild, express respect and support for *both* parents. Listen to their thoughts and feelings in an accepting, understanding and nonjudgmental way. Allow your grandchild to unburden her heart. She will be dealing with many issues, such as divided loyalties, blame, fear, and hurt, and she will feel much safer if she sees you as nonreactive and on everyone's side. Remind all family members that the storm will pass. Your grandchildren need you to be the rock to which they can cling.

However sad you are about the divorce, don't be too grim with your grandchild. Have fun with her. Go out of your way to arrange and attend upbeat events at home and at school, especially during the holidays. Be sure to take care of yourself physically, emotionally, and spiritually. Your family needs you.

After the Divorce

Adjust to the changes in your family. For example, your daughter may now be an overwhelmed single mother. If your son is divorced, it is likely that his ex-wife will have the children. (After all, 30 percent of households in the United States consist of a single adult with children, and 80 percent of those adults are women.) Reach out and ask what you can do to help her, now that she no longer has a husband around to help.

There may come a time when you will be asked to provide respite for your family. Sometimes a newly divorced parent may want to move in with you until he or she can make a new start. If this happens, it is best to discuss well in advance the length of the stay, financial terms, household responsibilities, baby-sitting arrangements, parenting and grandparenting responsibilities, and the need for private time. Your grandchild will be especially sensitive to how you and his parent get along at this juncture.

Let the parents and your grandchild know that you are available to help. Offer to take your grandchild to give your child a much-needed break. Be sure to discuss the parents' rules with your grandchild and, aside from perhaps a little normal grandparental indulgence, provide a consistent structure (see Chapter 27, "Spoiling Grandchildren"). Depending on the involvement of the parents and how often your grandchild sees them, make sure to leave a space for the parents in the daily routine. Talk about the parents frequently, place a picture of them at your grandchild's bedside, and make time for your grandchild to be with them as often as possible.

Grandparents and the Divorce Agreement

Because the quality of human relationships is ever changing, and the person who has custody of your grandchild holds the key to your relationship to your grandchild, it is important for you to ensure that access will continue after the divorce. Ask the divorcing parties to request their lawyers to make provisions for your visitation rights in their divorce agreement (see Chapter 42, "Legal Issues"). This is particularly important if your child does not have legal custody.

Be aware that failure to make these arrangements may result in your being denied access to your grandchild if your relationship with the child's custodian goes sour. Syd, sixty-two, was "very friendly," with her ex-daughter-in-law, Jackie, for several years after Jackie's divorce from Syd's son. When Jackie, who had full custody of her children, remarried and moved to another state with Syd's two grandchildren, Syd had little legal recourse to win access to her grandchildren because there was no mention of her visitation rights in the divorce agreement. As Jackie started her new life, Syd's role evaporated and she lost the opportunity of seeing her grandchildren grow up; in her words, "I lost my grandmotherhood."

On the other hand, Damon, a sixty-five-year-old attorney, had his grandparental rights inserted into his son's divorce agreement. His ex-daughter-in-law, Missy, said she was "happy to have them in the divorce agreement because I like Damon and Irma very much. I didn't divorce them; I divorced their son."

Peggy, fifty-three, is happy that she had her visitation rights written into her daughter Allie's divorce settlement. She and her son-in-law, Garth, forty-one, never got along. When Garth divorced Allie, who was ill at the time, he got custody of the three children. But Allie would not agree to the divorce unless her parents' visitation rights were assured by the agreement. When Garth remarried, he tried to block Peggy's visits with her grandchildren. Peggy invoked her legal visitation privileges outlined in the divorce agreement, and the court agreed that Garth had to make time for Peggy to see her grandchildren.

GUIDELINES

If one of your children is divorced, or is planning a divorce, here are some time-proven guidelines that will allow you to be as helpful as possible to all concerned. In this way you will minimize the stress and emotional turmoil of your grandchild.

- Acknowledge, evaluate, and work through your own feelings about the divorce.

- Handle your feelings that come up in an appropriate and healthy manner.
- Be compassionate, understanding, loving and supportive to your child and your ex-in-law. Remember that they are *both* your grandchild's parents.
- Shelter and support your grandchild through this painful process.
- Reach out to your peers for support.
- Think before you act. Make sure your actions do not create new conflicts or problems.
- Understand that the effects of divorce are lifelong for your grandchild. The issues involved have to be understood and dealt with.

CONCLUSION

Divorce is complex. As a grandparent, your role is to limit the damage and be as supportive as possible. You have a special responsibility to help your grandchild deal with what may turn into lifelong feelings of pain, confusion, fear, anger, and disillusionment. Don't forget to help them see the good side of life while going through this difficult period.

RESOURCES

www.parentsplace.com/family/divorce

www.info4parents.com—the Children's Rights Council provides assistance for parents who feel excluded from children's lives.

www.grandparentsrights.org

The Essential Grandparent's Guide to Divorce: Making a Difference in the Family, by Dr. Lillian Carson. Health Communications, May 1996

CHAPTER 38

When Grandparents Divorce

A | s you know, parental divorce is quite common today. It may surprise you to find out that because of increased longevity grandparental divorce is becoming quite commonplace as well. When grandparents divorce it can be particularly shocking to a grandchild. Especially a youngster who views her grandparents as the stable heads of the family.

As I pointed out in Chapter 37, when parents divorce, grandparents should strive to be objective and offer their support. Children expect them to do so. But when grandparents divorce, it shakes the foundations of the family. And although parents may understand the circumstances of the divorce, they are apt to be emotionally upset. Grandchildren have to deal with their parents' upset as well as what is happening to their grandparents through the divorce and even remarriage. With their support system in turmoil, children often have to look to the other set of grandparents (see Chapter 34, "Between Grandparents"). Whether you are a divorced grandparent, or have a grandchild whose other set of grandparents is divorced, the following information will assist you in getting your grandchild and her parents through this tough period.

Effects of Grandparent Divorce

As I mentioned earlier, the increase in human longevity is an important factor in the rising rates of grandparental divorce and remarriage. The longer lifespan also makes for an increased opportunity to study what happens to divorced grandparents and their families over the long term. We are learning more about what happens when divorced grandparents remarry and become stepgrandparents to their new spouse's grandchildren. We are also learning about what happens to divorced grandparents who do not remarry. Our studies have shown that grandparents who divorce must deal with not only the reactions of their own adult children to their decision, but also the reactions of their grandchildren. This is no easy task.

Explaining grandparents' divorce to grandchildren can be a difficult and complex undertaking. To do it most effectively it is important to know exactly what the grandchild is experiencing. Studies show that the grandchild undergoes a modified version of the same thoughts and feelings he might experience if his parents were to divorce. What is added is a deep tear in her idea of family continuity, traditions, and place (whether the changes involve the grandparents' traditional home or a new geographic location). The child's image of the grandparents can also be altered. It is the grandparents' job to understand this process and to help the grandchild deal with the changes in family system.

What follows is a sampling of what children say about the experience of seeing their grandparents divorce. If you are a divorced grandparent, what they say may give you insight into their thoughts, feelings, and needs; hopefully what you learn will help you to support your own grandchild as effectively as possible if you are dealing with the circumstances of your divorce.

What Grandchildren Feel

When grandparents divorce, children's feelings range from confusion and emotional upset if the grandparents are very close, to less intense emotions if the grandparents are distant. These can also vary according to the degree of acrimony involved in the divorce. Children may have more concerns about one grandparent than the other depending on their closeness and how vulnerable they perceive the grandparent to be. "When my grandparents divorced I was fifteen," says Myra, now twenty-five. "I always felt worse for my grandmother because I knew her better than my grandfather. He was never around because he traveled so much. He just up and left her and she was devastated. There she was, an abandoned woman who had to support herself. She had given him the best years of her life. Grandpa still calls me and I love him, but I guess I am still very angry with him. I've tried all this time to get over it, but I don't know if I ever will. My mother never did."

The main impact on the grandparent-grandchild relationship is the way that the grandparents' divorce affects the ultimate availability of the grandparents for the child as well as the grandparents' understanding of the grandchild's personal experience.

Mourning / Disappointment / Disorientation

Because grandparents play many roles that indicate stability and continuity, divorce brings grandchildren sadness and disappointment as well as what can only be described as a deep sense of family disorientation. Sixteen-year-old Vanda says she grieved for one year when she learned about her grandparents' divorce. "I knew they fought a lot, but I would never have thought they didn't love each other anymore. I am so sad about it because they kind of represent the family. Now—I can't explain it—I feel lost. My world is topsy-turvy. The whole family is sad about Grandma and Grandpa. We don't know what to do about holidays, who to invite. It is like all of the things we did every year stopped. You would think they were too old to want to get divorced. I looked up to them."

Insecurity

The deep disorientation of the child often is translated into a sense of family insecurity—especially if the parents are divorced too. Carl, twelve, was concerned about Thanksgiving without his grandfather. "The whole family always spends Thanksgiving and Christmas together. It's true that Grandpa did get drunk and that's why Grandma didn't want to be married to him anymore, but he never hurt us. He was silly when he drank. Now he won't be at Grandma's for the holidays any more. I am sick about what happened. I hope this doesn't happen to my parents. I always thought that my parents and grandparents would always be together. Now I worry about my parents getting divorced, too. Can I count on any adults to stay together?"

Need for Reassurance

The insecurity the child experiences when grandparents divorce leads to an increased need for stability. They need to know how and why this happened, and what they can count on. When Glen, sixty-four, decided to get divorced he sat his three grandchildren down and explained to them exactly what was going on. His granddaughter Tillie, nine, now says, "I was happy my grandfather talked to us kids and told us that he still loved all of us. He said he and Grandma didn't want to be married anymore, but they still liked each other. He asked us to tell him how we felt and we told him we were sad and everyone started crying, even Grandpa. He told us to call him to talk anytime. But I feel scared about marriage. If my grandparents get divorced what does that say about getting married? Will this ever happen to me?"

Identity Issues

Children have trouble seeing their grandparents in a different light after the divorce takes place. Elia, fifteen, attended a party where his divorced grandfather brought a date. Elia was upset when he saw his grandfather smooching openly with this stranger. "I couldn't look at him, " Elia said. "My grandfather making out like that. And my grandmother was there too. I felt bad for her. My mother was really mad. What a mess." It's important that grandparents remain "grandparental" when children are around.

Staying Neutral

Children most often want to maintain a relationship with both parties in a divorce and do not want to choose sides. That is why it is so important that divorced grandparents support their grandchild's relationship with their other grandparent (although I imagine Elia's grandmother would be hard put to do so). Twelve-year-old Billy and his grandfather are close. He was very upset when his grandparents became divorced and his grandfather moved out. Billy told his grandmother, Clarice, that he was angry with his grandfather for divorcing her and marrying a much younger woman. Clarice recognized Billy's sadness and his confusion about how to deal with the grandfather he loved. Instead of criticizing his grandfather, Clarice, in a most considerate and loving way, told Billy that his grandfather loved him and what had happened was between *both* grandparents. She told Billy it had nothing to do with him. Clarice's words were comforting to her grandchild; he had been overly concerned about protecting his grandmother because he viewed her as more vulnerable than his grandfather. With time Billy was able to forgive his grandfather and even became close to his new stepgrandmother.

Children want to know *why*. Grandparents should keep in mind that they must explain their reasons for a divorce in a way their grandchildren can understand. Children are able to understand the idea that people grow out of or away from one another over the years, that sometimes people have a good life together until a certain point and then decide to move on. Each grandparent needs to take the time to explain the situation to his or her grandchild. A positive change for the divorcing grandparents may turn out to be a good thing for everyone in the long run.

Helping the Parents

Often children will mimic the attitudes, feelings, and actions of their parents toward certain events or situations. That's why it's important that all family members be on the same page when grandparents divorce. Often, however, this is difficult to accomplish because the parents' reactions are so vociferous toward their parent's divorce. This naturally colors the child's feelings. Rob, twelve, says he felt sick when he heard that his grandparents were divorcing. "My parents got really angry and upset and started yelling at my grandparents. They were so upset I couldn't say how I felt because I felt sorry for my parents. They said they were ashamed. But my grandparents explained to them why they were getting a divorce. They said they had wanted to get a divorce for a long time, but they'd waited until the children grew up. They made my parents feel better and that made me feel better." If you are involved in a divorce, make every attempt to take everyone's feelings into consideration.

Being Available

The most important thing a divorced grandparent can do for their grandchild and family is to be available to listen to their thoughts and feelings about the divorce situation. *Don't expect approval; just listen.* Only time will heal the wounds. Being available to share the pain and confusion that accompanies divorce, and to act appropriately, helps to decrease its destructive effects. Lara, seventeen, says, "It took four years for me to get over my grandparents' divorce. I wasn't used to seeing them without each other. However, whenever I called them they responded. Both of them would drop whatever they were doing to see me. They both remarried, but they are always there for me when I need them. This was so important for me because they told me that things wouldn't change between us after they got divorced, and then they showed me they meant what they said."

GUIDELINES

A divorced grandparent will likely encounter difficulties when trying to get things back on an even keel. If you are a divorced grandparent or you are acquainted with a divorced parent or grandparent who can use your counsel, here are some guidelines to help.

- Understand that a grandparent divorce has severe repercussions for all family members, especially grandchildren.
- Evaluate, acknowledge, and work through your own feelings about the divorce situation.
- Formulate a plan for damage control and healing.
- Initiate your healing plan. Let family members know the facts of the divorce, and listen to their thoughts and feelings. Let children know only what is appropriate.
- Respect the grieving process of all family members.
- Set an example. Be respectful of, and do not interfere with, family members' relationship with the divorced spouse.
- Do not place family members in the middle of disagreements with the divorced spouse.
- If your grandchild asks specific questions answer frankly according to your position in the family and her age and need to know.
- If you are a divorced grandparent who has become involved with another person, be very sensitive to timing the introduction of the new person correctly (see Chapter 46, "Stepgrandparenting").
- Take care of yourself during this difficult time. Seek professional help from a therapist or member of the clergy if necessary. It is essential that your family see you as working hard to make the best of a painful situation and striving toward healing. Include them in all aspects of this process.

CONCLUSION

When grandparents divorce, the repercussions of their actions trickle down to affect all family members. Keep in mind that the better you cope with the situation, the better your children and grandchildren will cope. If you allow your family to share in the process, everyone will heal more quickly and move on.

CHAPTER 39

Gay and Lesbian Issues

P ublic awareness and discussion about gay and lesbian issues has increased in recent years. As a result, I have begun to study how these issues affect grandparents and grandparenting.

Whether they want to or not, grandparents become deeply enmeshed with gay and lesbian issues by

- having a gay or lesbian grandchild
- having a gay or lesbian child who becomes a parent
- the "coming out" of a grandparent (a grandparent who reveals that he or she is a homosexual)
- supporting a grandchild whose parent "comes out" after living a heterosexual lifestyle

I will address each of these situations in this chapter.

Having a Gay or Lesbian Grandchild

In most instances, homosexuality, like heterosexuality, is not a matter of personal choice. Nor is it a pathological condition, according to mental health experts.

Research has shown conclusively that gays and lesbians have the same incidence of mental illness as that of the general population as well as equal rates of criminal behavior.

When the child is young, the parents may have some inkling that he or she has identity issues. Indicators might include of a variety of modes of behavior, including his or her play preferences. It is adolescence however, that, for most youngsters, is an especially confusing, painful, and fearful time. This is when they first have to deal with being *sexually* attracted to people of the same sex. They address this issue by a personal choice either to publicly acknowledge homosexuality or to go "in the closet," meaning to hide the condition from the world and attempt to live a "traditional" life. This is an extremely difficult and painful process that involves not only dealing with one's own turmoil, but also the feelings and attitudes of friends and loved ones.

Fortunately, this process is a bit easier today than it was in the past when homosexuality was much more of a social taboo and gay and lesbian individuals were more widely persecuted. Today many people reject the notion of remaining in the closet about their homosexual orientation. Public acceptance is increasing. Many parents now publicly profess their love and support for their gay and lesbian children (see Betty DeGeneres's excellent and groundbreaking books in the resources at the end of this chapter).

All this new support does not completely spare young people who may suffer terribly while coming to terms with their homosexuality. This is a time when grandparents are needed and can help enormously. They can support the parents through the period of adjustment, and they can be nonjudgmental, compassionate, loving, accepting, and understanding toward their grandchild. To do this successfully requires a great deal of maturity, knowledge, and education about a gay or lesbian grandchild's experience.

Grandparents need to know that a child struggling with this realization may not feel able to share her feelings with anyone and therefore may experience a great deal of anxiety and even depression. Among the things a youngster in this situation might feel are guilt, shame, fear of their loved ones' criticism, alienation from the social mainstream, rejection by peers, and fear about being vulnerable to HIV and other sexually transmitted diseases. As a result many teens withdraw from friends and activities and may feel they hate themselves. They may even have suicidal thoughts. This is where grandparents come in.

Attention must be paid early on. As the child grows, and his homosexuality becomes evident, grandparents should be alert to what parents are feeling and how they are dealing with it. Parents may become defensive if someone else makes a comment about the child's behavior. It is not uncommon for one parent or another to deny the reality that their child has an identity issue. This can generate family disagreements and blame. It is important for grandparents to stay out of the fray, to be available to listen to and support parents, and to continue a loving and affirming relationship with their grandchild.

They achieve these things through open and free-flowing communication with the grandchild (see Chapter 22, "Adolescence"). Some children, who are too upset to share their feelings with parents will talk to grandparents if they have an emotional and spiritual context within which to do so—a close, nonjudgmental and accepting relationship, what I call "unconditional love" (see Chapter 23, "Attention"). For example, when Carmela was sixteen she was able to share with her grandmother her discovery of her homosexual feelings. "I told her I was in love with a classmate and when we took a shower after gym I wanted to look at her body and I got sexy feelings and bad thoughts. I wanted to touch her. I was so upset. I was sick. I felt I was weird. I wanted to kill myself. I moped around and my grandmother saw me moping and asked me what was wrong. Grandma always knows my feelings. I burst out crying and sobbing. I told her I think I like girls. She said that many people feel like that and not to worry. She acted like it's no big deal. She also told me that one of my uncles liked people of the same sex and that that's the way it was, and he had to make the best of it. 'It won't change the way you really are,' she told me, 'or how much I love you.' And that saved my life."

Like Carmela's grandmother, if you have a gay or lesbian grandchild it is important to be loving, accepting, and available. To do so may require a major change in your attitudes. But it's worth it, because your love for your grandchild should be unconditional. That's what grandchildren expect from their grandparents. To demonstrate love and acceptance, to better understand their feelings, and to affirm their grandchild, many grandparents have joined support organizations for families of homosexually oriented people. Becoming part of the gay and lesbian family community is very helpful (see the resources listed at the end of this chapter). Some grandparents serve as mentors for groups of gay and lesbian students in colleges or in academic or church communities. Even if you don't condone homosexuality, keep an open mind and educate yourself about the issue. At the very least this will dispel any false ideas or prejudices you have been taught by society. Once educated, you can then enlighten others about the true aspects of the issue and show your love and dedication to your grandchild.

GUIDELINES

Here are some guidelines to follow if you have a gay or lesbian grandchild.

- Educate yourself about gay and lesbian issues.
- Think about your own attitudes and prejudices concerning gay and lesbian issues.
- Identify how these attitudes interfere with how you deal with your grandchild's homosexuality.
- Assess how your grandchild's parents are dealing with the issue. Are they rejecting of the child? Accepting? Emotional and confused?
- Discuss the issue with the parents openly and freely. Ask how you can help.
- Help the parents deal with it too.
- If the parents want to have your clergy or other professionals to investigate your grandchild's homosexuality (via counseling or clinical psychiatry), try to get involved for learning purposes and to support your grandchild through the process.
- Let your grandchild know that you are accepting of him no matter what. Your love is unconditional.

- Spend time with your grandchild. It might be helpful to go on a trip or spend some time together while your grandchild is beginning to wrestle with homosexual feelings, and to talk about it—and mostly *listen*.
- Help your grandchild communicate with his or her parents if necessary.
- Join a support group or get involved in some aspect of your grandchild's social life.

Because much of the low self-esteem that young gay and lesbian individuals may feel early on in their discovery process is linked to fear of loss of love, you can reassure your grandchild that your love is forever. That is the greatest gift you can share. You will learn a great deal and stretch your capacity for love, understanding, tolerance, and compassion.

When a Gay or Lesbian Child Becomes a Parent

An unprecedented number of gays and lesbians are becoming parents through adoption or reproductive technology; in fact, between 8 and 10 million children are being raised in gay or lesbian households. As a result, one of the most positive, indeed extraordinary, events affecting grandparenting during the past few decades has been the creation of a new generation of "unexpected" grandparents.

This remarkable situation has not only brought newly minted gay and lesbian parents into mainstream parenthood, but it also has helped many of them reconcile past differences with their own parents. Let me illustrate with a case study.

An Unexpected Gift

Early in his life, Jason felt he was different from other boys. "As soon as I could think, I knew my interests and sensitivities were different," he now claims. He had his first homosexual affair in high school and came out during his last year at college. His very traditional and loving parents' suspicions about his homosexuality grew stronger during Jason's teen years, but nothing was said. When he told them he was gay they were "horrified." They reacted to Jason's revelation by withdrawing and becoming morose. After college, Jason moved to a far-away city to work in the fashion business. After several years of separation from his family (and professional success as a clothing designer) Jason went home to visit a sister who was ill. During the visit, he edged emotionally closer to his mother. But his father remained embarrassed and distraught. He was struggling inside of himself with how to deal with the son he loved—not an easy task for a man of his generation.

Time went on. Jason entered into a long-term relationship with Phil. After five years together in what he calls "a stable and committed relationship," Jason expressed to Phil that the greatest misery about being gay was that he wasn't going to be a parent. Phil asked why not. Two years later, after researching the issue carefully, and discussing the possible effects of parenthood on their relationship, they decided to adopt. Their first child, originally called Ramon, was born of a teenage crack addict.

When Jason's parents heard about his intention to adopt, they became very concerned. His father and mother both wondered how he could raise a baby with no mother. After Ramon arrived, Jason found a church that would accept his relationship with Phil, acknowledge them both as parents, and baptize the baby within his religion. He invited his parents to the baptism. Here is what Jason's father said about his experience of attending Ramon's baptism (during which the baby's name was changed to Joseph).

"When I saw that baby, and how Jason looked at me when I held Joseph, my heart melted. He named the baby after me, Joseph. I knew my son was telling me something. He was making me a grandfather, in a roundabout way, of course, but I *felt* like a grandfather. And I immediately bonded with Joey—*immediately*. All of my fears and emotions about Jason flew out the window and I knew things would work out." Jason's mother, Eleanor, agreed, with reservation. "Jason will be a good father, and I adore Joey. Things are almost back to normal. But I am concerned about two men raising a baby. I guess I will have to get involved more. Joey is an unexpected gift for which I am grateful. He will make me change some of my old views. It's started already."

A Common Experience

Eleanor and Joe's experience is similar to thousands of other grandparents whose gay and lesbian children have become parents. They acknowledge, for the most part, reintroducing their sometimes-alienated child into the family again. There is in general a new beginning, a striving toward reconciliation, or at least an attempt at resolving old conflicts and problems. The arrival of a grandchild is a joyful experience, one that is usually welcomed with open arms. And because this situation can be so unexpected, the new grandparents are challenged to revisit intolerant attitudes and to expand their sense of tolerance, compassion, and understanding toward their child's life choices. They may also have to help other family members deal with the same kinds of feelings. In fact, siblings of a gay or lesbian child will often look to their parents for an example of how to deal with the situation. When great-grandparents and grandparents set a positive example, younger people follow.

Grandparents face other challenges in these situations. They will, for example, have to deal with their child's partner, their grandchild's "other" parent. These are primarily parent-child issues too complex to deal with here. However, if you want to learn more about this, see Stephanie A. Brill's book (listed in the resources at the end of this chapter). This is an excellent resource to learn about gay and lesbian parenting and different family configurations. (For a gay father's view, see the books by Dan Savage and Jesse Green, also listed at the end of this chapter.)

Many new grandparents of children whose parents are gay or lesbian find that they change their attitudes and become supportive of their child's role as a parent. Many such grandparents even become advocates for them. In fact, rising consciousness has led to the formation of PFLAG (Parents and Friends of Lesbians and Gays) and other national support organizations (see the resources at the end of the chapter).

Benefits to Children

Many grandparents involved in these diverse family arrangements are especially concerned about the effects of their grandchildren having same-sex parents. Advocates of this type of arrangement, supported by emerging research, say that children living in a family with same-sex parents who are caring and loving have as good a life as children who have more traditional families. Other research (Patterson 1998) points to the importance of having grandparents who offer opposite gender roles.

For me, a loved child is a well child. I prefer not to take the path of controversy. The fact is that gay and lesbian individuals have adopted many children who have been thrown away by society. They have given these children wonderful lives. Furthermore, there is no clinical evidence to show that children brought up in loving and caring homosexual homes have an increased incidence of homosexuality—after all, most gays and lesbians have opposite-sex parents.

Of course, there are complications and difficulties. Based on my interviews over the years, most of the children of gay and lesbian couples who have provided stable homes had the normal complaints about their parents. Those from disrupted homes had complaints similar to those of children from disrupted homes who were raised by parents of the opposite sex. What children complained about most was having to explain their family situation to their peers, and others. Most of them seem to handle this well, talking openly and honestly with their peers and meeting other children in similar situations through organizations such as COLAGE (Children of Lesbians and Gays Everywhere—see the resources at the end of the chapter). They usually seek out more broad-minded friends and society. It also helps when they have relatives in "traditional" family arrangements too. That's why it is so important that they be welcomed into the extended family—and that grandparents take the lead in making this happen!

If their lives are good, problems are more easily addressed and resolved. "When I was ten years old and played soccer," said Greta, twenty-six, who was raised by two mothers, "my birth mother, Momma, always brought me to the games. Then one day she was sick so my other mother, Mother, brought me. The kids were all confused and asked me where my father was. I said I didn't have a father but I had a grandfather. So, when the kids started to tease me about not having a father I asked my grandfather to come to the games with me. And he did. That blew the kids' minds because they could not figure out how I had a grandfather but no father. Anyway they stopped teasing me."

GUIDELINES

If you have a child with a homosexual orientation who is thinking of making you a grandparent, or a friend or relative in a similar situation, here are some guidelines to follow to be the best grandparent possible.

- Get involved in the process early.
- Be there when the grandchild comes along (see section on "Birth of a Grandchild" for details).
- Get involved in your child's and grandchild's world (PFLAG and COLAGE, for example).
- Take the initiative to welcome your child and grandchild into the family.
- Then just fulfill all of your grandparent roles.

The Gay or Lesbian Grandparent

There are two ways that gay and lesbian grandparents come into being. First, when a gay or lesbian parent's child becomes a parent. This notches up the gay or lesbian parent into grandparenthood. When this happens grandparenthood unfolds in a traditional manner and, for the most part, is devoid of the sexual issues and complexities that resonate through gay parenting. The second way is when a traditional parent comes out late in life, announces his or her lesbian or gay status, and becomes a grandparent.

The Making of a Later-Life Lesbian or Gay Grandparent

It is not uncommon today to meet people who, after having suppressed their homosexual feelings and longings throughout the early decades of their lives, suddenly acknowledge their homosexual orientation to their families and the world.

Often these are people who entered into traditional marriages, became parents, raised children, and were deeply involved in family and community life. Whether they are married, widowed, or divorced at the time they announce their homosexuality, the news usually causes a great deal of turmoil and consternation in the family, and perhaps the community as well. Their family members, some accepting, others rejecting, most bewildered, react to the news according to their belief system, the makeup of the family, the number of children and grandchildren involved, and other personal and social factors.

When the children of these late "announcers" grow up, marry, and have children, they make their own parents into gay and lesbian grandparents. That is where the confusion and often the trouble can start. I want to emphasize that what happens from this point on is highly individualized. What ensues depends on the individuals involved, and how the family accepts Grandma's or Grandpa's coming out in the first place.

After Milton, sixty-eight, was widowed, he announced to his family that he was gay. His shocked and embarrassed children reacted by shunning him. Milton feels despondent about the situation but is helpless to change things. "I have two great kids and three wonderful grandchildren and now it's all lost. They want nothing to do with me. Although I had homosexual relationships while I was married, I kept it quiet. I waited until my wife died to come out publicly. I probably never would have come out if she'd lived, but I did and I have paid a terrible price. I don't know how this will end." Hopefully Milton will persevere and try to reconcile with his family. I suggested he let things cool down and offer to get involved in family therapy with at least one of his children.

Sometimes the loss is only partial. Ed, for example, is a sixty-five-year-old grandfather of six who came out when he was fifty-five years old, much to his wife's surprise. After his announcement, he divorced his wife and moved in with his partner. His three sons were very angry at him at first but relented over the years and now are on speaking terms with him. The oldest two have six children between them. Ed has been an involved grandfather with his oldest son's children although his partner is barred from seeing them. He has less contact with his second son's children because his daughter-in-law disapproves of his lifestyle. Ed is naturally unhappy about the situation but has decided to wait to see how things develop. His partner Will said he would like to be involved with Ed's family but that he is persona non grata. Ed is respectful of his children's feelings. "This was a big step for me and I understand how everyone feels. But I couldn't live a lie any more. I don't want to force anything on my family so I'll take what I can get. This is the price I have to pay. It's nothing new. I've had to pay a price all my life for something I didn't want to be in the first place. But this is what I am and I have to embrace it and do the best that I can. And my children will have to learn to understand that I'm still their dad."

On the other hand, Evelyn, fifty-nine, who has three grown children and one grandchild, says her relationship with her children wasn't affected at all when she moved in with another woman after her husband died. "I always knew I had homosexual tendencies," she says, "but I loved my husband a lot, and my life, and my children, so I just put it out of my mind. After he died and I met my partner Pella in church, I decided the hell with it, my kids could take it so I started a relationship." In fact, Evelyn's children are close with her and Pella. As the youngest says, "Mom was always a bit different but a wonderful mother and a great person. If she is happy I'm happy." Seely, Evelyn's daughter, gets together with them as much as possible. "My mom is as wonderful a grandmother as she is a mother and my son is lucky to have her. I don't know what he will think about her relationship with Pella; right now, she is 'Auntie Pella.' We'll cross that bridge when the time comes but I'm not worried because he is so attached to both of them and love will tell."

GUIDELINES

Here are some basic guidelines for gay and lesbian grandparents to smooth the family waters and be the best grandparent possible (also see Chapter 46, "Step-grandparenting").

- Assess the family situation. Identify the challenges and supports. If you had a prior good relationship with children and grandchildren, all the better.

- If you have just come out, be patient and allow family members to digest the news. Allow them to react and cool down. Listen to what they say and respect their reactions. Understand what they may be experiencing as a result of your announcement. If there is alienation let reconciliation take place at an appropriate pace.
- Try to have as many one-to-one meetings with family members as possible to deal with the facts and place in perspective any emotional overreactions.
- Ask to keep the grandparent-grandchild bond as unaffected as possible. The younger the child, the easier it will be. In fact, younger children don't need to know anything concrete until they ask directly and are able to comprehend the situation fully.
- If a partner is involved, have him/her wait in the family wings and gradually come into the family's life (see Chapter 46, "Step-grandparenting," for more).

Make it clear that your sexual orientation is only a part of you and that you are still a parent and a grandparent and want to fulfill these roles.

When a Parent Comes Out

When a parent unexpectedly announces his or her homosexuality and decides to live a different life the children involved often feel devastated and socially embarrassed. Although adults know that the individual abandoning a marriage does not necessarily abandon the children, that's not what the children feel. They suffer a great deal of pain, turmoil, embarrassment, and confusion.

The adults involved in such situations need a great deal of time and energy to work through their own issues. Therefore, it is critically important that grandparents be available to help their grandchildren weather the emotional storm. In fact, grandparents will be all the more needed if the parental breakup was unexpected.

Not only do grandparents have to help in the ensuing divorce process (see Chapter 37, "When Parents Divorce"), but they can also help the grandchildren understand and deal with the revelation of the sexual orientation of their parent. This also involves helping the child to keep her own feelings from those of the abandoned parent (who most likely will feel betrayed and angry). Grandparents can help children work out their own feelings directly with the parent and keep the lines of communication open. This is a lengthy process and requires that the grandparent do the work necessary to separate his or her own feelings from the child's.

CONCLUSION

Grandparents can make an important difference in loving and accepting their children and grandchildren who might feel any negative personal and social effects resulting from being a gay and lesbian individual in society today. As a grandparent and parent, you will want to become educated about any situation that arises, draw close to your loved ones, and work toward tolerance, equality, and justice.

RESOURCES

PFLAG—www.pflag.com

Family Pride Coalition—familypride.org

colage.org—supports young people with gay, lesbian, bisexual, and transgender parents

The Queer Parent's Primer, Stephanie A. Brill. New Harbinger Publications Inc., 2001.

Love, Ellen, Betty DeGeneres. Rob Weisbach Books, 1999. *Just a Mom*, Betty DeGeneres. Advocate Books, 2000.

The Velveteen Father, Jesse Green. Villard Books, 1999.

The Kid, Dan Savage. Dutton, 1999.

The Gay and Lesbian Parenting Handbook, April Martin, Ph.D. Harper Perennial, 1993.

CHAPTER 40

Religious Differences

D o not be surprised to find that your grandchild is being raised with religious beliefs that differ from your own. For some grandparents, this is a nonissue. For others, who may feel confused, disappointed, or even deeply saddened by the loss of religious continuity in their family, it can be quite a serious problem. This is especially true for those people whose grandparenting involvement hinges on religious issues. As one researcher noted, "Religious grandparents are involved grandparents because they are generally more greatly involved in family and social ties" (King 1999). If you are concerned that your grandchildren are being raised with religious beliefs different from your own—or with no religion at all—be aware that the manner in which you handle this delicate issue can either strengthen or divide your family.

It is not unusual today for grandparents and parents to differ about their religious beliefs. A high rate of religious intermarriage along with 700,000 interracial couples and nearly 5 million multicultural children in the United States (according to U.S. Census estimates) means that all diversity is on the increase. Differences arising from such diversity often generate disappointment or even negative feelings among family members. With mutual respect people can usually come to terms with their differences. But when they are intolerant of the other's beliefs or diversity it can cause great turmoil to family members. In this chapter I will focus on problems related to religion.

Family Disconnection

"I am a devout Catholic," says Alice, a fifty-nine-year-old grandmother of four. "Although two of my grandchildren are being raised Catholic by their parents, my daughter Kelly has chosen to raise her two children with no religious education at all. I really do not approve of that. I think my grandchildren need to be brought up with Christian values, especially in today's world. Her choice has hurt our relationship. I feel disconnected in some way from my child and grandchildren."

Kelly, thirty-five, is sad about being alienated from her mother. "My mother has the right to her beliefs," Kelly says, "but I don't believe in her religion for a lot of reasons, some personal, others intellectual. I am not going to expose my kids to what I consider narrow thinking. To me God is everywhere and I want my children to have a broad view of spirituality. Religion is personal and I think my mother is overreacting. If she wants to make a big deal out of it, well, then we are going to have worse problems."

When religion is entwined with cultural history, the disconnection can be doubly painful for grandparents. Studies show that the sharing of beliefs, customs, and traditions between grandparents and grandchildren is extremely important (Kornhaber 1998, Wiscott 2000). Saul is a seventy-two-year-old Jewish grandfather whose family escaped Germany during the Holocaust. His religion is very important to him. His son, Al, married Cheryl, a Catholic. They have three young children. Saul is distraught about his grandchildren losing their religious and cultural heritage. "People have been trying to wipe the Jews out for centuries, but we have always endured. Our strength is in our religion and the Jewish community. Now it is over because my grandchildren won't have my religion and my family's religious traditions are going to be erased. My religion is the center of my world. Never in my wildest dreams would I have thought I would not have Jewish grandchildren. My wife passed away two years ago. When I die, my family's religious traditions will disappear with me."

Lee, a sixty-four-year-old Chinese grandfather, was concerned that his grandchildren's lack of religion has severed their connection to their ancestors—himself included. "My daughter married an American. They are raising my grandchildren with no religion. This is sad because respect for one's ancestors is woven into the consciousness of my religion. You see, my ancestors are very much alive for me. I talk with them every day. But now I will no longer be a part of my grandchildren's lives after I am gone. Will they ever talk with me after I am gone?" His daughter Mai, a self-described realist, dismisses her father's feelings. "For gosh sakes," she says, "we don't live in China anymore. I'm an American. That's the old life and doesn't mean anything to me. I am not a *roots* person. Father's feelings have no place here in this country, or in these times. I adore him but his religion and ancestor worship is old stuff and has no relevance to my children. I am too busy to talk to my ancestors now; I am working twelve hours a day trying to get my website off the ground. Father can do what he wants to do, but my kids have to deal with reality."

Reconciling Differences

If your grandchild is being raised with a religious belief system different from your own, there is only one path for you to follow to make the best of the situation. That is the *path of acceptance*. Hard as it may be, you will have to stretch your arms wide enough to include all your loved ones in your embrace. Here is what you will have to do to make the best of what, for you, might be a painful and difficult situation.

Before you do or say anything, take the time to understand what the parents think and feel. They have legitimate reasons for making this important decision regarding their child's religious upbringing. Listen to them and respect their decision. Do not sabotage yourself by allowing your own disapproval or disappointment to erode the positive aspects of your relationship with them and your grandchild.

Let the parents know how you feel as well. Share your feelings in a kind and nonconfrontational way. Tell them why you think it would benefit your grandchild to be exposed to your religious and cultural legacy. Communicate to the parents that this is a marvelous educational opportunity for their child, an opportunity that will provide her with a positive image of diversity and tolerance. If you make them understand that you would like to share your religious teachings and traditions with your grandchild rather than convert her, most parents will embrace this chance to broaden their child's spiritual horizons.

Do not act without the parents' consent and take your grandchild's religious upbringing into your own hands. If you do, you will risk alienating the parents and your grandchild as well. You and the parents can set a wonderful example for your grandchild by respecting one another's differences. Avoid proselytizing about your religion. When you respect the parents' beliefs, the chances are good that they will respect yours.

The Importance of Respect

When parents or grandchildren are pressured by a grandparent to choose one religion over another, they are apt to act in a defensive way and want to avoid the problem—and sometimes the grandparent too. When people respect and understand each other's points of view, things often can be worked out (more or less) to everyone's satisfaction.

Unfortunately, this is not always the case. In Alice's case, which I described earlier, she approached Kelly and let her know how strongly she felt about wanting to impart some religious teachings to her grandchildren. Kelly, however, remains adamant. "I love my mother but I can't give in to something I don't believe in," she says, "and I am not going to feel guilty about it." In such an intractable situation, Alice has to do her best to isolate the issue of religious differences from all of the other positive aspects of her relationship with her daughter and grandchildren. "I don't like it but I'll have to do it," she says. "And I'll keep on praying."

Fortunately, most families find ways to work out the issue one way or another. In Saul's case, for example, his daughter-in-law Cheryl is open-minded and respectful of Saul's religion as well as her own parents' religion. She tries to accommodate the grandparents' desire to teach their grandchildren about their religious beliefs. "Although I don't want to attend a synagogue myself, I do not object to Saul teaching the children about Judaism. They are well aware of the fact that their father is Jewish, although Al is not a practicing Jew. And once in a while, my parents take the kids to church so that they can learn about *their* religion. We try to find similarities in our beliefs. For example, Christ was a Jew. We try to share holidays. My family spends Christmas at my parents' house and Passover at Saul's house. When the kids are old enough, they can make their own religious choices."

Saul is grateful for the compromise. "Well, what can I say? They are not Jewish, but they know I am—and what it means to me. That is better than nothing. And I get to show them off in the synagogue once in a while."

Likewise, Lee and his family were able to reach a positive arrangement. Lee called a family meeting and made his feelings strongly known to Mai and his son-in-law Ken. To Lee's surprise, it was Ken who empathized with Lee and took the initiative to resolve the situation. With Mai's reluctant consent, he urged the children to learn more about Lee's religion and their own Chinese heritage. Lee was able to teach the children about his religious rituals. "If I get through to even one child," he said, "I'll have someone to talk to after I'm gone." Mai responds with a shrug. "It's between Father and the children. If they are happy, OK. I'm out of it," she says.

GUIDELINES

Here are some guidelines to help you bridge the diversity gap, especially if your grandchild is being raised in a belief system that differs from your own.

- No matter how strongly you may feel on the subject, respect the fact that your grandchild's religious education or lack thereof is the parent's call.
- Show your grandchild that you and the parents respect one another's beliefs. Never undermine the parent's religious teachings

to the child. Above all, you do not want to place your grandchild in the middle of a family disagreement.

■ Have a family conference to develop a policy toward dealing effectively with your differences. Explain what your religion means to you. Explain that you are open to learning about other religions. Then what you do with your grandchild will have the support of the parents.

■ Learning about different belief systems is educational. Become a student of other religions and include your grandchild, with the parents' consent, in this process. For example, attend services at different houses of worship with your grandchild.

■ Do not pitch your religion to your grandchild. Always teach and show. Your grandchild will understand how your own religion affects your attitudes and behavior.

■ Celebrate other family members' religious holidays with them.

■ Set the example for the family concerning acceptance, tolerance, understanding, and respect.

CONCLUSION

Mutual respect and understanding are the keys to turning this highly charged issue into a wonderful learning opportunity for your grandchild. Exposure to different ways of thinking, believing, and worshiping can be very educational. Your grandchild will learn understanding, tolerance, and diversity. And you will do the same by learning more about other cultures and religions. There is no better example of tolerance and understanding as part of a spiritual legacy to leave your grandchild.

CHAPTER 41

Raising Grandchildren

T hroughout human history there have been examples of grandparents raising the young while parents supplied the basic needs for survival. Parents
and grandparents have served as a family team to support and nurture the
young. In the modern world, however, the family dynamic has become increasingly complex. The result of this complexity is that large numbers of children
are being raised by grandparents, on either a full- or part-time basis.

Here are some statistics that will give you an idea of the extent of the issue.
A recent report from the U.S. Census (which only partially reflects the widespread nature of this issue)[1] made the following comparison. In the year 1970,
there were 2,214,000 children under the age of eighteen living in grandparent-
headed households; the mother was present in approximately half of these households. By the year 1997, the number was reported as 5,435,000, or 7.7 percent of
all children in the United States. The majority of these children are raised by
two grandparents, or a grandmother alone, with various degrees of parent
involvement. Since 1997, the number has increased even more.

---

1. 1997 U.S. Census. See www.census.gov.

In families that have both grandparents and grandchildren, the grandparents are the head of the house 75 percent of the time; in the remaining 25 percent the parents head the household.[2] In the former arrangement, half of the families have both grandparents present. The rest have a grandmother with no spouse. The majority are under sixty-five and employed. Half of the grandchildren are under the age of six, and 28 percent are between six and eleven; many have neither support nor health insurance. These factors underline the financial as well as the emotional burden for grandparents. Although official census estimates made in the year 2000 indicate that the number of children being raised by their grandparents is more than six million, it does not present the full picture. I estimate that the number of children being raised by grandparents in America today—part- or full-time, permanently or temporarily—is now close to eight million.

A Growing Challenge for Grandparents

Taking on the full- or part-time care of a grandchild involves a life-changing decision. After all, it is no easy thing to dedicate one's life to raising a child at a time in life when people typically look forward to more leisure and less responsibility (Minckler & Roe, 1993). The rise in grandparent-headed households reflects both an understandable parental need for help with childcare and, in the worst-case scenario, parental failure.

This chapter discusses some of the reasons for the explosion of the grandparents-raising-grandchildren trend, its repercussions on the family and society, and what is being done to help grandparents accomplish the job. For example, as a result of the increase in the number of grandparents raising grandchildren, numerous support organizations have been created. If you are raising your grandchild, lots of resources and support groups are available to help you do the best job possible; some are listed at the end of this section and can also be found on websites such as www.grandparenting.org and www.aarp.org.

---

2. Bryson, Ken, and Lynne M. Casper. "Coresident Grandparents and Grandchildren." U.S. Census Bureau, 2000, p. 23.

The more children you have, the greater the chance you will be caretaking a grandchild at some point. If you are currently raising a grandchild, or even caring part-time for a child, there is a lot you need to know.

Raising a grandchild is a complicated matter. You will have to know about emotional, financial, health, legal, and educational matters. In what follows I will discuss these matters and some emotional and psychological aspects of raising grandchildren that you need to know about. Let's start at the beginning.

The Cause: Parental Need or Failure

When parents falter, children often fall into the laps of their grandparents. Caring for a grandchild may be temporary—for example, when a parent is ill or in turmoil. It can also be permanent, as in the case of death, serious substance abuse, or incarceration. Following are some of the common circumstances that place children in jeopardy, forcing them to seek the sanctuary of their grandparents.

- Abandonment of the child by the parent
- Parental illness (mental and physical)
- Teenage pregnancy
- Substance abuse
- Unemployment
- Homelessness
- Incarceration
- Death of a parent
- Divorce
- Family violence
- Child abuse and neglect
- Poverty

The Effect: Grandparents to the Rescue

Many grandparents are ambivalent when faced with raising a grandchild. They become concerned about the welfare of their own child (the parent) as well as their grandchild. They also have to deal with the reality that taking on such a responsibility will turn their lives topsy-turvy. This decision is further influenced by personality type, values, priorities, life circumstances, the amount of time and effort required to raise a grandchild, the amount of support from their family and society, financial status, health, housing situation, and level of authority.

Some grandparents view taking on a parental role late in life as a blessing. They are grateful for the opportunity to form a deeper bond with their grandchild. Other grandparents resent the responsibility and attendant inconveniences that come with raising a grandchild. The effects of raising a grandchild depend on the basic health and vitality of the grandparent. Some grandparents say that raising a grandchild, although stressful and tiring at times, has increased their vitality and zest for life (Caren 1991, Kornhaber 1996). Others say their health is adversely affected (Minckler 1999). Most researchers agree that more study is needed in this area (Bower 1991).

Many grandparents in this situation are forced to deal with their resentment toward the grandchild's parents for thrusting the responsibility upon them. Others view the failure of the parent as their own failure and feel overwhelmed with guilt. Others express concern about the fate of their grandchild in the event of their illness or death.

The degree of resentment or acceptance they experience is closely related to whether or not they have a choice in the matter. Raquelle, a forty-seven-year-old grandmother, was awakened at three in the morning by a knock on her front door. On the front steps she found her two-month-old grandson neatly wrapped and sleeping in a small basket. Her drug-addicted daughter had left her baby there. "I had to take the baby in," Raquelle says. "My daughter was back on the street, and there was no one else to care for her. I don't like it, but what alternative do I have? I am not giving my grandchild over to strangers to raise."

When their daughter and son-in law were killed in an auto accident, Peter and Gloria automatically took in their four grandchildren. "They are my grandchildren, my flesh and blood," said Peter. "Who else is going to care for them the way Gloria and I do?"

For some timing is a challenge. Della, sixty-seven, was ready to retire when her son, who was divorced and had just joined the Air Force, deposited his two children at her home. "I wasn't happy about it," she says, "but I had no choice except to raise them."

Naturally, the lives of grandparents undergo great change when their grandchild moves in with them. Instead of spending time with their friends, they become immersed in the social life and schoolwork of their grandchild. And it can be especially difficult when a grandparent has a grandchild with emotional or behavioral difficulties. Some complain about being tired and overworked and resent it. Others feel that raising a grandchild has given their lives new meaning, which compensates for the fatigue they feel. If you are raising your grandchild, expect to have many different feelings. You will undoubtedly have to sacrifice a certain amount of your freedom. On the other hand, you may be saving your grandchild's life.

Legal Considerations

The legal status of children raised by grandparents can be tenuous. For example, many children who live with their grandparents because of intermittent parental substance abuse problems are often fearful because their parents still have legal custody. Bouncing back and forth between grandma's house and a frequently relapsing parent can be very disruptive to children. According to Sylvie de Toledo, LCSW, who started Grandparents as Parents (GAP), a California-based support system for grandparents raising grandchildren, this syndrome is common. Parents with unresolved drug problems reclaim their children when they are in a period of remission. Then, when they experience a relapse, they abandon the youngster once again. The child eventually becomes confused about where he belongs and fearful that his living routine will always be disrupted. That is why grandparents raising grandchildren should obtain some kind of legal custody for their grandchildren until they are assured the parent is able to be responsible.

One eight-year-old was shuttled back and forth between her mother and grandmother's homes seventeen times in just three years. She said, "My mother goes into rehab and she's all right for a little while. Then she leaves the hospital, takes me from Grandma and brings me to her house. In a week or two she's back on drugs. Then I go to Grandma's and Mom goes back to rehab." Barbara Kirkland, a pioneer in the grandparent-caretaker movement, has stated that if parents aren't available, grandparents should be given the legal means to provide the stable environment children need. Ms. Kirkland told me, "Arrangements should be made for children to get on with their lives, not remain in limbo. All children deserve a future of belonging."

That is why a grandparent's legal status is so important (see Chapter 42, "Legal Issues"). To have total responsibility and authority for your grandchild you may choose adoption, full or temporary custody, or guardianship. You can pursue full custody if your grandchild's parents are dead, abusive, incarcerated, or terminally ill. With legal custody you gain rights and benefits that may not be offered with other caretaking arrangements, such as subsidized health insurance, Temporary Assistance for Needy Families (TANF), Social Security Survivor's Benefits, Medicaid, social services housing, and school enrollment. Full custody is necessary if you wish to protect your grandchild from a parent's permanent dysfunction, or to be free to raise your grandchild in the event of the parent's death. If the parent is living and you have custody be aware that a situation might arise where the parent may attempt to regain custody of their child. This can be a bad or good thing depending on the parent's competence.

Other legal arrangements, such as adoption (which terminates a parent's rights), temporary custody, and obtaining foster-parent status, serve you with a measure of legal security that will help you maintain a balance of power between yourself and the parents. If you have no legal recognition of your caretaking status, you may have difficulty accessing social support systems or medical, educational, or financial services.

Coping

You can expect a radical change in your lifestyle when you raise a grandchild full-time. You will experience lifestyle changes that can affect your work life, friendships, daily activities, and retirement plans. You will have to be involved with your grandchild's health, education, and social life. If you are single, or have economic or health problems, you will need personal support as well as help from social service agencies. You will have to deal with issues such as your legal rights, your grandchild's education, attitudes of insurance companies toward insuring grandchildren, financial strain, health problems, and problems with parents.

The quality of your relationship with your grandchild's parents and the terms of your arrangement with them will depend on the degree of your responsibility as your grandchild's caretaker. For example, if you are parenting a child and grandchild at the same time, you will have constant, but varying, responsibility and authority (Jendrek 1993).

You may have other grandchildren who need your attention too. If you are providing regular day-care while parents work, you can send your grandchild home at the end of the day. You can also provide a stopgap. For example, providing sanctuary for a teenager having difficulty with her parents is a temporary situation that ends when parents and child are reunited.

Although grandparents raising a grandchild full-time recognize the benefits of their position, they are also aware that the role can be time-consuming, fatiguing, and often financially and emotionally burdensome. In one study of grandparents and great-grandparents rearing their children's children as a consequence of parental drug addiction, Burton (1992) concluded that while "respondents found parenting their grandchildren an emotionally rewarding experience, they also incurred psychological, physical, and economic costs in performing their roles. Some grandparents resent the disruption in their lives caused by their grandchildren's needs for time and attention. Others raising debilitated grandchildren—children addicted to cocaine, afflicted with fetal alcohol syndrome, malnourished, or suffering with other health, behavioral, or learning problems—may be resentful of the extra care the child requires."

Support for grandparents raising grandchildren is vital for successful caretaking. Studies show that grandparents who cope well with their situation are those who seek out other family members and support groups to help them deal with their concerns. Others use their strong spiritual beliefs to bolster them. It is important that grandparents take care of themselves physically, emotionally, and spiritually to be effective caretakers of their grandchildren.

Dealing with Social Agencies

Grandparents raising a grandchild must learn how to deal with organizations and institutions to obtain the support they so desperately need. In the past, society's institutions did not support grandparents' efforts to obtain adequate funding, health care, education, or respite resources for their grandchild. Neither was help available to grandparents raising grandchildren who were concerned with issues such as their own illness and mortality, their level of authority, control, the generation gap, sibling rivalry among the grandchildren, sense of isolation, and abandonment. Because of the efforts of dedicated advocates, today there is a great deal of help available for grandparents from social agencies. Joining a local grandparent support group is a great way to get the latest information as well as support from other grandparents who are in similar situations. You can get a list of available services from organizations such as Generations United and the AARP Information Center (see the resources at the end of this chapter).

If you choose to join a support group, here are some of the issues and problems that you may want to discuss with your peers.

- There can be great difficulty in obtaining medical attention without formal custody. Many insurance companies do not allow grandparents to carry their grandchildren as dependents.
- Many schools will not admit a child unless the child's parent is living with the grandparent; thus grandparents are denied authority concerning their grandchildren's schooling.
- Grandparents often cannot obtain emergency medical care for their grandchild unless they have legal custody.
- There can be problems with obtaining adequate financial assistance. Many funders give money to foster parents but not to grandparents.
- The households of caretaking grandparents do not conform to the traditional definition of family as set forth in zoning laws; thus they may be excluded from living in a community that is zoned for single-family living.

- Grandparents cannot help their grandchildren in mental-health or substance-abuse treatment centers without parents' permission.
- Caregiving grandparents who lack legal custody must give up their grandchildren to the parents with or without assurance of the child's health or well-being.

Grandparents whose grandchildren live with them full-time yet who do not have custody may have to pay for their grandchild's education and medical needs as well as day-to-day support. Although the state offers financial support to parents and foster parents through the Aid to Dependent Children program, such help may be hard to come by for grandparents. Furthermore, grandparent groups claim that some government agencies have been negligent in seeking counsel from grandparents concerning the disposition of an abandoned child. There have been cases in which state agencies, ignoring the wishes of grandparents seeking to raise their own grandchild, have placed the child in the care of a series of strangers.

Parent or Grandparent?

Caring for your grandchild challenges your generational identity. The tricky balance is to maintain your grandparent identity while acting as a parent. My experience, and that of others (Kennedy & Keeny 1988) shows that children raised by grandparents would prefer their grandparents to remain grandparents. Even if they want to, children cannot banish their parents from their minds and hearts; it is common knowledge that children who lose their parents create dreams and fantasies to deal with the loss, such as idealizing their parents. Just as they may project anger onto a custodial parent as a result of the pain of divorce, children may rationalize the loss of parents and even blame grandparents for that loss. Therefore, grandparents must be very careful not to be caught in the battle zone between their grandchild and the psychological work he or she has to do to resolve issues with the parent.

Whatever his or her experience, your grandchild has a need to have a healthy and loving parent. As a grandparent who is aware of this fact, try to defer your own needs to those of your grandchild. Demonstrate flexibility by moving in and out of the various roles you may be required to play, such as nurturer, mentor, role model, playmate, and parent. Your support and love can help your grandchildren work through the difficult issues they may be grappling with.

The extent to which you play the parent will be affected by a number of factors; for example, the presence of other young children at home, your age, whether or not you have legal custody, and so on. Providing children with a sense of stability and continuity is critical. Whether or not you play the role of parent for your grandchild, it is reassuring to know that, having learned from your own mistakes, you will be more competent at parenting a second time around. Daisy, a fifty-five-year-old grandmother, says, "I feel good that I'm not making the same mistakes with my grandchild that I did with my children." Her husband, Olin, sixty, agrees: "I never gave my own children the time and attention I give my grandson. I wish I had my own family to raise again. I would be a much better father."

Grandparents acting in a parental role often ask me about what happens to the magical ingredients of the grandparent-grandchild relationship—the unconditional love, playfulness, spoiling, and loving conspiracy. When you raise a grandchild, you may have to relinquish some of your grandparental prerogatives. Children need behavioral limits and, because they don't have a parent to enforce the rules, you must step in and lay down the law. If your grandchild has behavioral difficulties, you may have to play the role of enforcer even more than usual. Remember that a loving and flexible grandparent responds to the needs of the child. Be whatever the child needs you to be in the moment.

How Your Grandchild Feels

I have found that children raised by grandparents tend to be less rebellious and more understanding and grateful than other children. Christine, twenty-one, was raised by her grandmother. She says, "When I was a teenager most of my friends stayed out well beyond their curfew and often fought like hell with their parents. Not me. I knew my grandparents were doing all they could to keep things together. I didn't want to give them any grief so I always tried to come home on time."

Studies[3] hint that children without serious preexisting problems who are raised by grandparents are healthier than children in single-parent or remarried families, have fewer behavioral problems, and are better adapted socially. On the other hand, most studies recognize that many children do have problems that began before their grandparents took over. In that case as well intentioned as the grandparent may be, the problems still need to be addressed.

Most grandparents realize the importance of what they are doing; they are quite aware they are saving their grandchild. Few have reservations about what they have given up to achieve this. "Not for one second," James, fifty-two, answered when asked if he had any hesitation about raising his grandchildren after their parents were killed in a car crash. "It's natural to take them. That's what grandparents are for." His six-year-old grandson Ralph concurs. "If my grandparents didn't take care of me, I'd be dead."

Dealing with Parents

If you are raising your grandchild, you must not forget you are still the parent of your grandchild's parent. Even though you may be very angry and have lost respect for your child, it is very important to recognize your child as your grandchild's parent and to help your own child as much as possible. Your ability to be kind and forgiving may well be taxed, but always remember that people do grow and change. Maintain a hopeful attitude; at the same time, always look reality in the face. Assure your child that there will always be a place for her in the family. This behavior on your part sends a great message to your grandchildren, who will be observing how you relate to their parents. For their sake, keep the lines of communication to the parents wide open. This will help you to avoid being blamed by your grandchildren for their parents' mistakes!

---

3. Ibid.

Grandparent Support Groups

To help grandparents raising grandchildren manage their responsibilities, a plethora of local support groups and national organizations have sprung up all across the United States as well as other countries. Support groups such as The AARP Grandparent Information Center, Generations United, Grandparents Raising Grandchildren, GAP (Grandparents As Parents), and ROCKing (Raising Our Children's Kids) can help (see the resources at the end of the chapter for more support organizations).

GUIDELINES

If you are raising a grandchild, I urge you to join a local support group. In acting as an advocate for your grandchild, you may even feel a surge of activism about certain issues. Here are some guidelines to follow to increase public awareness about this issue and the quality of services available in your community. Share these ideas and suggestions with local agencies.

- Establish community-training courses for grandparent caregivers and group support systems for grandparents and their grandchildren.
- Research the effects of current grandparent-caregiver support groups to adapt them to your specific population and then upgrade their quality.
- Establish uniform qualitative standards for grandparent caregiver groups by providing a basic standardized curriculum and training course that may be locally adapted.
- Form a network of group leaders to interface with local and state organizations. Convene on a regular basis to discuss changing needs, enhance and update the curriculum, and plan, advocate, and implement policy.
- Document and assess benefits derived by caregiving grandparents. (In this way you encourage others to take responsibility for their grandchildren.)

- Establish uniform federally mandated legal rights and social privileges that support the efforts of caretaking grandparents and kin.
- Research the effect of caregiving on the mental and physical health of grandparents and grandchildren. Elders who are cut off from other generations are more likely to suffer from depression than those who remain actively involved.
- Demonstrate to society, by the means of social programs, the importance of the grandparental role and intergenerational relationships as emotional and spiritual work that elders can perform for their families and society.

CONCLUSION

Raising a grandchild can be challenging. It can also be highly rewarding. After all, what greater gift could a grandparent receive than the love and respect of a grandchild who appreciates the sacrifices made on his behalf so that he could grow to be a happy, healthy person?

If you are raising a grandchild, you have an added responsibility to educate others about what you are doing so you are supported and respected for your efforts. Make the effort to join together with other grandparents raising grandchildren and urge government agencies, the legal system, schools, insurance companies, social agencies, and religious institutions to recognize the good you are doing and to help lighten your burden as much as possible. To begin this effort, get in touch with one of the organizations I have listed in the resources section.

RESOURCES

Resources for grandparents raising grandchildren have proliferated recently. For information about local resources, it is best to do a search on the World Wide Web. Contact your state agency on aging for help. The following organizations and agencies are very helpful too.

The AARP Grandparent Information Center (www.aarp.org) lists support groups for grandparents raising grandchildren and publishes a helpful and informative bulletin.

Boston Grandfamilies Home, (617) 266-2257, caters to grandparents raising grandchildren.

Brookdale Center on Aging
Grandparent Caregiver Law Center
425 East 25th St.
New York, NY 10010
(212) 481-4433

Generations United
122 C. Street NW
Suite 820
Washington, DC 20001-2109
(202) 638-1263
www.gu.org

Kinship Care CWLA
(202) 942-0288

ROCKing Inc. (Raising our Children's Kids)
P.O. Box 96
Niles, MI 49120
(616) 683-9038

www.grandparenting.org—contains links to international websites

CHAPTER 42

Legal Issues

T he first section of this chapter deals with grandparents' legal rights. The second addresses important legal aspects of custody and different types of powers of attorney that grandparents need to know about when caring for their grandchildren.

Grandparents' Legal Rights

Surprising as it may sound, prior to 1970 grandparents had no status under the law or, for that matter, any legal rights at all. In the last several decades, however, the legal system has been forced to consider the legal status of the grandparent-grandchild relationship. Children suffer greatly as a result of parental failure or strife between parents and grandparents. Many people now believe that because the grandparent-grandchild relationship is a separate and unique human attachment, grandchildren should have the legal right to maintain a relationship with their grandparents even in the face of problems between parents and grandparents.

There has been considerable progress at the state level to ensure the integrity of the grandparent-grandchild bond, particularly in the area of legal caretaking issues and dysfunctional family situations. In spite of this progress, the law still does not wholeheartedly support the natural, intergenerational family system in parentally intact families. The law does not *specifically* recognize grandparents as either important members of the family or as positive forces in the lives of their grandchildren.

Grandparent Visitation Laws

Until only recently, the term *grandparents' rights* could not be found in any law book. Indeed, before 1970, aside from a smattering of archaic "grandfather clauses" in contracts referring to legal exemptions or privileges (such as the dedication of titles or property zoning), there were virtually no laws enforcing grandparents' rights.

Grandparent visitation laws today are a reflection of an unfortunate fact of life, which is now referred to as *visitation disputes*—situations in which the parents do not allow grandparents access to their grandchildren. Most often, parent-grandparent visitation disputes exist in families involved with issues such as divorce, death of a spouse, and remarriage. But these disputes also occur in families with intact marriages where a spectrum of fractious issues between parents and grandparents can range from personality squabbles on one end to outright abuse on the other.

Parent-Grandparent Conflicts

Parent-grandparent conflicts and problems are not uncommon (see Chapter 33, "Between Parents and Grandparents"). Often they are a result of a parent-child problem that simply becomes notched up into the next generation as a parent-grandparent problem. In-law conflicts are also quite common, especially in a divorce situation. Even when a couple establishes a cordial post-divorce relationship with one another, there can be plenty of tension and confusion about visitation, especially where the grandparents are concerned. A seemingly simple issue, such as trying to agree on where a child spends holidays and vacations, can flare up into a major battle. When the divorce is contentious, former spouses who remarry and want to start fresh with a new spouse may sometimes deny grandparents visitation with their grandchildren altogether. Any problem a grandparent may have with their grandchild's parent, for whatever reason and however justified, can potentially affect their access to the grandchild.

Normal conflicts and problems—the everyday emotional cost of doing business in family life—can grow out of proportion. When this occurs it can result in a family feud that escalates to the point where parents banish grandparents from the family dynamic. In such a case, when the family is *intact*—the legal term for a married couple whose children reside with them—most state laws allow a situation in which grandparents have no right to visitation. In other words, grandparents whose children are divorced stand at least a chance of retaining their vital connection to their grandchildren. On the other hand, grandparents whose children are married have no legal recourse when the middle generation banishes them from the lives of their grandchildren. If the parents of the grandchild were never married, grandparents' legal standing is even less defined.

Because any family can experience conflicts and problems, it is important for grandparents to be educated about their legal rights. The following is an overview of the evolution of grandparents' rights. Included also are some step-by-step guidelines to follow if you are concerned about being denied visitation, or are presently being denied visitation with your grandchild.

Grandparents' Rights

As mentioned above, it was not until the late 1970s that states began to pass legislation enabling grandparents who had been denied contact with their grandchildren to petition local courts for visitation with privileges. Prior to that time grandparents had no legal rights whatsoever. Even social services and adoption agencies ignored grandparents as potential caretakers, and looked to paid or professional foster care or institutions to care for children. When states first began enacting grandparent-visitation legislation, the new and provocative term *grandparents' rights* was coined.

It is only recently that society has begun to examine the repercussions of divorce on grandparents and grandchildren (see Chapters 37, "When Parents Divorce," and 38, "When Grandparents Divorce"). My description in the early

1980s of the silent distress of grandparents when their children divorced came as a surprise to many[1] and inspired grandparents to become vocal about getting their children to include grandparents' visitation privileges in divorce agreements. Over the years, this has proved to be a great benefit to grandparents and grandchildren whose relationship could have been adversely affected by a parent's remarriage and subsequent focus on a new life and a new family.

Today grandparents' visitation laws are in flux. Although established in many states, some are being challenged (to see the current status of laws in your state check the resources at the end of this chapter). What is most important however is that today there *are* visitation laws and a grandparent and grandchild's right to have a relationship with one another has been legally acknowledged. For this we have to thank hundreds of grandparents and organizations across the country. A few national advocates among many worthy of mention are: Lee and Lucille Sumpter, founders of Grandparents-Grandchildren's Rights; Ethel Dunn; Patricia Slorah; the pioneering work of attorneys Robert Foster and Doris Freed (1979), Leonard Loeb, and Richard S. Victor.

What the Visitation Laws Do

When a grandparent is denied access to a grandchild, the law gives grandparents the right to petition the court for visitation. But this does not automatically assure the grandparent the right to visit their grandchild. First they have to win. Often winning is not easy. In addition to the organizations that advocate for grandparents' visitation laws, there are also parent-advocacy organizations that dub grandparents' visitation laws an unconstitutional intrusion into the parents' lives. These organizations keep up a steady campaign to repeal the visitation laws. Also, the courts are often ignorant of the value of the grandparent-grandchild relationship; consequently they frequently uphold the parents' position in an attempt to put an end to the turmoil.

---

1. Kornhaber, A. "Grandparents: The Other Victims of Divorce." *Reader's Digest*, February 1983.

Because families often keep grandparent visitation issues private, there isn't much in the way of valid statistics about this issue. Nevertheless, experts estimate that more than one million families in America are dealing with this problem. With certain exceptions, it seems that the reasons are usually rooted in dysfunctional early parent-child relationships, divorce and remarriage situations, or in-law personality clashes. Most often both parents and grandparents carry some degree of responsibility for the problem. Sometimes one party is more blatantly at fault than the other.

Being a grandparent is not an automatic qualification for sainthood. Grandparents make mistakes. There exist self-centered grandparents who are completely uninterested in their grandchildren. And there are certainly some grandparents who should be temporarily or even permanently restrained from being with their grandchildren because they have serious mental or behavioral problems. But most grandparents who are denied visitation are average people suffering the painful circumstances of having their grandchild's caretaker refuse them access to their grandchild. This "punishment" of being denied access to their grandchildren—leaving no room for change, forgiveness, or restitution—is harsh for grandparents; it also has unfortunate repercussions for the grandchildren and the parents.

Parents' justifications for denying visitation take many forms. Many parents deny visitation because they are angry with their own parents and do not want them, as one young mother said, "to screw up my child like they did me." Others are angry because their parents rejected their spouse. Some hold permanent grudges over things their parents did in the past and decide to punish them by not allowing them access to their grandchildren. Parents also deny visitation for legitimate reasons when grandparents break trust or are abusive.

It is important to note that in most cases, children suffer, most often silently, from the emotionally toxic spillover generated by feuding between their parents and grandparents. Thus, children are often forced to choose between them and, out of fear, feel forced to ally with the parents in spite of how much they may love their grandparents. This is a terrible thing to do to a child; it is always destructive to the parent-child relationship.

Specifics of the Grandparent Visitation Laws

The specific conditions of the grandparent visitation laws are different from state to state. Many statutes are narrowly drawn. To date, grandparents may sue for visitation in the following circumstances (depending on the state where the grandparent lives):

- Death of a parent
- Parents are unmarried
- Dissolution of parents' marriage
- Annulment of marriage or parental separation
- Adoption of a grandchild by a stepparent

Some states allow grandparents to pursue visitation rights if the grandchild has lived with the grandparents for a statutorily defined period of time beyond twelve months. To date, no courts have found clear substantive rights for grandparents to be with grandchildren if the parents' marriage is intact. Lamentably this does not consider an intact family as including grandparents, which is extremely shortsighted and, to my mind, even senseless.

Where is it written that a family consists of only two generations and that the parents have total and undisputed say over the lives of their children? In reality, children are raised and influenced by many people. In fact, family should be broadly defined as a bio-psycho-social-spiritual continuum of related kin of all generations. Shouldn't our laws be crafted to fit the reality of our family systems? Ironically, a family that excludes grandparents is not intact at all; it is a dismembered family. Another discrepancy in this thinking is that whether or not a marriage is intact is certainly no indicator of the *health* of a marriage, nor of its possible toxicity to a child.

Of course, most parents are caring and loving to their children. But in extreme cases those who are abusive or destructive and seek to forbid grandparents' access to their grandchildren can hide behind the law. Therefore, when abuse occurs, grandparents are rendered powerless to step in and help. Indeed, it is well established that many grandparents who "blow the whistle" on abusing parents are then banished by the parents from seeing their grandchildren.

Grandparents' rights are also limited because of the U.S. Constitution, which has established and maintained the freedom of parents to raise their children as they see fit. This bars grandparents with great-grandchildren, grandchildren adopted by a stepparent, grandchildren born out of wedlock, or grandchildren taken into custody by child-protection agencies from successfully suing for visitation in most states.

Certain child experts who want to spare children the suffering of being caught in the emotional crossfire between their parents and grandparents support the parents' rights in these situations. Derdyn (1985) noted that, "Visitation laws and visitation determinations by courts are reflective of difficult, contentious situations. The visitor is affecting an entry forced over the resistance of the custodial parent. . . . The adult's anger and residual resentment can make for some very difficult situations for children." This view has some merit but accepts too easily the permanent disruption of the grandparent-grandchild bond. This is unfortunate because many of these conflicts are temporary, and given a chance, could be worked out over time.

Should the grandparent-grandchild bond be permanently torn asunder because of a temporary family problem? I believe that unless a grandparent is truly toxic, the grandparent-grandchild relationship should not be disrupted while parents and grandparents are working through their issues (unless there are truly pathological circumstances).

Of course the grandparent-visitation laws should not have to be invoked at all if the family members work out their problems in a rational and principled manner. Using visitation laws should be a last resort. Unfortunately, when all efforts toward reconciliation fail, grandparents have no other recourse. Fortunately, with increasing awareness about the importance of grandparents in children's lives, more and more child experts today are supporting grandparents who are forced to take the drastic measure of suing for visitation. These experts have greatly evolved in their thinking and are beginning to recognize the value and importance of grandparents to a child's healthy development and well-being. Even the legal system has made strides in acknowledging grandparents as a vital force in their grandchild's lives. Blau (1984) noted "awareness on the part of the court that grandparents and grandparenting may be a significant factor in actualizing the best interests of the child."

In truth, the term *grandparents' rights* simply refers to a grandparent's right to enjoy the privileges and fulfill the responsibilities of grandparenthood and parenthood. Perhaps just as importantly, it refers to the children's right to have a beloved grandparent in their lives.

History of the Grandparent Visitation Laws

Although the legal issues are too extensive and complex to explore in depth here, you should become familiar with some of the background and current legal developments in the grandparents' rights movement. This section offers a brief overview of the legal history of this movement. (For more historical and legal details, see the resources listed at the end of this chapter.)

The first American statute allowing grandparents the opportunity to petition for visitation with their grandchildren was passed in 1970. By 1988, every state had enacted a law providing for some form of grandparent visitation rights in cases of death, divorce, or stepparent adoption. However, laws still vary from state to state; they are typically limited in scope and inconsistent in application. The current debate centers on the question of whether or not a grandparent has any rights to petition the court for visitation if the grandchild's parents have an intact marriage. As I mentioned earlier, if a parent's marriage is intact in the eyes of the court, the law prevents grandparents from intervening at any time. This is especially troubling in a situation where a grandchild is being abused or neglected by the parents and the grandparent is the only one the child can turn to for help. Because of widespread sexual and substance abuse and divorce and serial remarriages, this is not as uncommon a situation as you might suppose. Today, even if a grandparent witnesses substance, sexual, or physical abuse in his grandchild's family, if the parents' marriage is "intact" they can forbid the grandparent from seeing the grandchild; in such a case, the grandparent has no legal standing to petition the court for visitation. All the grandparent can do is report the situation to the authorities. If this happens and the authorities do not act (which is most often the way things go) the grandparent is permanently banished by the parents from ever seeing the child again.

In reaction to this horrendous injustice, grandparents and organizations have been pressing to enact wide-open grandparent visitation statutes that would apply whether a family is considered intact or not. As of today, grandparents in several states have succeeded in having some statutes passed. There is still considerable resistance to these new laws, though, and parents are challenging them on the books. In fact, some laws have even been rescinded based on the argument that the statute amounts to an unjustified infringement on a fundamental constitutional right of parents to raise their children as they see fit.

The fight continues.

How the Laws Evolved

Missouri statutory law states that visitation can be pursued when a grandparent is unreasonably denied visitation with his or her grandchild for a period exceeding ninety days, provided the court finds that visitation would be in the best interest of the child. To support this opinion, the court stated that although parents have a constitutional right to make decisions regarding the upbringing of their children, the magnitude of the infringement is a significant consideration in deciding whether a statute is unconstitutional. The court goes on to state that the grandparent visitation it was approving was a "less than substantial encroachment on a family situation." (Herndon 857 S.W. 2d, at 206).

The court cited King vs. King (1992), a Kentucky Supreme Court case that upheld the constitutionality of a similar statute to the Missouri statute that dealt with a comparable family situation. The King case stated that one of the purposes of the statute was to prevent family disputes from disrupting the beneficial relationship that exists between grandparents and grandchildren. The Missouri court elaborated on this statute. Under Missouri law, visitation can only be granted to a grandparent if that grandparent has unreasonably been denied visitation for more than ninety days, and only if visitation is in the best interest of the child, will not endanger the child, and will be minimal and subject to reasonable restrictions and conditional to the discretion of the court.

In September 1989, the Illinois legislature amended the state's grandparent visitation statute and declared it "wide open," thus allowing a grandparent to file a petition for visitation privileges regardless of the parent's marriage being intact or not. Mississippi supplied the "viable relationship" option to their statute; a viable relationship is defined as a relationship in which the grandparents have voluntarily and in good faith supported the child financially in whole or in part for a period of not less than six months before filing any petition for visitation rights, or if the grandparents have had frequent visitation or occasional visitation with their grandchild for a period of not less than one year.

In 1993 New Jersey passed a bill allowing grandparents to seek visitation under almost any circumstances. This bill enumerates the following evaluative criteria:

- The relationship between grandparent and grandchild, current and prior
- The relationship between the grandchild's parents and grandparents
- The lapsed time between last grandparent-grandchild contact
- The effect that visitation would have on the grandchild-parent relationship
- The time-sharing arrangement between divorced parents
- The good faith of the grandparent seeking visitation
- Any history of abuse or neglect by the grandparent
- Any other factor relevant to the best interests of the child

A grandparent applying for visitation rights in New Jersey has the added burden of proving, by a preponderance of the evidence, that granting visitation is in the best interest of the grandchild. However, the court concedes that a grandparent who has been a full-time caretaker of their grandchild in the past is prima facie evidence that visitation is in the grandchild's best interest. (NJ statutes Ann. 9:2-7.1. West Supp. 1994)

A Florida law stated that grandparents could petition the court for visitation if their grandchild were a minor still living with both natural parents who were still married to each other, whether or not there was a broken relationship between either or both parents and the grandparents, and either or both parents had used their parental authority to prohibit a relationship between the minor child and the grandparents. (Florida Statutes 752) This law has been repealed as of this writing.

One reason the courts have been inconsistent concerning visitation rights in intact families is because there are so many questions that must be addressed, such as:

- Does the grandparent have the ability to care for the child?
- Is the grandparent physically and mentally fit?
- What is the child's preference?
- What is the effect on the child of the parent-grandparent dispute?

Failure to Establish a Uniform State Visitation Law

A hugely frustrating factor for grandparents who have won visitation in one state is that their visitation rights might be abrogated when their grandchild's caretaker moves to another state. To alleviate this situation, the Visitation Rights Enforcement Act was signed into law by President Clinton on November 12, 1998. This law guarantees that grandparents can visit their grandchildren anywhere in the United States, as long as any state court has provided for the visitation. Although the law sounds good, its practical implementation can be difficult at best. Already emotionally and financially exhausted from their first hard-won battle, grandparents must often reinstitute the expensive legal proceedings and once again fight to hold on to their right to see their grandchild in his or her new state of residence. Because of this problem with the legal system, many grandparents are pushing for visitation laws that are uniform and equally honored in each and every state. In spite of a protracted effort, this has not yet happened.

In 1984, a United States Senate subcommittee held a hearing to assess the possibility of passing such a nationwide uniform grandparent visitation law. This resulted in the passing, in 1986, of House Concurrent Resolution 67 calling for a uniform state act to be developed and enacted. The House and the Senate adopted the resolution. Nothing further was done until 1991, when a follow-up hearing was held. In spite of a heated debate, a uniform state law was never enacted. This effort failed because politicians believed that such a law would infringe upon the rights of the parents to raise their children free from interference—a concept that politicians are traditionally hesitant to challenge. The legislative argument against the uniform law holds that although Congress can use indirect methods to influence the policy of individual states (by withholding federal funding, for example), it does not have the power to legislate family law issues.

In commenting on the complexities of the proposed uniform state law, the Commission on Legal Problems of the Elderly of the American Bar Association stated the following.

- Statutes vary a great deal from state to state.
- They differ on who is authorized to petition for visitation.
- The statutes vary regarding when a grandparent may petition for visitation.
- Most statutes allow courts to hear visitation disputes only in specific family situations, the most common being parental divorce, death of a parent, or in cases where a child has resided with a grandparent.

Current grandparent visitation laws are clearly in flux. The courts are only beginning to test the efficacy of the various statutes and to define the aspects of grandparent visitation rights not clearly addressed by the statutes. Thus, in most states, a grandparent trying to obtain visitation with a grandchild has the same standing as any other nonparent interested in maintaining a relationship with that child. One positive result of the enactment of the grandparent visitation laws is that they support kinship care (see Chapter 41, "Raising Grandchildren") by protecting the close relationships of children and grandparents.

Enforcement of Grandparent Visitation

There are a number of practical problems concerning logistics and visitation enforcement that arise for grandparents who are awarded visitation privileges. As mentioned above, even if a grandparent obtains a court order for visitation, a parent can thwart visitation by not conforming to the arrangements made by the court or by moving to another state.

There are issues related to grandparent visitation legislation on a more subtle level as well, such as children's rights. While courts implicitly recognize the importance of a parent's relationship with a child, the language of most laws contains no recognition of the unique relationship between a child and a grandparent, or even of the child's need for a grandparent. Yet, by its very existence, the concept of grandparents' rights implies that there are also grandchildren's rights. In recognition of this factor, many courts are placing importance on the degree of closeness of the grandparent-grandchild relationship prior to separation as a condition for visitation. In spite of all that remains to be done, the advent of grandparent visitation legislation represents a giant step in the direction of validating the grandparenting role in the family.

Visitation Guidelines

In past years, guidance was hard to come by for grandparents contemplating litigation as a last resort to see their grandchildren. Professionals were unfamiliar with the problem, laws were different from state to state, and the courts (busy enough with other issues) were generally unfriendly to grandparents. Fortunately, things have changed a bit for the better as pubic awareness about this issue has increased. To help grandparents contemplating litigation, the American Bar Association, as well as many grandparent groups, have suggested some guidelines for grandparents and professionals. These include suggested procedures and policies to follow for judges, attorneys, and mental-health professionals dealing with grandparent visitation issues. These guidelines are important for you to know.

- Attorneys should try to refer the disputants to mediation. The judge should also direct the parties to mediation if he or she feels this is a viable option.
- The state legislature should supply the court with specific criteria to help evaluate if grandparent visitation is in the best interest of the child.
- Establish the degree of closeness that exists within the grandparent–grandchild relationship.
- Establish whether the child's psychological development would be promoted or disrupted by visitation.
- Assess whether visitation will cause friction between the child and the parent.
- Assess whether visitation will supply the necessary stability and support to the child in the aftermath of the breakdown of the child's family.
- Evaluate the ability of the adults involved to compromise and cooperate with each other in the future.
- The child's wishes should be taken into consideration.
- Closely examine any other relevant factors.
- Perform an individual case-by-case assessment.

Children's Reactions to Grandparent Visitation Issues

Over the past thirty years, I have spoken with children of all ages who have been entangled in the grandparent visitation issue. What they think and feel about their feuding elders is important for disputing parents and grandparents to know. More and more grandchildren, some now grown into adulthood, are coming forward to talk about the experience of losing their grandparents. They relate how painful it was for them when they were unwillingly separated from their grandparents. They express concern for the children of today who are going through the same ordeal. Many who are no longer minors, and are thus free of parental restraints, are making the effort to seek out and reconcile with their long-lost grandparents.

Ella, now twenty-one, was separated from her grandmother at the age of six when her mother, an exotic dancer, moved from California to Nevada. "After we moved I continually asked my mother if I could call my grandmother, but my mother told everyone that my grandmother was a terrible person, and I was forbidden to contact her. You see, my grandmother did not approve of my mother's lifestyle and my mother hated her for that. One day my mother told me my grandmother was bad because she was trying to go through the courts to see me. Then, soon after that, my mother told me my grandmother was dead. Later, when my mother admitted that she had lied to me, I was completely shocked. I really needed my grandmother and when I got older, I searched and found her. I went to college right near my grandmother so I could be with her."

Many people whose grandparents went to court for visitation express feelings of pride and happiness that their grandparents loved them enough to fight to keep them in their lives. Those who loved their grandparents never expressed such feelings to their parents. Others express the pain and disappointment they felt in the way the adults in their lives were acting.

I have also spoken with parents who cut off all contact between their children and their parents. Many were unhappy about the situation but felt they had no alternative. Others regretted having separated their children from their parents or parents-in-law. Some parents have even made an effort to repair their past damage by reuniting their parents with their children.

It took Juan and Rosita ten years to give their children permission to contact Rosita's parents again. Rosita married Juan against her parents' wishes. They thought Rosita could "do better." After a year of marriage Juan and Rosita's first child was born. This happy event did not alleviate the tension between Juan and his in-laws. Eventually Juan would not come home if Rosita's parents were at the house. After two more years and another child, Juan told Rosita she would have to choose between her parents or him. At the time, the children and the grandparents were very close; the grandparents were the primary caregivers during the day while Rosita and Juan worked. Rosita was forced to tell her parents that they couldn't come over any more. In the ensuing years, Juan and Rosita allowed them no contact with the children, although the grandparents did see the grandchildren now and then on the sly. Rosita's parents implored Juan to start over, got the local priest involved, and asked other relatives (including Juan's mother) to help. But it was all to no avail. When Rosita's father became very ill, Juan softened and allowed his children to see their grandfather. By this time the oldest child was thirteen. Now, many years later, Juan is not happy about the way he separated his family. He is also concerned about what he taught his children during those years and how they will act toward him in the future. But at the time he felt he had no choice. "My in-laws were controlling my life," he says. "Now I have enough confidence to deal with them. I am sorry that Rosita and the children had to suffer."

Grandparent Visitation Laws Under Fire

Laws that support grandparents' visitation rights are not etched in stone. In 1995, certain parents' rights groups succeeded in convincing high courts in Florida, Tennessee, Georgia, and North Carolina that grandparent-visitation laws were unconstitutional. The courts made their decisions on the basis of upholding two doctrines: the liberty interests parents have in their children's upbringing and excessive interference by the state in familial relations. To keep abreast of new changes in the laws and what the challenges are, visit www.grandparenting.org and other websites mentioned in this book.

Mediation

In spite of the fact that grandparents can now petition the courts for visitation in every state (and the fact that the threat of being taken to court often serves as a deterrent to caretakers intent on severing the bond between grandparents and grandchildren), resolving parent-grandparent battles in the courtroom is far from the best solution. Although laws that give grandparents the opportunity to petition for visitation provide hope for many grandparents who would otherwise have no chance of ever seeing their grandchildren again, grandparents should view court as a last resource and should attempt every other means of dispute resolution available.

For most grandparents, the negative aspects of bringing family conflicts into the courtroom far outweigh the benefits. Going to court is the equivalent of walking into a lion's den. While there is always the chance that the court might decide in their favor and grant visitation, there is ample evidence that grandparents and grandchildren more often lose one another in the courtroom. Nowhere will the negative aspects of family conflicts seem more intractable, and nowhere will family members be more sharply divided against one another, than in the courtroom. When people go to court, family strife escalates.

Fortunately, there is *mediation*, an alternative method to resolving conflicts. Mediation has proven especially useful in resolving family issues. (For a more in-depth discussion on this topic, see Chapter 44, "Mediation.") My experience shows that court-mandated mediation is the best way to *sentence the family to healing*—and to ensure that healing does indeed take place.

When the Courtroom Is the Only Recourse

When all other avenues of reconciliation have been exhausted, taking the case to court is the only option. Once in the courtroom, there are certain things grandparents should understand, and steps they can take, to best support their position.

The most important thing to remember is that everything should be geared toward ensuring the ultimate well-being of the child. Once a family dispute is brought into the legal arena, it can be difficult to keep this in perspective. But it is the cardinal rule to which all attorneys, therapists, counselors, and judges will adhere, and as such it must be the foundation of the grandparent's case. *A grandparent should go into court on the premise that visitation is the grandchild's right, not the grandparent's.* This is a much easier position to sustain, since the court has no obligation to look after the well-being of the grandparent but is obligated to look after the best interests of the child.

Unfortunately, it may be difficult to demonstrate that maintaining a relationship with the grandparents is in the best interest of the child. Traditionally, the criteria used by the courts have focused on the convenience and wishes of the parents while altogether ignoring the deep genetic and spiritual bond between elders and their grandchildren. This is particularly sad in light of the fact that my research has shown that the relationship between grandparents and grandchildren is separate and distinct from the relationship of parents and children. It has a character and purpose all its own and can exist separately from the parents-grandparent relationship. To deny a child access to his heritage and to prevent him from carrying that legacy into the future is a tragedy that inflicts profound psychological wounds on all family members. Yet, in most cases, the law continues to use only the most superficial definition of "the best interest of the child," often ruling that grandparent visitation should not be granted if it disrupts the parents' lives. This, in my view, is most definitely *not* in the best interest of the child and is in fact abusive toward the him.

It is also important for the grandparents to state that they want to achieve reconciliation with the very person that denies visitation. Grandparents should display a desire to help and heal the situation; they should take the lead in being selfless, tolerant, and forgiving. This positive attitude provides a good example and an excellent beginning to a positive mediation process. Being older, and allegedly wiser, grandparents must lead the way and reach out a forgiving hand to parents.

The best grandparents can do in court is to state their case as truthfully and sensitively as possible while emphasizing that their relationship with their grandchild is beneficial on many different levels. They should also pray for a judge wise enough to reason not only with the mind, but also with the heart.

If you are a grandparent who has decided to take your visitation case to court, here are some practical guidelines to get started.

Finding an Attorney

The first step is to find a good attorney. Even if you already have a family attorney, he or she may not necessarily be the best person for the job. Richard S. Victor, president of GRO (Grandparents Rights Organization), is an attorney in private practice with extensive experience in grandparent visitation cases. He urges that a grandparent looking for representation should seek out an attorney who specializes in family law with an emphasis on custody and visitation matters.

To help you find an attorney, contact one of the support groups listed in the resources at the end of this chapter. If you find that attorney fees are too high, limited legal aid may be available to you. Your local legal-aid service or bar association can tell you how to go about securing legal aid, but be aware that this process is usually a lengthy one.

Preparing for Court

After you have chosen representation, it is then up to the attorney to get the ball rolling. You should remain involved in every step of the process, however. Your attorney may request numerous meetings with you to get all the facts of the case. Do not be afraid to ask your attorney for frequent updates and opinions as to your chances of winning your case.

You should also ask your attorney to keep you apprised of any alternatives to direct litigation as they arise. Even after you have gone this far, some alternatives may still exist. For example, if the visitation issue arises from a case involving divorce, the divorce agreement may contain elements that allow for grandparental visitation. Even if a final divorce agreement has not been entered, it is possible that grandparental visitation could still be written into it. In that case, it would be up to your attorney to contact the other attorneys involved in the case to try to work out an agreement. Also, attorneys themselves may make attempts to get you and the other feuding parties into mediation one last time before going to court.

If all parties agree to one last attempt at mediation, the attorneys themselves may serve as mediators, or they may refer you to other mediators or even collaborate with another mediator. In a divorce case, for example, a mediator may be brought in to work out the logistics of grandparental visitation and then collaborate with the attorney to have these written into the divorce agreement.

In some cases, however, participation in the mediation process is not a matter of choice. Some states have passed grandparent visitation laws that allow the

judge to order an embattled family to enter into mediation to resolve their conflict. These laws are definitely in the best interest of the family because they
deemphasize the adversarial process typical of courtroom proceedings and make
it a policy to sentence even the most contentious people to mediation. In this
way many people are able not only to work out visitation schedules, but also to
attempt to resolve all of their pertinent issues. People in these states who refuse
to mediate are ruled in contempt of court.

There is a particularly heart-warming case I like to describe in which mandated mediation worked wonders. A couple named Leon and Ellen Wade went
to court to try to arrange for visitation with their grandchild, and their ex-son-
in-law's attorney tried to draw out the case as long as possible, knowing that the
Wades' funds were limited and that they could not afford legal services for very
long. The judge hearing the case saw the inequity in the situation and decided
to appoint a family therapist to interview the family members and make recommendations to the court.

The therapist probed further into the complexities and ramifications of the
situation than could ever have been done in an adversarial courtroom setting.
He interviewed friends and relatives of the family to determine the degree of
closeness between the Wades and their grandchildren. This sort of information
would have been far too time-consuming and costly to elicit in court, yet it was
crucial in achieving an equitable solution to the problem. Because of the technique used to settle this case, the therapist was able to bring about a negotiated
visitation agreement that spared all family members the pain and suffering that
could so easily have resulted from a continuation of the courtroom battle.

Of course, not even mandated mediation succeeds in all cases. If litigation is
unavoidable, it is imperative that you are prepared for the courtroom and that you
and your attorney present the information the judge will need to decide your case.

What to Expect in the Courtroom

On the surface, the courtroom experience may seem to be a logical procedure.
Two opposing attorneys will try to show the judge that their own clients are "in
the right." Each attorney will submit evidence, call in witnesses to testify, and

cross-examine witnesses called by the opposing attorney. The trouble is that once the proceedings get underway, the intense emotions and passions of those involved can easily cloud issues and distort facts. Again, it is important to focus on one thing and only one thing throughout the courtroom battle: the best interest of your grandchild. That is what the attorneys will be trying to establish, and that is the basis from which the judge will ultimately decide.

Attorneys recommend keeping a level head in the heat of battle not only because it will help the legal proceedings to run more smoothly, but also because it reflects more positively on your case. It is to be expected that bitter, vindictive feelings may surface during the proceedings, but it will work in your favor if you keep a lid on them. One judge I know, who feels strongly that it is not in the best interest of the children to be exposed to violent feelings, looks harshly upon those who foment turmoil. Grandparents should beware of revealing too much hostility in the courtroom; opponents will use this to their advantage. Often parents will try to label the fight as a custody battle, but grandparents stand a better chance of winning if they limit their aim to visitation rights. It is essential that grandparents present themselves as rational, practical persons by making it clear to the court that the only goal in pursuing litigation is to achieve visitation with a grandchild, not to "win" a battle against parents.

After many years of courtroom experience, Richard S. Victor emphasizes that the most important aspect of a grandparent's visitation case is to show the court that the grandparent's request is to provide the minor child involved with the ability to continue and maintain the close and continuing relationship that previously existed. The best strategy is to show that the grandparent is not fighting this action for herself but rather for and in the benefit of the minor child.

Here are a few tips from the experts about what grandparents and their attorneys should present to the court.

- A well-conceived plan for visitation
- A well-documented visitation history between the grandparent(s) and the grandchild
- Proof that the visits were satisfactory and beneficial to the child

The Best Interest of the Grandchild

The attorneys involved in the case will most often use the testimony of the grandparents and others who are familiar with the case. Expert witnesses may also be called to try to establish what is in the best interest of the grandchildren. Lawyers with extensive experience in family issues usually have access to one or more mental-health professionals who can interview the children and make recommendations to the court. If a grandparent is important to a child, such an interview will demonstrate it. In addition, the attorney may call other therapists and counselors to have them testify as to the importance of grandparents in the overall family dynamic in general. The judge may also interview the children *in camera*—that is, in his or her chambers in a relaxed setting—to determine the wishes of the children.

An attorney will also call other witnesses, such as friends, baby-sitters, and relatives, to help establish the nature of the grandparents' relationship with the grandchildren. Grandparents should be prepared to provide the attorney with the names of witnesses who can testify about the stability of their relationship with their grandchildren (occurrence witnesses) and about their own emotional stability (character witnesses).

The attorney may call the grandparents to the witness stand. To prepare for this potentially nerve-wracking experience, Richard S. Victor suggests that when a grandparent takes the witness stand in a hearing, the attorney representing the grandparent should have reviewed with the grandparent the state law language that defines the phrase *best interest of the child*. He feels that advance familiarity with statutory language is very important for any grandparent who will serve as a witness.

Usually the attorney reviews questions he or she will ask the grandparent before calling him or her to the witness stand. The grandparent may be asked to compile information regarding his or her home life, habits, activities, work life, and religious affiliations. It is also helpful to have at hand any information about the parents' previous marriages, other familial relationships, and the grandparents' marital relationship.

But the most important information grandparents need to have is hard-core evidence that their relationship with the grandchild is real, thriving, and stable. The best plan is to prepare a written summary that clearly demonstrates the degree of closeness in the relationship. This summary should include these important elements:

- Whether the grandparent was present when the grandchild was born and how often they saw each other from that time on.
- The activities they shared, such as reading, excursions, trips, and how often they visited the grandparent's home
- How often the grandparent baby-sat the grandchild
- The grandparent's familiarity with the intimate details of the grandchild's life, such as the names of friends and pets; favorite colors; and favorite games, stories, foods, and TV shows

Grandparents should also be clear on what has led them to the courtroom in the first place and the underlying issues that are affecting the continuation of their relationship with their grandchild. Remember that the ultimate goal in a visitation hearing is to show that the relationship with the grandchild is healthy, thriving, and necessary to the mental and emotional well-being of the grandchild.

Once the summary is completed, it is essential that the grandparent is familiar with and clear about this information because there may be hostile cross-examination by the opposing attorney. There is no surefire way to prepare for this experience. The best strategy for a grandparent, experts agree, is to relax, be honest, and simply explain the situation. Most questions will center on issues that were already covered, such as the extent of the relationship with the grandchild and the nature of the relationship with the parents and other family members.

The Guardian *ad Litem*

If a case involves young children, it is not unusual for one or both parties or the court itself to request that the court appoint a guardian *ad litem* (GAL) to look after the interests of the child. The GAL is an attorney who represents the child's viewpoint, even if the child is in the care and custody of his or her parents.

In effect, the GAL speaks for children who cannot, because of their age or situation, speak for themselves. Because parental rights are secondary in importance to the best interest and welfare of the child, the GAL even has the power to sue the child's parents if the GAL perceives that their behavior is detrimental to the child.

When the Courtroom Battle Is Done

After all the testimony has been given and the dust has settled a bit, the parties wait for the judge to render a decision. If the court decides to allow visitation, it is then necessary to agree on the specifics of the visitation order. One of the most important things to look for in a visitation order is flexibility. Does the order allow for increased visitation over time? Visitations in the child's home can be difficult and/or uncomfortable; therefore, it is best if the order allows for a variety of visitation locations. If the court does not decide in favor of visitation, and the grandparents are able to withstand the additional expense and anguish, they may want to file an appeal. The attorney can supply information on how the particular state appeals court system works.

No matter how the court decides, there will be deep emotional wounds that will need to be healed. It is to the benefit of all parties involved in the case to seek out professional counseling. The most important thing after a combative, divisive courtroom battle is for the family to regain emotional stability as soon as possible. Only then can the grandparent-grandchild bond, and indeed *all* the family bonds, become what they should be.

Remember that family problems do not have to be permanent. An essential part of our humanity is that we grow and change. With growth and change comes increased wisdom; with wisdom comes understanding; and with understanding comes an ever-increasing capacity for tolerance and forgiveness. This applies not only to the grandparents, but also to the parents. Always proffer a loving and accepting hand to everyone in your family. It sets a wonderful example for your grandchild.

Avoiding Parent-Grandparent Conflicts

Prevention is the best medicine. Here are some guidelines to help you avoid future grandparent–parent conflicts.

- When conflicts occur, focus your energy on getting rid of the *problem*, not the people you are having the problem with. This includes seeking professional help if necessary.
- Many of the attitudes and situations leading to problems between parents and grandparents are temporary. People grow and change, and forgiveness of others' past transgressions is essential. Our experience and research has shown that over time many parents regret that they separated their children from their parents.
- Alienation between parents and grandparents is painful for all; it rips the fabric of the family. Actively search for solutions that keep the family together.
- Regardless of the problems between parents and grandparents, strive to continue the grandparent-grandchild relationship. When parents forbid their children access to their grandparents, it serves as a very negative example of problem solving. Many children wonder if their parents will also get rid of them if they are not "good." It also forces children who love their grandparents to live a double life. They live in fear of telling their parents that they love and miss their grandparents. Ultimately, the way the separation is handled may cause children to lose respect for their parents.
- Many children wish to reconcile with their grandparents and will attempt to do so when they come of age.
- Keep in mind that children need both their parents and grandparents. Feuding parents and grandparents must put aside their feelings and place the child's welfare above the anger they may feel toward one another. Except in cases of abuse, the

grandparent-grandchild bond should never be ruptured. Parents should know that research shows grandparents rarely inflict on grandchildren the conflicts and problems they may have inflicted on their children.

■ Litigation should be regarded as a last resort. It can create a devastatingly permanent resolution for what might only have been a temporary problem.

Custody

If your court case involves gaining custody of your grandchildren, you will want to familiarize yourself with the different types of custody that exist. The following list can serve as a baseline.

■ *Informal custody* means living together without a legal arrangement. In this situation, the parent retains full legal rights.

■ As a *foster parent*, the grandparent lacks legal custody, but has physical custody of the child, including the right to enroll the child in school and attend to all medical needs.

■ Aside from adoption, which terminates parental rights, a grandparent can obtain full legal and physical custody through *guardianship*, which temporarily suspends parental rights.

Power of Attorney

If you plan to take a trip with your grandchild, or if you are temporarily caring for your grandchild, you will need to have power of attorney. Power of attorney is a document signed by the custodial parent(s) that gives you the right to make decisions on behalf of your grandchild. A special power of attorney is limited in scope and restricts your authority in certain situations and areas, such as those dealing with your grandchild's medical care. General power of attorney gives you the same broad authority as a parent in dealing with your grandchild's care.

A power of attorney requires the notarized signature of all-custodial parents or guardians. Custodial parents can revoke the power of attorney by signing another document to that effect. A single power of attorney can apply to more than one grandchild and can grant power to more than one grandparent, as long as the relevant parties' names are listed on the document. A power of attorney is of limited duration and can be renewed.

Childcare Authorization

The childcare authorization grants another person or institution temporary custody of a child. For example, if a parent will be separated from her child for a few days, she may wish to grant certain powers to the child's temporary caretaker regarding the child's basic needs. Sometimes a Childcare Authorization may be needed to provide a child's teacher, school, or other organization with the authority to take the child on a field trip or other outing. A parent may name more than one caretaker on a childcare authorization—for example, a married couple.

Letter to School

The letter to school provides notice to school officials of the identity of the caretaker(s) and the scope of the authority that has been granted. It is important to understand that the letter to school does not grant any authority to the caretaker(s). It simply provides notice to the school officials.

Childcare Instructions

The childcare instructions document provides important phone numbers, medical information, and special instructions to baby-sitters, day-care providers, and other caretakers responsible for a child's care on a short-term basis. If the caretaker is in need of other specific powers, he should use the childcare authorization document.

RESOURCES

For Grandparent Visitation Law updates, visit www.grandparenting.org and click on the "Grandparent Visitation Laws" link. For an on-line comparative chart of state-by-state grandparent visitation laws, go to www.aarp.org/litigation/table .html.

For the latest information on laws and local support groups contact:

Grandparents Rights Organization (www.grandparentsrights.org)
100 West Long Lake Road, Suite 250
Bloomfield Hills, MI 48304
(248) 646-7191
Richard S. Victor, Esq., Founder, Executive Director
Kathleen A. Germaine, Assistant Director
www.RichardSVictor.com

National Coalition of Grandparents
137 Larkin Street
Madison, WI 53705
(608) 238-8751

American Bar Association
Center on Children and the Law
740 15th Street NW
Washington, DC 20049
(202) 662-1000

CHAPTER 43

Long-Distance Grandparenting

H ow many of your friends, colleagues, and neighbors actually live near all of their children and grandchildren? Not too many, I am sure. This makes day-to-day, hands-on grandparenting very difficult. In fact, studies show (and common sense would tell us) that being geographically distant from grandchildren is grandparents' number-one complaint (Kornhaber 1996, Peterson 1999). According to a recent AARP survey, only 33 percent of grandparents live near enough to one grandchild to see him or her once or twice a week. This is why it is so important that you and your family brainstorm together and devise strategies to be together as much as possible. This is the challenge of long-distance grandparenting.

Because we are a nation on the move, the situation is not going to go away. We know that distance can adversely affect grandparents' relationships with their children and grandchildren. But if everyone works together, the negative effects can be minimized. Living a long-distance from a grandchild need not relegate a grandparent to a token role in the grandchild's life. There is good news. Thanks to technology, today's grandparents—now more than ever before—have the opportunity to narrow the distance-related emotional gap between themselves and their families.

The Effects of Distance

Geographic separation can impede three of the strongest emotional and spiritual existential aspects of the connection between grandparents and grandchildren:

- Intimate time together. Undivided attention between grandparents and grandchildren can be difficult when they live apart.
- General time together. Daily contact within the context of the extended family.
- Grandparents and grandchildren need to be part of one another's daily lives, especially in the child's early years. Distance makes this type of continuous personal contact impossible.
- Common experience. Grandparents and their grandchildren need to feel that they live in the same world and react to the same people, places, and situations.

Children grow and change so quickly. They require regular contact with their grandparent to forge a strong relationship. When grandparents and grandchildren have not had contact for a while the child feels strange and "out of synch," (as a teenager said) with the grandparent. That is because continuity has been lost and they are no longer familiar with one another. As ten-year-old Tyler put it, "Every time my grandmother visits she treats me like I was the last time she visited. But I've grown up. So she treats me like another person for a while until she catches up."

When people who live far from one another do get together, they need to carve out time to be alone. When people get together infrequently there is so much to do and so little time to do it. Grandparents' time with their grandchild is often limited because other family members need time and attention too. However, there is still a great deal a long-distance grandparent can do to keep the relationship alive and vibrant in spite of distance. The key is to maintain the attachment to your grandchild by becoming as much a part of her *everyday life* as possible. Adhering to two principles can help: (1) Try to keep *continuous con-*

tact with the grandchild; and (2) arrange your life to offer to as much *one-to-one attention* as possible in the time you spend together. This isn't easy to accomplish in today's times, but it's not impossible either—thanks to technology.

Staying in Touch

The remedy for the problems that distance inflicts on your relationship with your grandchild is to stay as close as possible in body, mind, and spirit. The best way to do this is to make wise choices about the occasions when you are with your grandchild. If you are a long-distance grandparent, prioritize your choices to be there for the important events in your family's life: the birth of your grandchildren, religious ceremonies, recitals, holidays, and graduations. Spending time alone together traveling or visiting at your home is very important too (see Chapters 30, "Traveling with Your Grandchild," and 32, "When Your Grandchild Visits").

Technology to the Rescue

The Internet can help to bridge the distance between you and your grandchild and keep you in touch on a daily basis. Although technology will not allow you to physically soothe a grandchild's fevered brow or lend a hand to an overworked parent, it can foster ongoing communication between you. No matter how far apart you may live this is the most indispensable factor in keeping you close. The Internet can help you welcome a new grandchild into the world (with the help of a videocamera), tutor a grandchild in any subject, or play games with a grandchild who lives thousands of miles away. When you communicate regularly with your grandchild via the Internet, you limit the gaps in your experience of one another. Therefore, when you do physically visit together, you are up to date on each other's lives. For example, you may already know exactly how your granddaughter felt last week after she won her track meet because when she returned home that evening she sent you an E-mail telling you all about her day and scanned her medal so that she could send you a picture of it.

Any kind of undivided attention strengthens a relationship. Time alone with your grandchild is the ideal situation, of course, but the two of you can spend very meaningful time together in cyberspace, too (see Chapter 36, "Cybergrandparenting").

Computers

Using the computer should be an important part of your strategy. There is a lot of new and easy-to-use technology on the market now. The computer is a wonderful tool for you to stay in touch with your grandchild on a continuing basis. Most children today are computer literate. If you are not, take a class or have a friend teach you how to use a computer (see Chapter 36, "Cybergrandparenting"). The cost of a computer is significantly less than it has been in the past. The opportunities afforded by E-mail and even videoconferencing—which enables you to talk to your grandchild face-to-face—are nothing short of amazing. You can send recipes, jokes, family stories, or even the latest gossip to your grandchild. Playing computer games with your grandchild over the Internet can keep your contact vibrant and relevant. You can even create your own home page on the World Wide Web. Log onto www.grandparenting.org to see what a home page looks like.

Fax

Faxes are useful for sending printed material that cannot be sent via E-mail (for folks without a scanner). One grandmother we know gave each of her grandchildren a fax machine so they could keep in touch on a daily basis. Jokes, report cards, and drawings can be faxed back and forth between grandparents and grandchildren. Another grandmother, Hilda, seventy-eight, makes a point of faxing all three of her grandchildren a little note of encouragement a few times a week.

Telephone

Telephone contact is important, too. It is nice to hear the voices of loved ones. Remember that your grandchild wants to feel special, so when you call, ask to speak to your grandchild and when your conversation is over, hang up. Do not talk to others during your grandchild's time. Save that for another phone call so that everyone can feel special. It's best to call at a time when you know your grandchild is not rushed. Some grandparents make a regular phone appointment to talk with each of their grandchildren.

The telephone allows for intimacy. One grandmother, a retired librarian, reads her grandchildren a nightly story on the telephone. She is selective in her choice of books, "safeguarding little minds and stimulating them with good literature." Lists of age-appropriate reading material can be accessed at your local library or at www.familyedge.com.

Letters

It's not very high-tech, but there is something deliciously intimate about a personal letter. So don't forget about good old-fashioned letter writing—or "snail mail," as it is referred to today. Little notes are a nice way to reach out and remind your grandchild that he is in your thoughts. Younger kids especially love receiving letters. It makes them feel important and grown up. Encourage your grandchildren to write to you as well. Ask them to send you their drawings, family photographs, or letters describing their daily lives. It is a way of letting them know you care. Including a small token, a photograph, a piece of chewing gum, or a small check always helps. Letters can be read over and over and then tucked away in your family treasure chest.

Family Newsletter

As the living ancestor and family historian of your family (see Chapters 2, "Ancestor," and 5, "Historian"), you can serve as the heart of the family communication system by editing your own family newsletter. This can be done simply on the computer using a publishing program that converts your newsletter into a print or E-mail version. This is one way to keep everyone up on the latest family developments. Many grandparents use their grandchildren as correspondents and have them mail in news items for publication. Publishing a family newsletter shows your family you care about them all as individuals and as members of the family.

Family Website

It is easy to start a family website today. A website can keep family members in touch, post photographs and family letters. This is especially good if you have family members in the military service on duty in faraway lands. Have a family bulletin board. Post a family history, create and maintain a family tree, and more. The limit to what you can do is bounded only by the limits of your imagination.

Videotape and Photographs

You can record yourself on videotape singing a song or telling a story and send it to your grandchild. Give your grandchild a video camera or tape recorder so they can do the same. Make sure that someone is recording each grandchild's growth and development on videotape. One grandmother I know collects all the family tapes and edits them into a story complete with music. Such videotapes can be included in a family archive.

The new digital cameras take excellent pictures that can be downloaded on to a computer and E-mailed to the family the same day. This is especially good for important occasions (marriages, graduations) or other events.

Audiotape

Make a recording that will put your grandchild in touch with her roots (see Chapter 5, "Historian") by talking about your joys and sorrows growing up in the old days. Remember to have fun with it. One grandfather recorded Irish music as background to his description of coming over on a boat from Ireland. Don't forget the jokes or humorous anecdotes. To keep your grandchild's interest, vary the pace and tone of your reading. Balance a serious story with a funny one. You might just want to record your favorite music or read your favorite story or poems to your grandchild.

It is possible to broadcast your videotapes and audiotapes over the Internet so that your extended family has access to them. Your imagination is the only limit. This is a legacy you can create for your grandchildren no matter how far away you may live. It is a gift your grandchildren will treasure and pass on to their grandchildren as well as other family members.

GUIDELINES

If you are a long-distance grandparent, there is plenty you can do to maintain continuity with your grandchild between the times you spend together in person. The principles involved are to maintain continuity and to be as much a part of your grandchild's daily life as possible under the circumstances. Following are some guidelines to help you formulate strategies and develop a plan to make the best of the situation.

- Be there when your grandchild is born.
- Sit down with the parents and grandchildren to discuss the importance of maintaining family bonds over distance. Let everyone know it's important to you.
- Identify the issues and discuss the pitfalls and problems of being geographically apart.
- Make a family commitment, and a plan, to minimize the difficulties inherent in the separation by keeping in constant communication and being physically together as much as possible.
- Pledge family financial resources to support the family's commitment and the plan. Allocate resources to specific activities, such as paying for Grandma's airfare to visit while Mom and Dad go on vacation or purchasing a computer for Grandpa so that he can E-mail everyone regularly.
- Make it a point to attend major events and celebrations (family, school, religious ceremonies, etc.).
- When you *are* physically together, allow for as much grandparent-grandchild alone time as possible (see Chapter 23, "Attention").

Coordinate visits, parent vacations, and so on. Plan to go on outings alone with your grandchild when you visit. Make it a point to share as much of your grandchild's world as possible when you are together (school, friends, etc.).

CONCLUSION

To minimize the negative effects of long-distance grandparenting, try to be as much a part of your grandchild's daily life as possible. Use your ingenuity to keep your grandchild emotionally close. Grandchildren truly appreciate it when grandparents make the effort to love and care for them even though they live far away. (When the grandchildren are older and able to travel by themselves, they often repay the favor by visiting their grandparents!) "My grandmother really loves and misses me," said Louella, ten. "Even though I live really far away, I hear from her almost every day. She calls and writes and spends her money on coming to see me, so I know she cares."

Mediation

E very family needs a mediator at one time or another. And grandparents, by virtue of their experience and wisdom, are well suited for this role. After all, as parents they mediated the disputes of their children. And now, one generation removed, their skills have been honed by years of experience.

Most conflicts and problems between family members can be worked out through mediation. In an extreme situation however (for example, a dispute over a grandparent's visitation rights), outside help is necessary. Of course as they get older (and hopefully wiser), grandparents can learn and use mediation techniques to prevent, resolve, and heal hurtful family situations. This is a traditional role of the wise man and wise woman. And as grandparents tend to inherit this role, it is important that you learn about mediation and how to apply some of its reasoning and techniques in your own life.

Mediation is a process of conflict resolution whereby people at odds with one another strive to solve their differences. Put simply, "Mediation is a cooperative dispute resolution process in which a neutral third party tries to keep the contesting parties talking while steering them to a mutual settlement of their differences" (Pearson, 1981). Experience has proven that the mediation process is most often respectful, private, and fair. The settlements achieved are more often adhered to than settlements reached through litigation. Another benefit is that mediation is much less expensive than litigation. In fact, it is often the threat of an expensive trial that motivates most families to enter into mediation.

Because there may come a time when you or someone close to you may be called upon to mediate a dispute, it is helpful to be informed about the process. This chapter contains more information about it and includes some examples of how professional mediators work.

The Mediation Process

The mediation process involves gathering data, sharing and verifying the data with all parties, using the data to define a neutral party statement, developing options to solve problems, and then negotiating over the precise options to fulfill the needs of both parties. The mediator moves the parties toward agreement by using questions to provoke them, pointing out similar perceptions and opinions, seeking common ground, and then directing the parties' actions toward the future. Sound familiar? It should. This is exactly what you do whenever you settle an argument.

However, in serious disputes more objective help is needed. For example, professional mediation is increasingly being used to settle grandparent-visitation issues. Learning how this works will help you hone your own mediation skills.

The Advantages of Mediation in Parent-Grandparent Legal Disputes

The courts are beginning to recognize the advantages of mediation over litigation with regard to family feuds. Without mediation, all the court can offer is an attempt to judge who is right and who is wrong in family disputes. Given the complex and convoluted nature of family conflicts and problems, this is often an impossible task. Although mediation requires a great deal of time and effort, the vast majority of family counselors, social agents, and even attorneys consider it the best alternative to litigation for resolving grandparent-caretaker conflicts (American Bar Association, 1989).

Mediation is different from the legal process, which is by definition adversarial. The goal of any legal proceeding is to determine a winner and a loser. A court considers "facts" derived from what it considers to be objective reality. To discern these facts, the court uses a prescribed set of procedures, considers evidence, and makes a purportedly objective judgment. It will then attempt to resolve the issue, usually according to legal precedent.

While this method works fairly well in cases concerning burglary or tax evasion, it is not as adaptable to family problems. Where family conflicts are concerned, it is almost always impossible to determine objective truth. What is fact to Grandma is not necessarily fact to Aunt Sally. Most facts within the family context are actually personal opinions based on people's own perceptions of themselves, their perceptions of one another, and their reactions to these perceptions. Every individual is a separate universe, with his or her own idiosyncrasies. When these separate universes collide, anything can happen.

That is why mediation is the best method to settle family issues and prevent permanent decisions about what often turn out to be temporary problems. It is also why grandparents who inquire about the feasibility of petitioning for visitation with their grandchildren are frequently offered mediation as a first option. Leonard Loeb, a distinguished family law attorney, says, "At the very least, an attorney considering filing a grandparent visitation suit should discuss the alternative of mediation as a means of resolving the dispute before the actual litigation process begins" (personal communication, 1987). The American Bar Association (1989) recommends that "attorneys, court personnel and other professionals should be encouraged to refer persons involved in grandparent visitation disputes to appropriate mediation services. If possible such referrals should be made prior to the filing of any court action."

Mediation can also ensure the enforcement of decisions, an element that is often missing from court-issued judgments. Even when grandparents win visitation rights in court, that does not always mean they will actually spend time with their grandchildren. The truth is that the grandparents' access to their grandchildren remains dependent on the cooperation of the grandchildren's caretaker, who controls how, when, and where visitation will take place.

With mediation, compliance is assured because family members' participation in the process is closely monitored. Appearance at mediation sessions and compliance with the agreements reached there is reported back to the court by the mediator. Any infractions in visitation can be dealt with swiftly by the court, which assures continuity of grandparent-grandchild contact in some form or other.

Mediation in Action

Personal mediation, initiated by a friend or professional also works when it is applied to the day-to-day trials and tribulation of family life. Here is an example. Buzz, ten, was involved in a web of family conflicts that was making him very depressed. He had lost his father in an industrial accident several years before the trouble started. His mother, Sissy, a mother of four, had a very good relationship with Buzz's grandparents, Jack and Beth, before her husband was killed. After the death of their son, they helped Sissy a great deal financially and also helped with child care.

Two years after the death of her husband, Sissy met and married Cal, a former high school sweetheart. Cal had also lost his wife and had no children of his own. Sissy maintained a close relationship with Jack and Beth while she was grieving the death of her husband and while she was dating Cal. But, unfortunately, from the outset, Cal did not like Jack and Beth. After Cal and Sissy were married, Cal increasingly resented Jack and Beth's "intrusion" into his new family's life. After three years of marriage, Cal legally adopted Sissy's children. Soon afterward he decided that he didn't want the children to spend as much time with their grandparents. He felt that Jack and Beth reminisced too often about the children's deceased father and that they continually compared him to Cal. This made Cal insecure; he reasoned that if he allowed the kids to continue to see their grandparents, they would never accept him as their new dad. Jack and Beth were confused and distraught. Because they did not understand why Cal didn't want them to talk about their son to their grandchildren, they continued to do so. Sissy just wanted peace.

The conflict escalated. Cal finally forbade Jack and Beth to visit their grandchildren at all. Cal told Sissy and the children not to talk to Jack and Beth. When Jack and Beth telephoned, Cal hung up. He sent back their gifts and eventually had a lawyer write Jack and Beth a letter saying that Cal would sue them for harassment if they continued to pursue seeing their grandchildren. Buzz, who had been very close to his grandparents, was devastated.

Jack and Beth, panic-stricken, went to a lawyer who told them there was not much to be done. The laws in their state would not support visitation because Sissy and Cal's marriage was intact (see Chapter 42, "Legal Issues"). Jack and Beth consulted Father Phil, their priest, a friendly, caring, and respected member of their community. Fortunately, Cal was actively involved in Father Phil's church, too. The priest spoke with all the parties and recommended they enter into mediation in an attempt to iron out their their differences.

Sissy readily agreed to this because she knew how important Jack and Beth were to her children. Cal reluctantly agreed because he wanted Sissy to be happy. Jack and Beth were relieved that there was some hope that they would be able to be grandparents to their grandchildren again. The children, needless to say, were very happy that someone was going to keep the adults from squabbling. By agreeing to mediation, this family made a commitment to confront the problem and to begin healing.

In the first session, the mediator pointed out that they all had something very important in common: their love for the children. From that positive starting point, the mediator and the parties worked over many sessions to resolve their problems. The mediator also dealt with each family member individually. Eventually, as a result of brief personal therapy, Cal was able to identify and deal with the reasons underlying his dislike of Jack and Beth. It actually had little to do with them; Cal realized that he had to look more closely at his own feelings about Sissy's previous husband and the fact that Sissy's children were not his own. Cal's own parents were authoritative and not supportive and he assumed Jack and Beth would be the same.

Because of mediation, Jack and Beth learned to respect Cal as an individual; they stopped comparing him to their own son. Instead they began to support and befriend him. It took more than a year to get to this point. In the meantime, Cal allowed Jack and Beth more and more time with their grandchildren. At first, visits were confined to the grandparents' home and were supervised by Sissy. Then, as Jack and Beth became supportive of Cal, he allowed them to spend time alone with their grandchildren. By the end of the year, the children were spending entire weekends at Jack and Beth's home.

One of the most worthwhile and surprising results of this whole affair was the children's increased respect for Cal. As Cal changed his attitude toward Jack and Beth, the children were gradually taken out of the difficult position of having to choose between people they loved. Buzz described his feelings: "I hated it whenever Mom and Cal talked about my grandparents, and I hated Cal. Before, I could not stand being around them when they were all together and watching them act so angry and weird. Now Cal drives me to my grandparents' house and he talks to them really nice. My grandparents are more careful to be nice to him. I don't know what everyone was fighting about, but now they're happy and I know they all love me."

This case demonstrates how well the mediation process can work. As soon as a mediator steps in, the destructive tailspin that characterizes so many family conflicts can be halted. Involving a mediator shows everyone that there is a chance for a positive solution to their troubles. Hopelessness is dispelled and healing can begin.

GUIDELINES

You can personally mediate many of the day-to-day conflicts and problems that may arise between you and your family. Here are some guidelines to help:

- The first step is to work at building a strong relationship with your children and children-in-law in the early stages. This will ensure a foundation that will give you the trust and respect you need for the mediation process (see Chapter 21, "Effective Grandparenting").

- Listen to all sides of the issue, identify common ground, help the feuding parties to see the disagreement from the other person's point of view, and work things out.

- Keep in mind, however, that family members and friends are likely to lose their objectivity and sometimes cause more problems than they solve. Professional mediators, on the other hand, because of their training, detachment, and authoritative position, are more objective in family disputes than even the most well-intentioned amateur mediators.

- If needed, there are mediation therapists in private practice as well as nonprofit family service agencies with sliding fee scales to suit your financial situation. Check your telephone directory or ask your clergy for a referral. For more about working out family problems, see Chapter 33, "Between Parents and Grandparents."

CONCLUSION

The mediation approach to solving family conflicts, no matter how severe the problem, is the most useful, least harmful, and least expensive method of conflict resolution. You can serve in the role of mediator when other family members are feuding—and you will be especially effective if you follow the examples outlined in this chapter. If you are a party in the conflict, however, find someone else to mediate.

CHAPTER 45

Mistakes Grandparents Make

A s the common lament of the older and wiser among us goes, "If I knew then what I know now." After all, we learn by our mistakes. And the older we grow, the more aware we are of our present and past mistakes. The good news is that grandparenting gives us another chance to learn from our mistakes and do it over again—and correctly this time! All this is to the benefit of the grandchild.

To Err Is Human

Don't fret over past mistakes. If we *learn* from our mistakes, then it was worth having made them. For example, hindsight can be a useful tool for grandparents to understand themselves as parents. Reviewing mistakes and not repeating them with our children is a positive and growth-enhancing process. Emma, seventy-six, has four children. When she treated her eldest daughter's husband in an aloof and unaccepting way she learned that if she continued to do so she would alienate her daughter and set a bad example for the other children. So, in her words, she "became the best mother-in-law in the world."

However, hindsight does not work for grandparenting because it is a new role, a constant discovery. Besides, grandparenting differs from parenting in many ways. It brings its own unique benefits, challenges, and problems.

Every grandparent needs to know that to quickly resolve mistakes and learn from them, the mistakes must be freely acknowledged. Grandparents must solicit forgiveness from the one who was hurt and attempt to reestablish trust. Other family members must do the same. If these steps are followed, in most cases the mistake will not be repeated.

On the other hand, when a grandparent does not acknowledge, or even denies, making a mistake, this behavior can seriously impair his or her family relationships, eroding trust and respect and creating emotional distance. Learning about some of the common mistakes made by grandparents may help you to avoid making the same ones yourself.

Mistakes Grandparents Make with Themselves

Grandparents may be unaware that grandparenthood involves a transformation in terms of their identity, roles, and relationships. Not recognizing such changes, including the changes in attitude and thought that take place within their own psyche as well as a changing relationship with their child as a new parent, can cause problems. To avoid such a mistake prepare carefully for grandparenthood by assessing your own feelings about the role as well as the expectations of your grandchild's parents. This way your expectations, as well as those of your own child, are clear and realistic (see Chapter 33, "Between Parents and Grandparents").

Understanding Grandparenthood

Another common mistake grandparents make is not taking the time to learn and understand what being a grandparent is all about. Grandparenting requires learning to adapt to a particular family situation as well as knowing the basics—the roles grandparents play, how to support the grandchild's parents, and how to relate directly to a grandchild. It also requires awareness of how the role is valued within society and how social attitudes affect personal grandparenting (see Chapter 1, "Grandparent Roles").

Keeping Up to Date

A grandparent who maintains out-of-date attitudes and opinions can widen the gap between family members. Many grandparents who do not keep up with modern times may find their grandchildren treating them as out-of-it when it comes to talking about current events and trends. That's why continual self-examination is necessary. Make sure to ask your family for feedback on your behavior too.

Having Available Time

Make sure to prioritize your schedule so that you have time for grandparenting. You do not want to say no to your child and grandchild on a continuing basis. Ask your family members what they need from you. Do your best to give them the things they ask for.

Mistakes Grandparents Make with Parents

Many grandparents would do well to keep in mind that parents are the linchpins of grandparents' relationship with their grandchildren. Be sure to work at maintaining a solid relationship with parents and in-laws. Let parents know how important they are to you and how much you appreciate their support of your relationship with your grandchildren.

Respecting the Parent's Right to His or Her Own Mistakes

Grandparents err when they fail to respect the parents' right to make their own mistakes and learn from them. A grandparent who is rigid about attitudes and behavior will certainly alienate parents. To avoid these mistakes yourself, keep current about childrearing practices. And be sure to be as kind, understanding, compassionate, nonjudgmental, supportive, and caring as possible.

Ignoring the Importance of Their Example

Grandparents set the tone in conflict resolution, often serving as family mediators. Therefore, make sure to be impartial in conflict situations. Spend time alone with each member of your family. Fairness is critically important. On a positive note, take the lead in showing your interest in the lives of family members. Share their world, listen to them, visit their workplace, and join them in activities that interest them. Get to know their friends. If family members do not feel you are interested in them, they will not be interested in you. Show them you care. Then when a conflict arises you can readily understand each person's point of view. Understanding is the bedrock of conflict resolution.

Mistakes Grandparents Make with Their Grandchildren

When it comes to grandparenting, making mistakes is a fact of life. Know that you will make mistakes with your grandchildren. Also keep in mind that it is up to you to learn from those mistakes.

Acting Like a Parent Instead of a Grandparent

Grandchildren already have parents. They need their grandparents to act like grandparents. Don't get the two roles mixed up. Understand the difference between parents and grandparents. If you are confused about this, ask your children for help. Be especially aware that younger parents need your confidence and support. Pia, twenty-two, has two young children. She and her husband live on the same street as her mother. Until she learned better, her mother, Pauletta, forty-eight, brought breakfast to Pia's house every morning. Once in the door, she "precipitated" on to the children, often brushing Pia out of the way. When

Pia finally got up the courage to tell her mother not to come over in the morning and that she was not letting Pia be the mother, Pauletta was devastated and took to her bed. Pia, guilt-stricken (because she saw her mother as a good, although overzealous, person) became depressed. It finally took Pauletta's younger sister to intervene, read Pauletta the riot act, and make her realize that she was overwhelming Pia with love and caring. Pauletta courageously asked Pia to forgive her, and now she asks Pia what she needs, and does it.

Failure to Understand Your Importance to Your Grandchildren

Your grandchildren want to love and adore you. Understand how your grandchildren value you and your functions for them (see Chapter 1, "Grandparent Roles"). Learn about how the grandparent-grandchild bond is different from the parent-child bond. And, above all, listen to your grandchild's thoughts and feelings about your relationship.

Failure to Spend Time Alone with your Grandchildren

Try to give your grandchildren personal attention—even when parents or other family members are present (see Chapter 23, "Attention"). Understand that grandchildren have the need to absorb their grandparents' essence and legacy. Giving your grandchildren your undivided attention is the best way to let this happen.

Failure to Relax with Grandchildren

Many grandparents focus too much on entertaining their grandchildren instead of relaxing and enjoying one another. You don't have to work hard at being a grandparent. And you don't have to worry that your grandchild will find you boring. You, your essence and your spirit, are enough. Relax and be spontaneous. On the other hand, expand your mutual interests with your grandchild by sharing everyday activities. Visit your grandchildren's school. Take them to the doctor's office. Take them to concerts. Meet and get to know their friends. Learn about what music they listen to and which TV programs they enjoy.

Ignoring How Fast Children Change

Children, and especially young children, change rapidly. Often grandparents do not recognize these changes. This generates hurt and anger. It is all too common in long-distance relationships. So keep in close contact with your grandchildren. Keep up with their development. Know their clothes sizes. Especially if you are a long-distance grandparent, keep up with your grandchildren's lives by phone, fax, E-mail, or regular mail. Exchange photos, videos, and audiotapes. And, of course, make it a priority to spend as much time together as possible (see Chapter 43, "Long-Distance Grandparenting").

GUIDELINES

Here are some guidelines to help you learn from your mistakes.

- Remember that mistakes are normal.
- If you make a mistake, own up to it and ask for forgiveness.
- Treat others' mistakes with understanding, love, and forgiveness.
- Work hard to keep the family safe, secure, and loving. This environment easily absorbs the mistakes of family members.
- Make sure to listen to others' views and opinions. Be open to new attitudes and ideas.
- Dealing well with your own mistakes gives a powerful message to your grandchildren and the rest of the family.

CONCLUSION

No grandparent is perfect. If you are a new grandparent concerned about making mistakes, do not worry. Mistakes are a natural part of the learning experience and of being human. It's how you handle them that matters. In any case, make sure your relationship with your family is based on love, open communication, and mutual respect.

CHAPTER 46

Stepgrandparenting

One third of American grandparents have at least one stepgrandchild.[1] This situation is a consequence of longevity coupled with the high rate of divorce and remarriage in the United States today. As a result, the stepgrandparent has become an increasing and significant presence in the American family. People become stepgrandparents when their own child marries someone with children, or when they themselves marry someone with grandchildren.

Becoming a stepgrandparent can be a blessing for you and your stepgrandchild because it offers both of you a potentially loving relationship. Keep in mind

---

1. It has been estimated that there are over 50 million stepgrandparents in the United States today. The Stepfamily Foundation reports that stepfamilies are growing by approximately 50,000 a month. Every day in America 1,300 couples with children under 18 remarry. Approximately one-half of all Americans are currently involved in some form of stepfamily relationship. Seven million children, or one out of six, live in stepfamilies. By the recent turn of the millenium, more Americans were living in stepfamilies than in nuclear families. Here's why:

- It is predicted that 50 percent of children in the United States will experience their parent's divorce before the age of 18.
- One out of two marriages end in divorce.
- 40 percent of second marriages fail, according to the U.S. Census Bureau.
- 66 percent of marriages and cohabitation situations dissolve.

that geographical distance need not keep you from developing a loving relationship (see Chapter 43, "Long-Distance Grandparenting"). As a stepgrandparent and stepparent, you can be a valuable addition to everyone in your stepfamily.

Being an Effective Stepgrandparent

For many people, making the adjustment to stepgrandparenthood requires a great deal of self-examination and maturity as well as emotional and spiritual savvy. Unless you had a stepgrandparent when you were a child, you are probably unfamiliar with how one enacts the aspects of this role. That is why, to be most effective in this role, it is essential to evaluate your feelings about becoming a stepgrandparent, and to understand and listen to your partner's feelings and those of your stepgrandchild and your new stepfamily.

Understand Yourself

Your first priority as a stepgrandparent is to get in touch with how you feel about this new role. Spend some quiet time alone and reflect on these questions:

- Do you want or need this role?
- Are you enthusiastic about its possibilities or do you see it as just another obligation, even a burden?
- Do you have the time and desire to maintain a lifelong relationship with your stepgrandchild?
- Are there family issues that may prevent you from establishing a good relationship with your stepgrandchild?
- What is your partner's attitude toward your involvement with your stepgrandchild?
- Are you and your partner in agreement about the type of relationship you want to have with your stepfamily?

After you have reflected on these issues, you will be ready to learn a bit about the dynamics of your new stepfamily and your stepgrandchild's situation.

Does Your Stepgrandchild Need You?

Just *wanting* to be a committed stepgrandparent offers no guarantee that you will enjoy a close relationship with your stepgrandchild. The degree of closeness the two of you achieve also depends on your stepgrandchild's *receptivity* to the relationship. When your stepgrandchild first comes into your family, step back and observe her situation as objectively as you can.

Age Is Important

If your stepgrandchild is a baby, that's a plus. As a baby, she is ignorant of any negative family dynamics and is at a developmental stage where she will welcome all who adore her. The older the child, the more you have to look at her personality, experience, family issues, and developmental state. A five-year-old will relate to you much more easily than a teenager who is certainly preoccupied (if not obsessed) with school, friends, and activities. If she does not seem ready, do not push it. At this point, any open expressions of your desire to establish an emotional attachment are best kept to yourself. Of course, if your stepgrandchild reciprocates your advances, then you can throw yourself wholeheartedly into establishing your relationship.

Shareen, a seventy-six-year-old grandmother who participated in our Grandparent Study summed up the benefits of "the younger the better" syndrome this way: "I got my stepgranddaughter before she could even walk. I'm the only grandmamma she ever had. So I had no competition at all. She needed me, and I needed her. And her parents needed me as well. We all fit together very nicely."

Connecting

There is a time for everything. Be alert to the receptivity of your stepgrandchild. Often eager efforts to forge a bond with an unreceptive stepgrandchild can backfire. "I pushed too hard to get close to Randy," says June, fifty-five, whose stepgrandson is eleven. "I don't have any kids of my own and when he came into my life I was ecstatic. I sent him cards, telephoned, and tried to spend time alone with him when I came to visit, but he just never warmed to me. He lost his mother in a car accident and was still mourning her when I came along. And he had other grandparents he was already close to. He treated me like an intrusive stranger so I finally just backed off. It hurt, but you cannot force someone to love you. I'm hoping when he's older he'll learn to accept me."

Patience is a great virtue. At this stage, patience is your finest virtue. Many childless or grandchildless elders are thrilled to have a stepgrandchild unexpectedly appear in their lives. They immediately plunge into building a relationship with their stepgrandchild, without first evaluating whether their stepgrandchild is receptive to this new relationship. June's example demonstrates that she could have avoided rejection if she had first put herself in Randy's place and recognized that he was dealing with great personal loss on top of adjusting to a new stepfamily. She would have seen that Randy was not open to or available for a new relationship at that time.

Be Aware of the Child's Age and Development

Be especially sensitive to developmental and psychological factors that affect receptivity. For example, if you do become a stepgrandparent to a teenager, expect resistance with issues concerning authority (see Chapter 22, "Adolescence"). That is why stepgrandparents of adolescents have a particularly difficult time when they assume any disciplinary functions. Expect added resistance if a stepgrandchild is still grieving a parent's divorce. On the other hand, as we mentioned earlier, younger children are much easier to establish a bond with. If the parents are very busy, you are a readymade caretaker for the young child.

Be Aware of the Child's Psychological State

Your stepgrandchild may be dealing with many profound psychological issues, including:

- Grieving and emotionally processing a parent's death or divorce
- Accepting first the remarriage of their parent and then the new stepparent

- Divided loyalties because of this remarriage
- Adapting to a family configuration of new siblings, aunts, uncles, and stepgrandparents

These powerful psychological processes can be a significant burden for a child to bear. They can severely impact his receptivity by diminishing his emotional reserves. There will not be much left over for you. In this instance, be careful not to saddle an already emotionally overburdened child with your own needs and expectations. Filled with pain, an older child may resent you as an invader in her family life. Whatever her age, your stepgrandchild needs you to be patient, supportive, and loving. If your stepgrandchild is unreceptive to your overtures, let her come to you. Do not try to win her over or buy her love with gifts. Be there for her when she *is* ready. If you are consistent and reliable, in time you will become an important person in her life.

Understand the Parents

Boris, a forty-two-year-old father, said, "When I remarried, my new mother-in-law told my wife and me that she wanted to be a real grandmother to my kids. I was very touched because up to that point my kids did not really have any grandparents. And I especially liked that she asked our permission first. That showed she respected my feelings. Now she takes the kids out to the movies, goes to their school plays, takes them to the park, even hiking! It's great, too, because my wife and I get time alone together which is a treat. And the kids just love her. She's a great lady. I wish *I'd* had a grandmother like that."

Parents May Be in Turmoil

Boris was lucky to have his mother-in-law step in and help his remarriage get off to a strong start. Stepgrandparents must be sensitive to the great amount of emotional change the parents are undergoing. Death or divorce of a loved one is traumatic. Remarriage, although a happy occasion, also requires a huge emotional adjustment. Sometimes stepchildren will not accept their new stepparent and this can be hard on everyone in the family. Offer your support by being available to listen and give counsel when necessary. Be careful, though, not to force your opinions or ideas on the parents. Make sure parents approve of your relationship with your stepgrandchild. Avoid criticizing your new in-law's parenting techniques. This is counterproductive to establishing closeness with your new family, as you will only end up alienating yourself from everybody involved. The closer you are to the parents, the closer you can be to your stepgrandchild.

Where Does a Stepgrandparent Fit In?

As a stepgrandparent, you might sometimes be confused about how you should act or where you fit into the family picture. You are not alone. Your stepgrandchild will no doubt share your sense of disorientation. Other family members, too, will be overwhelmed and confused when dealing with new steprelationships. It can be awkward and even painful if you and your new in-laws do not share the same expectations about your role in the new family. That's why, without clarification of their position, stepgrandparents can be confused and consequently flounder about and never quite connect with their stepgrandchildren.

Hal, sixty-eight, explains his experience as a stepgrandparent: "I'm sort of in the family, yet kind of outside it. I'm free from some of the hassles of being too close. But I'll throw myself into the thick of things when I feel like it." Mai, a fifty-five-year-old stepgrandmother who spends a great deal of time with her four stepgrandchildren, says of her outsider status: "The children know I love them, but they also had a history together before I came on the scene, and I will never be part of that history. So I am trying to be part of their present and their future. That way, when they're grown up, I *will* be a part of their history."

Assess Your Availability to Your Stepgrandchild

Your desire to establish a bond with your stepgrandchild combined with your physical proximity and emotional availability can affect the strength of your bond. Livia, a fifty-eight-year-old stepgrandmother, is fortunate to live within walking distance of her nine-year-old stepgrandson and has a wonderful relationship with him. "I work at home so every afternoon on his way from school, Paul comes to my house for milk and cookies. His parents work and his real grandparents live far away. If it were not for me, he'd be a latchkey child. I love having him around. He brightens up my day. I know one day he's going to go away to college and I'm sure going to miss him. But for now, he needs me and I need him."

Assess Your Stepgrandchild's Family Situation

A positive relationship between you and the members of your stepgrandchild's family will have a positive influence on your relationship with your stepgrandchild. You need the family's permission to stepgrandparent your stepgrandchild. Esther, eight, is very close to her stepgrandmother, Patricia, fifty-nine, who married her widowed grandfather. In fact, Patricia was Esther's other grandmother's best friend. Patricia fit right into the family because everyone already knew her and loved her. "I lost one grandma, but then I got another one," Esther said. Esther's mother and two aunts were equally happy to welcome Patricia as a stepgrandmother. "I know our situation is kind of rare. I just stepped right in and tried to take up the slack. I already knew Esther so it was very natural for me to become her stepgrandmom. I'll never take the place of her grandmother, but what we have is pretty special, too."

On the other hand, if the family soil is toxic, conflicts and problems may interfere with your relationship with your stepgrandchild and may even end all contact between you. "I like the parents of my new stepmom," says David, eleven. "My new grandpa used to be a professional basketball player. But I'm not allowed to play with him because my mom hates my stepmother and her whole family." Louis, the "new grandpa," says, "I do like David and would enjoy spending time with him, but it would make trouble for my daughter and all hell would break loose. Maybe by the time he's older things will change. Being a stepgrandparent is a tricky thing."

Your Stepgrandchild's Other Grandparents

If your stepgrandchild already has a strong relationship with grandparents, it's important that you respect these relationships. The child's grandparents may feel jealous of the time you are spending with their grandchild. Some grandparents might even feel envious of a stepgrandparent's contact with their grandchild if they themselves are deprived of this contact because of divorce or distance (see Chapter 34, "Between Grandparents"). In this case it is important to discuss this issue with the parents, and, if possible, the other grandparents. Tell your stepgrandchild's other grandparents that you would like to coordinate gift giving during the holiday season and ask them what would work best for them. Demonstrate that you respect their relationship with their grandchild and that you want to add to, not detract from, family harmony. Share your desire to establish a relationship with your stepgrandchild openly with her other grandparents. In most cases, they will appreciate that you reached out to them and are probably even sympathetic to your cause.

If your stepgrandchild has no living grandparents, or lacks a grandparent of the same sex as you, there is a vacancy waiting in this child's heart and soul for you to fill. If your stepgrandchild happens to be your partner's grandchild, your bond with your partner can be strengthened by your shared love of the child.

Family Problems

As a stepgrandparent, you will be challenged by conflicts and problems within your new family, as well as circumstances, such as geographical distance, which can have a negative impact on your family life. I have already mentioned how a good relationship with your stepgrandchild's parents can facilitate a healthy bond between you and your stepgrandchild. But if the parents see you as an outsider or on the wrong side of an acrimonious divorce, then, through no fault of your own, problems can arise. If such a situation exists, it is critical to avoid unrealistic expectations concerning your position in the family on a short-term basis.

Remain flexible, and maintain an optimistic outlook on the future. Many step-grandparents discover that over time their family situation changes for the better as people heal or mature.

Be Part of the Solution

If family problems exist in your stepfamily and parents are resistant to your efforts to have a relationship with your stepgrandchild, sit back and wait until things change. Above all, don't fan the family fire. This might further alienate you from everyone as well as create problems between you and your partner. Stay hopeful and positive. Keep in mind that children grow up, people mature, and attitudes change. If the parents reject you, but still want to maintain their relationship with your partner, then just let it happen. Don't make your partner choose between love for you and love for his or her family. Showing that you are understanding and compassionate will help everyone and ease the situation for your partner. Separating yourself from the problem in this manner will help, rather than hinder, the situation.

Distance Is No Obstacle

Distance can be a formidable obstacle to maintaining close family relationships. Some stepgrandparents give up hope of establishing a relationship with a step-grandchild because of distance. But it is an obstacle that can be overcome, especially when a new stepgrandparent is as determined as Winnie, sixty-one, was when she married Walter, sixty-three. Walter's only child, a daughter, lives a thousand miles away from him. Before Walter married Winnie, he was a worka-holic who rarely saw his daughter and his two grandchildren. After his marriage, Winnie expressed to Walter her desire to visit his family. Walter grudgingly obliged and was surprised to see that Winnie and his family hit it off. Now Winnie visits the family several times a year, sometimes with Walter and sometimes alone. In fact, Winnie has taken the two children to the Foundation for Grandparenting's Grandparent-Grandchild Summer Camp[2] by herself for the past two years. "Walter may come next year," she says, "but it's really not important if he comes or not. This is my time with the kids. And their parents love us coming to the camp together."

Dealing with Your Partner's Attitudes and Behavior

Your partner's family relationships will affect you too. If your partner is feuding with a parent or a parent's spouse, it's probably going to be difficult for you to have access to a stepgrandchild or become close to the family. If your partner is removed from his or her family, it's likely that you will be too. But then again, some stepgrandparents have been of great help to conflicted families.

Lisa, for example, intervened directly to help her stepfamily. When Lisa, fifty-four, married Carl, sixty-seven, Carl didn't get along well with his only daughter, Alice. Because of this Carl was not as close to his grandchildren as he would have liked. When Lisa became friendly with Alice and her stepgrandchildren, it gave Carl an excuse to visit his grandchildren more often and he subsequently strengthened his bond with Alice as well.

Some people assume an attitude of watchful waiting. Roger, a fifty-six-year-old stepgrandfather, married Leslie, fifty-seven, who is feuding with her only son and his wife. Because Roger does not want to get caught in the crossfire he is waiting to approach his new stepfamily until things improve. "I don't want to cross Leslie, but I sure wish she and her son would work out their problems," he says. "I'd like to get to know him and his children. You know, be a family. I've been talking to Leslie about it and told her I'd like to hang out with the grandkids once in a while. She said she'd think about it. I think I planted a seed there. I just have to make sure I keep watering it."

By making an effort to understand the dynamics of your stepfamily, and by being aware of your own feelings as well as those of your stepgrandchild, you

---

2. For information about the camp visit www.grandparenting.org.

can make the best of what may sometimes be a challenging family situation. In most cases, however, there will be room for you as a loving friend in your stepgrandchild's life.

The Silver Lining

Research supports the notion that stepgrandparents can have a meaningful loving relationship with their stepgrandchild. Indeed, in one study, researchers asked twenty-five newly remarried couples about how their children and stepchildren got along with their spouse's parents (stepgrandparents). All the couples reported that everyone got along quite well. Most of the stepgrandchildren viewed their stepgrandparent not only as someone they cared for, but also as someone they respected. In fact, the study reported that "[many] stepgrandchildren maintain contact with their stepgrandparent beyond high school; the majority of respondents wanted more contact with stepgrandparents; almost half the respondents viewed their relationship to their stepgrandparent as important; the relationship was perceived both personally and socially" (Cherlin & Furstenburg 1986).

If you are having trouble forging a relationship with your stepgrandchild, take comfort because these studies show that even when children are slow to warm up, the relationship can still blossom. My own studies and clinical experience, the work of others in many fields, and the existence of intergenerational programs nationwide demonstrate that old and young people are naturally attracted to one another and share a mutual need for each other. This works to your advantage. If you go slowly and make yourself available without asking for any immediate reward or feedback, the chances are good that you will be able to fulfill your desire to be a lifelong friend, mentor, caregiver, and role model for your stepgrandchild.

GUIDELINES

Here are some step-by-step guidelines that will help you be an effective, loving, and involved stepgrandparent.

- Examine your thoughts and feelings about being a stepgrandparent. What are your own expectations, dreams, wishes, and needs? How much energy do you want to put into this role? What are the returns for you and for others in your family? How does your partner come into the picture?
- Educate yourself about stepfamilies and stepgrandparenting. Learn all you can about how stepfamilies work. Observe other stepfamilies in operation. Learn from their successes and from their mistakes.
- Assess the new family. Put yourself in everyone else's shoes. Ask your new family members individually how you can enhance the family system. Let them know you acknowledge, understand, and respect what they are going through.
- Objectively observe your own feelings and thoughts about your new family situation and the people involved. Separate your own biases and preconceived ideas from the reality of the situation. Remain nonjudgmental.
- Differentiate your stepgrandparenting role from the other roles you play.
- Remember that your relationship with the parents of your stepgrandchild will profoundly affect your relationship.
- Watch and wait. At first, stay calmly at the periphery of the family system. Let things settle down. Be an available presence. Remember that children have a difficult time after a parent's death, divorce, or remarriage; they are trying to make sense of their new family configuration.
- Be a source of peace and pleasure. Stay in a positive role. Be close and available to those who reach out or need you. Stay at a loving distance from those who are negative, but try not to react to or perpetuate their negativity. Maintain a relationship with the child's other grandparents and parents.
- Confront challenges and use them to grow. Set positive examples for the whole family to follow.

- If you already have grandchildren, you may not have the time or inclination to get deeply involved with a stepgrandchild. If this is the case, keep in mind that it can be very painful for a stepchild to be treated differently than her stepsiblings. When handing out gifts during the holidays, for example, make sure all grandchildren get something, including the stepgrandchildren.

CONCLUSION

The role of stepgrandparent is part learning, part perseverance, part commitment, and all love. It is also an adventure. When undertaken with sensitivity, tenderness, and compassion, stepgrandparenting can be a source of great joy for you and the children you will come to love.

RESOURCES

The Stepfamily Foundation, www.stepfamily.org, offers helpful information about all aspects of the stepfamily.

PART 6

Grandparents, Community, and Heritage

As grandparent consciousness grows, grandparents will have an increasing voice and role in their community and society. Over the years, the Foundation for Grandparenting has designed and implemented—both independently and in partnership with other organizations—many programs that involve grandparents nationally and in the community. Chapter 47 discusses the national holiday celebrating grandparenting. Chapter 48 describes several programs that grandparents can initiate in their local communities.

National Grandparent's Day

G randparent's Day was first established in 1978 and is celebrated every September on the Sunday after Labor Day. Designating Grandparent's Day as a separate and distinct holiday brings attention to grandparenting as an important role, identifies grandparents' importance as an emotional resource for the family, reinforces the public's consciousness of the vital connection between grandparents and grandchildren, and lends credibility to the value of elders in our society.

Since its inception, Grandparent's Day has become a popular holiday that, for the most part, has remained immune to commercialization. Some media, schools, communities, and a variety of religious institutions have implemented special festivities and observances. The low-key noncommercial nature of the holiday is a reflection of the intent of its founders.

History of Grandparent's Day

Although the origins of Grandparent's Day remain somewhat controversial, several key people have made a major contribution to the establishment of this official national holiday. The first recorded state-mandated Grandparent's Day came as the result of the outstanding dedication of Marian McQuade of Oak Hill, West Virginia. After witnessing too many neglected and ignored elders in nursing homes, she decided that elders needed more respect and recognition. In 1973, she convinced Governor Arch Moore to issue a proclamation establishing West Virginia as the first state with a special Grandparent's Day. She then embarked on a campaign to persuade politicians, including the president of the United States, of the need for this holiday.

At about the same time that Marian McQuade was on her crusade, Louella M. Davison, the founder of Grandparents Anonymous and a pioneer in the grandparent-visitation movement, succeeded in having a statewide Grandparent's/Grandchildren's Day designated in Michigan in 1977. Also at the same time, businessman Michael Goldgar became concerned that although most of the nursing home residents in his area were grandparents they were not publicly recognized, or honored, as such. Goldgar decided to join the campaign for a national Grandparent's Day. In the ensuing national networking effort, many other individuals and organizations joined the campaign. The Foundation for Grandparenting was one of them. In 1978, Mrs. McQuade prevailed upon President Jimmy Carter to designate the Sunday after Labor Day as Grandparent's Day. Today, Mrs. McQuade's family continues to promote the spirit of Grandparent's Day (see "Resources").

The Proper Spirit of Grandparent's Day

The philosophy and message of Grandparent's Day is a blend of love, caring, commitment, and selflessness—the basic ingredients of *grandparent power*. To be truly meaningful, Grandparent's Day should be a time for grandparents to celebrate their worth, savor their importance and demonstrate to their families and communities just how valuable they are. It should be a day to gather families together, to talk about their lives together, to examine new options, to forgive, and to heal old wounds. It is a precious time to reaffirm family connections and love.

Stepgrandparents and long-distance grandparents should take the time to reach out to their grandchildren and other family members on Grandparent's

Day, to let them know they are thinking of them, that they are conscious of their roles as grandparents within the family.

Grandparent's Day is a day for giving, not receiving. Although other holidays like Mother's and Father's Day have been highly commercialized, the founders did not want the same fate to befall Grandparent's Day. There are already more than enough holidays throughout the year for gift giving. Instead of store-bought gifts, think about giving a token of endearment, such as a homemade children's drawing, instead. These are more in keeping with the day's theme of emotional and spiritual celebration.

GUIDELINES

The next time Grandparent's Day rolls around here are some tips on how you can make the holiday meaningful and memorable for yourself and your family.

- Reflect on your role as a grandparent. What does it mean to you?
- Think about what you would like to do with your family on Grandparent's Day.
- Have family members gather together on Grandparent's Day. Share hopes, dreams, problems, and solutions.
- Plan for the future of the family and discuss the plan with family members.
- Forgive and forget. Make a commitment to heal old wounds.
- If you are a long-distance grandparent, contact your family on Grandparent's Day. Send your grandchildren something you made for them.
- Remember that mature grandparents are not concerned with what their family does for them, but rather with what they can do for their family. Try to support, offer encouragement, and help out. Caring and loving are what grandparents do best.
- Celebrate the holiday in your community. Start a Grandparent's Day celebration in schools, community centers, local organizations, and places of worship.

- Coordinate an act of charity on Grandparent's Day. Help the homeless, visit someone in a hospice, or volunteer to read to children at your public library.

CONCLUSION

Grandparent's Day is a day for reflection for grandparents and elders to give to their families and communities, and for families and communities to celebrate grandparents. When you devote this day to give of yourself; share your family's hopes, dreams, and values; and have fun with your grandchildren, you will set a marvelous example for future generations. This day offers a chance to focus; it's a time to think about yourself as a grandparent and the importance of this role in your life. Enjoy this special holiday.

RESOURCES

For more information visit www.grandparents-day.com.

CHAPTER 48

Grandparents and the Community

G randparents' presence in the community is indispensable. Included in this chapter are some programs that grandparents can implement at the local level. By implementing these programs you will raise public consciousness and rally other grandparents to identify community needs and respond to them. Whether you live in a city or a small town, you can bring grandparent power to bear in your community. By doing so, you will benefit all generations.

Grandparent's Day in the Schools

An exciting way to make a difference and raise grandparent consciousness in your community is to organize a Grandparent's Day in your local schools. This special day offers grandparents a chance to strut their stuff while getting a glimpse of their grandchildren's daily lives. It also offers grandchildren the opportunity to show off their grandparents to peers and teachers.

Ever since the holiday was launched back in the 1970s, many schools nationwide, and even internationally, have started to celebrate a Grandparent's Day (or week). If your grandchild's school does not have one, you can take the lead and start one. It is really quite simple and a lot of fun!

What to Do

Starting a Grandparent's Day in your local schools is easier than you think. That's because once the idea is announced, people are always eager to get involved. Even bureaucrats! Because they are grandparents too! So, if you are apprehensive about dealing with your local school's bureaucracy, you will be happy to learn that most school administrators are delighted to work together with parents and grandparents to create this event for their school.

Keep in mind that Grandparent's Day in the schools is a community event. Though the idea may seem intimidating at first, there are many people, many of them with expertise in areas you do not know about, who will pitch in and help you so that everything goes smoothly. There also are many agencies within your community that would be happy to sponsor such an event.

The first thing to do is spread the word and rally grandparents, parents, and grandchildren, as well as local businesspeople, media, and community agencies. Here are some suggestions that you can tailor to your own specific situation.

Classes

To rally the local grandparent community, you might want to offer some classes. Starting a grandparent class in your community is easy. You can even use this book as your text for the course. First, spread the word that you want to start a grandparent class. You can accomplish this through word of mouth in your neighborhood, a newspaper ad, posters in stores, or an announcement in your place of worship. Here are some hints for the class.

- Convene the class twice monthly. Each session should be two hours long.
- Use each chapter in this book as a topic for a class. You can go through the book sequentially or skip around.
- Open the class with a period during which people can share personal experiences or grandparent-related events in the news.
- Have a different class member assigned to present the topic each week.

- After the presentation, discuss the topic as a group. Have class members share personal stories and experience related to the topic.
- Close the class by appointing a class member to present the next topic. Alert the class to look for supplementary material (see www.grandparenting.org) or other sources (for example, newspaper stories).

Planning

Form a planning committee consisting of your grandchild, the school principal, teachers, the PTA, and assorted community leaders. Identify a date for the event. Make it at least six months away so that long-distance grandparents have the time to plan and make arrangements to attend. Get a publicity committee together and spread the word! Encourage teachers to discuss the event with the students and take their suggestions about how they can incorporate Grandparent's Day into their classes. This will get the children excited about the event.

Good teachers usually try and weave Grandparent's Day in the school into the educational process by involving children in special learning projects, creating showcase programs for students to enact for or with the grandparents, and allowing grandparents to teach and display their skills and talents. Art shows, plays, even a grandparent-grandchild choir are great ideas for this special day. Have children volunteer their grandparents to teach classes. A grandparent who is a physicist can teach a math class, a grandparent from another country can give a geography or language lesson, a grandparent who is also a war veteran can spice up a history lesson with firsthand accounts and personal experiences.

Communication

It is vital that everybody in the school district be excited about their Grandparent's Day. Get the ball rolling with your grandchild first. Have your grandchild and her classmates work with you in planning the day. Have a meeting at your home with the children or visit the classroom. Classmates can then encourage other children to invite their grandparents and ask them to teach, share experiences, tell stories, and show off their talents. Have the principal and members of the PTA write to all the students' families explaining the event and inviting all grandparents to participate. Furnish everyone with a list of potential activities in which grandparents might want to participate. Be open to suggestions and feedback. Remember that your enthusiasm is contagious.

Events

On the eve of Grandparent's Day, organize a kick-off dinner with children, parents, grandparents, teachers, and community members. This can be a catered, sit-down dinner or simply snacks and refreshments with music so that everyone can dance. Square dancing is a great activity for grandparents and grandchildren to do together. Be sure to invite interesting speakers and/or entertainers to liven up the proceedings and set the mood for Grandparent's Day. It is ideal if some of the grandparents provide the entertainment, but lacking that, hiring a small band or a DJ, is an option. Don't forget to invite the local press as well.

Opening Program

Begin Grandparent's Day with a school assembly. A speaker should give a brief, upbeat, humorous and inspirational talk. When the assembly has concluded, have children give grandparents a tour of the school. It is best to assign a central room where grandparents and grandchildren can congregate during the day. Following the tour, the children will have their normal day at school with grandparents attending classes and eating lunch with them in the cafeteria. End the school day with an outdoor barbecue, square dance, play, or other festive event.

The Day After

The day after the event, have teachers question the children about their experience and ask for input about making Grandparent's Day even better next year.

When Grandparents Cannot Attend

There are always grandparents who, for one reason or another, are unable to attend their Grandparent's Day in the school. Find out from teachers which grandparents will not be attending and assign other local elders to act as surrogate grandparents. Some grandparents who attend make it a point to "adopt" for the day a friend of their grandchild or another child whose grandparents cannot attend. Senior centers and community and religious organizations are great sources for older volunteers who might want to act as surrogate grandparents on Grandparent's Day.

GUIDELINES

Here are some guidelines for making your Grandparent's Day a success.

- Get local people excited about Grandparent's Day in the school.
- Organize your planning group.
- Coordinate your activities with the school curriculum.
- Plan your Grandparent's Day in the school well in advance so that long-distance grandparents can make arrangements to attend.
- Find out which children's grandparents cannot attend and arrange for another grandparent or elder to act as their surrogate.
- Reach out to others for the support and encouragement you need to make this special day everything it can be.
- Your enthusiasm is contagious. Spread it around.

CONCLUSION

Grandparent's Day in the school is a wonderful opportunity for the young and old to come together and have fun. If your local school does not already have one such a program, it is a relatively easy matter to get one started. Your grandchildren will be especially proud that you are the one(s) who started their school's Grandparent's Day!

CHAPTER 49

Making Memories

Keeping a Memory Chest

D o you have antiques that were passed on to you from earlier generations? Did your parents keep family photos and mementos? Perhaps they even bronzed your baby booties and passed them on to you. Do you like to forage through family memorabilia? If so, you are just the right person to create a wonderful memory chest for your grandchildren.

"My mother saved my baby bonnet," says Anne, sixty-nine, "and my granddaughter is fascinated with it. 'It's so small! How did it fit on your head?' she said when I gave it to her and told her to pass it on to her granddaughter one day." Mementos such as these are more than just conversation pieces for you and your grandchild. Indeed, they are memories from the past that can be passed on into the future. By building a memory chest, you create a lovely legacy for your grandchildren and the other generations to come.

Creating a Memory Chest

You can start building your memory chest at any time, even before you have grandchildren. To begin, choose an interesting or attractive-looking container— something with character. Antique stores, flea markets, garage sales, and estate sales are great sources for containers of this kind. You could even have one custom-built or build one yourself. The more it looks like a mysterious treasure chest the better!

Now you can begin your hunt for the keepsakes that will go inside your memory chest. These include memories of your own past and new memories from your grandchild's life. Objects with special meaning make the best memories. The more unusual the object, the more fun it is to share with your grandchild. It might be anything: a wedding ring, a high school diploma, a trophy, playbills from your grandchild's school plays, baby booties, a pacifier, baby blankets, family photos, historical memorabilia, record albums of favorite artists, a hundred-year-old tool, a videotape of a beloved movie, your grandchild's Little League uniform, theater ticket stubs, your granddaughter's prom dress (or even perhaps your own)!

Select items that will have special meaning to future generations. When a new grandchild arrives, commemorate the birth by buying a newspaper and stowing it in the memory chest. Purchasing special coins or a commemorative stamp on the day of a grandchild's birth and storing it in the memory chest is a good idea. Family photos and videotapes make a vital pictorial history for your great-grandchildren to enjoy.

A Lifelong Project

Memories are made every day. That's why it's a good idea to keep your memory chest growing as an ongoing activity for you and your grandchild. Have him add regularly to the chest. An object that reminds you both of a special time you spent together will be especially meaningful. Anne, twenty-two, says, "My grandmother and I spent a summer on Cape Cod when I was thirteen. We gathered seashells on the beach and when my grandmother got home, she put them on her bureau. She told me that way she would remember our trip every day. She kept those shells there until she died. Now I have those shells in a box I keep in my closet along with my grandmother's other things."

The next time your grandchild comes to visit, sit down and go through your memory chest together. Talk about each item, the meaning it has for you both in the present and its possible significance for future generations. She will always remember!

GUIDELINES

Here are a few guidelines to help you get started on your own memory chest.

- Communicate to your grandchild the importance of the memory chest.
- Shop for a "chest" together.
- Make the maintenance of the memory chest a shared activity with your grandchild.
- Choose the items you put in your memory chest with future generations in mind.
- Be creative and have fun!

CONCLUSION

Creating a memory chest is an enjoyable way to record your family history and ensuring that future generations will have firsthand knowledge of the items and objects that filled your and your grandchild's lives. Someday your grandchild will go through the chest with her own grandchildren and tell them all about you and the time you spent together. What better legacy is there?

CHAPTER 50

Legacy

N ow that you have read this book, I hope you are proud to be a grand-parent. I hope you feel more educated and informed about yourself as a grandparent. I further hope you have raised your own grandparent con-sciousness, forged a strong and meaningful grandparent identity, and recognize how important and influential you can be to your family and community. I trust that you have begun to shed any stereotypes about old age our society has taught you and that you are ready to look at grandparenting in a new way. After all, we have so much to do.

Our mandate is to show the way for future generations and to leave a legacy of love and commitment to our grandchildren. Ours is a new identity and image of grandparenthood for future generations. We must show our progeny what grandparent power is all about. To do this we have to accomplish some basic tasks.

First, grandparenting must be unhooked from the concept of old. Old is not viewed as a noble condition in our society. To be old in the United States today means to be useless. This is the wrong label for active and vital grandpar-ents. Our generation of grandparents must jettison this outdated notion. Grand-parenting is not a function of age; it is a state of vitality. And vitality has many forms—physical, emotional, and spiritual. Let us replace the notion of being old with the notion of being vital. And let's tell everyone about it!

Next, we must create a cultural rite of passage and celebration of grandparenting. Other cultures have noble denotations for grandparent. In Japan, grandmothers wear red to announce their status. We need something similar in the United States. A national annual Grandparent's Day is only a small beginning. *Every day should be Grandparent's Day.* Schools, religious institutions, and community agencies need to involve grandparents more and intergenerationalize their organizations. Grandchildren should be encouraged to talk more publicly about their grandparents and to invite them to participate in their world. Grandparenthood as well as grandchildhood must be understood as an important part of a person's psychological and social identity.

Then we need to find new areas in which to apply our grandparent power—this power of love, wisdom, caring, unselfishness, courage, and dedication—to make a better world for the generations to come. We must do this in the home, workplace, and community. Our job as grandparents is to care for our juniors, to assure the health and well-being of the young, to fight the good fight. To do this we must forge a strong grandparent identity, work hard to create a healthy family life, and improve our communication and relationships.

In conclusion, let us build our legacy by making this the century of grandparent power. Let us establish our place in the culture. As grandparents we must come to society's rescue. Let us assess what needs fixing and get to work to enhance the lives of our children, our grandchildren, and our friends and neighbors. By following our example, they will all become powerful grandparents, too.

We are an important hope to make the world a better place. What else are our later years for? We can only fulfill our promise by being conscious of our role, and persistent in our actions. Only then can we claim a hallowed place that grandparents deserve in society—a place earned through wisdom and dedication and maintained by deeds, not words.

Let's do it!

APPENDIX 1

Grandparent Books and Films

Other Books by Arthur Kornhaber

Those who are interested in the field of grandparenting, or just want to refamiliarize themselves with the basics, will benefit from reading Dr. Kornhaber's other works. His most popular books are available at libraries and bookstores and through on-line vendors (Amazon.com. and Powells.com).

Grandparent Power (1994) applies the results of more than twenty years of research into the grandparent-grandchild relationship. This easy-to-read book is full of practical advice to help grandparents understand the importance of their grandparent identity. The book addresses many situations facing today's grandparents: establishing a grandparent identity, being an effective grandparent, and understanding the diverse roles of grandparents.

Contemporary Grandparenting (1996), the first text of its kind, synthesizes the current knowledge about grandparents' identity, the drive to grandparent, and grandparents' roles in the family and society. Offering a contemporary and perceptive view, this comprehensive volume is especially written for grandparents who want to understand their role in depth, and also for professionals who deal with grandparent-related issues—teachers, therapists, attorneys, judges, and governmental workers. This acclaimed book is also used in academic settings and as a basic text for grandparenting courses. You can order a copy from Sage Press by calling (805) 499-9774.

Grandparents / Grandchildren: The Vital Connection (1980) explains and explores the unique emotional attachments between grandparents and grandchildren. It also examines the loss of those attachments and the effects of that loss on children, older people, and society. Dr. Kornhaber's contention—borne out by more than three years of in-depth personal interviews with more than three hundred children and as many grandparents—is that in terms of emotional power and influence the bond between grandparents and grandchildren is second only to the parent-child bond. The groundbreaking research in this book, in addition to raising grandparent consciousness and positive grandparent action, is used as a theoretical basis to support the grandparent movement in America as well as efforts to establish grandparent visitation laws and to recognize and support grandparents raising grandchildren. Initially published by Doubleday, the book is now available through Transaction Press. You can order a copy directly from the publisher by calling (732) 445-2280.

Between Parents and Grandparents (1986), published by St. Martin's Press, deals with the relationship between parents and grandparents and how it affects the grandparent-grandchild bond. Included are helpful hints about how to identify conflicts and problems and intervene to correct them.

More Grandparenting Books

The Grandfather Thing, by Saul Turtletaub. This is a very funny book by a comedy writer who is a multiple Emmy Award winner. You can order a copy directly from Tallfellow Press by calling (818) 865-1096. Highly recommended.

Attending Your Grandchild's Birth, by Carolynn Bauer Zorn. This book sets forth what you can expect and what you can do during the delivery of your grandchild. We have always recommended that grandparents be there when the grandchild is born as long as their presence goes along with the parents' wishes. This book provides pertinent information and guidelines about this process. The book is also available in virtual form at www.1stBooks.com.

Grand-Stories, compiled and edited by Ernie Wendell. This book honors the powerful bond between grandparents and grandchildren. There are 114 stories covering a gamut of situations and emotions in a multitude of categories. It's inspirational and entertaining reading. You can order a copy from Friendly Oaks Publications by calling (830) 569-3586.

Halmoni's Day, by Edna Coe Bercaw; illustrated by Robert Hunt. Jennifer's grandmother Halmoni is visiting all the way from Korea—and she has arrived just in time for Grandparent's Day at Jennifer's school. What happens is interesting and informative and carries a warm and loving message. This is a great book to read with your grandchild! The illustrations are lovely as well. We give this book our Foundation for Grandparenting's seal of approval. It is published by Dial Books For Young Readers (New York, NY: Penguin Putnam).

Learning from Little Ones: Tales from a Grandfather's Heart, by Gilman Smith. The author has learned that little children give us gifts when we interact with them. This book contains lovely and inspiring stories about these gifts. The spirit of the book is well summed up in the words of Dr. Linus S. Pecaut, who reflects "my Grandpa went fishing to be with me—catching fish had nothing to do with it." It is published by Papaco Press.

The 12 Rules of Grandparenting, by Susan Kettman. Checkmark Books brings us this straightforward book filled with advice on developing a positive attitude, baby-sitting, fun projects, dealing with grandchildren, dealing with family issues, and more.

The Joy of Grandma's Cooking, by Clarice Carlson Orr. Ah, the memories of dinner at Grandma's house in days gone by. Grandmother and old friend Clarice Carlson Orr stirs up those nostalgic memories with her new cookbook. The book is a collection of approximately two hundred recipes most of which are accompanied by short stories. For example, there's the story of how the hog growers association crowned Aunt Amanda the Pie Queen of Hanson County, South Dakota, for her piecrust made with lard. Apart from the high-calorie content, the book is excellent and perhaps will move you to pass on these, and some of your own recipes, to your children and grandchildren.

New-Fashioned Grandparenting, by Julia Nelson. Author Julia Nelson shows us an innovative way to become better grandparents. Using an entrepreneurial model she applies it to a practical delivery system for transferring one's wisdom and experience to grandchildren through a "birthday program." This book will be very helpful for grandparents who want to become proactive and involved in their grandparent roles. To order from Allyn Group Publications, call (800) 247-6553.

The Nanas and the Papas, by Kathryn and Alan Zullo. When the Zullos were going to be grandparents, they were thrilled. "What do we really know about being grandparents?" they thought. "We're nothing like our gray-haired grandmas and grandpas." To answer their questions, for themselves and other grandparents, they have written a fun and informative book. It is well written and full of heartfelt advice for dealing with today's adult children, different family forms, technology, and financial issues. This book will help you make the most of your relationship with your grandchild. It makes a great holiday gift for parents and grandparents. It is published by Andrews McMeel.

The Essential Grandparent: A Guide To Making a Difference, by Dr. Lillian Carson. The author, a psychologist in private practice in Los Angeles and Santa Barbara, gives plenty of practical advice on grandparenting. Chapters on "The Essential Grandparent" and "The Joys of Giving" make an important contribution to the grandparent literature. The book is published by Health Communications Inc.

Grandparent-Grandchild Interactive Books

Kelly Bear Books "Feelings," by Leah Davis; illustrated by Joy Davies. This book is designed for children and adults to read together. Kelly Bear asks questions that encourage children to share their thoughts and feelings. Reading this book with your grandchild can be fun—and useful. The book is published by Kelly Bear Productions. For further information log on to www.kellybear.com.

Grand Activities, by Shari Sasser. Grand Activities contains more than 150 fun activities for grandparents to do with grandchildren. With each activity, a keepsake is produced. Ideas are creative, simple and fun—for example, creating family portraits by drawing faces on cracked eggshells and growing grass inside for hair. Sounds like lots of fun! You can order the book directly from Career Press, 3 Tice Road, Franklin Lakes, NJ 07417.

Grandloving: Making Memories with Your Grandchildren, by Sue Johnson and Julie Carlson. This is a peppy, upbeat, easy-to-read sourcebook on how grandparents can have fun and make memories with their grandchildren. It is chock-full of suggestions for innovative and inexpensive activities for grandparents and their grandchildren to do together. You can order the book from Heartstrings Press, 20 Birling Gap, Fairport, NY 14450; or call (800) 262-1546.

Grandparents Raising Grandchildren

Second Time Around, by Joan Callander. This book is based on the author's personal and professional experience. Grandparents will find it both relevant and helpful. It is published by Bookpartners (Wilsonville, Oregon).

Grandparents as Parents, by Sylvie de Toledo and Deborah Edler Brown. This is an excellent resource book for grandparents who are raising their grandchildren. Helpful hints concerning getting through the red tape, support groups, and many other aspects of this unique, complex, rewarding, and challenging experience. It is published by Guilford.

To Grandma's House We . . . Stay, by Sally Houtman, M.S. This book guides grandparents through the turbulent waters of grandparenting—and acting as surrogate parents. The author describes the many aspects of this experience and offers helpful advice in dealing with the challenges that face grandparents who devote themselves to helping and healing their grandchildren. It is published by Studio 4 Productions.

Bubbe & Gram: My Two Grandmothers, by Joan C. Hawxhurst. This is a charming book about a grandchild with both a Christian and a Jewish grandmother. Full of love, understanding, and compassion, this is a great book to read with any grandchild. It is published by Dovetail Publishing.

Grandparenting: A New Challenge, by Helene Gonski. Psychologist Helene Gonski was born in South Africa and migrated to Australia in 1961 with her husband and four children. The grandmother of ten, she is well qualified to write this book. Created for an Australian audience, the book deals with a wide variety of issues; including joys, problems, communication, and more. You can order the book from Sally Milner Publishing Pty. Ltd., 558 Darling Street, Rozelle NSW 2039, Australia.

That's What Grandfathers Are For, by Arlene Uslander. This is a charming book of poetry that touches the core of what happens between grandparents and grandchildren. This poem speaks for the book. "I had an old, old fiddle from when I was a boy, and when I'd play a tune or two, your face lit up with joy. You clapped your hands and stamped your feet; we had a good old time. And if I played some sour notes . . . you never seemed to mind. No sooner did I play one song, and then you'd say, 'Papa, more!' So I'd raise my bow and tap my toe, (That's what grandfathers are for.)" You can order the book from Chicago Spectrum Press, 1571 Sherman Ave. (Annex C), Evanston, IL 60201.

Grandpa Told Me: Things Your Father Meant to Tell You, by Joe Baker. The author has written a creative book full of wisdom and down-to-earth relevant advice "not just to my grandsons, but also to those of you who did not get a chance to know your own grandfathers, and to those who knew their grandfathers but are not real sure of just what it was their grandfathers told them or were trying to tell them." There are sections giving advice on money, education, clothes, recreation, possessions, and lots more. The book is available from Joe Baker & Associates, 14152 Chagall, Irvine, CA 92714-1806.

Creative Grandparenting Across the Miles: Ideas for Sharing Love, Faith, and Family Traditions, by Patricia L. Fry. The author, a freelance writer and long-distance grandmother of six, offers suggestions to help grandparents keep their connection to their grandchildren over the miles. This book contains innovative tips for visiting, creative correspondence, and great ideas for how to keep communication going with fax, video, and E-mail. The section on maintaining family traditions is especially important. The book is available from Liguori. Write to One Liguori Drive, Liguori, MO 63057-9999.

From Grandma with Love: A Legacy of Values, edited by Toni Thomas. Experience is the great teacher. What we learn is passed on to the young as stories. Our personal stories are part of our legacy. This broad-ranging work contains stories from real-life experience, related by grandmothers from all over the nation, that celebrate enduring human values across gender, race, religion and ethnicity. The stories are warm, highly readable, and adaptable for reading to (or with) grandchildren. You can purchase a copy from ALTI Publishing, P.O. Box 28025, San Diego, CA 92198-1616.

The Long-Distance Grandmother, by Selma Wasserman. This 1998 book contains plenty of ideas about how to stay in touch with your grandchild over distance. It is highly recommended for all long-distance grandparents who want to remain an important part of their grandchildren's lives. It's available from Hartley & Marks Publishers, Box 147, Point Roberts, WA 98281.

Research and Professional Services

Handbook of Grandparenthood, edited by Professor Maximiliane E. Szinovac. This new book is chock-full of interesting articles covering a broad range of grandparenting topics. Especially important are chapters on ethnic grandparenting, gender variations, research, and grandparent programs. This book is a valuable resource for keeping up to date with the rapidly expanding world of grandparenting. It's available from Greenwood Press.

See also Dr. Kornhaber's *Contemporary Grandparenting*.

Films

Grandparent Productions offers films produced by the Foundation for Grandparenting to promote the importance of grandparents and intergenerational relationships. The following two films can be ordered from the Foundation for Grandparenting. E-mail your request to gpfound@grandparenting.org.

Kartenspieler. Produced in cooperation with the Foundation for Grandparenting and written and directed by Chantal Marie, this award-winning comic film chronicles how a simple card-shark grandmother, Maryasha, saves her grandson from the clutches of gamblers. The film stars Shifra Lehrer and Marty Ingels.

Click Three Times. Produced in cooperation with the Foundation for Grandparenting, this award-winning film was written and directed by Victoria Sampson. Isabel Sanford stars in the magical tale of a mentally challenged young woman who escapes her parents' incessant arguing by retreating to a garage where she draws rainbows. A bag lady appears on the scene, dons the identity of a fairy godmother, and saves the day.

The Foundation for Grandparenting: Origin, Purpose, and History

The Foundation for Grandparenting was born as a result of the important findings of the Grandparent Study begun in 1970. The Grandparent Study is the longest ongoing study of the relationship between grandparents, grandchildren, and parents. Over the years, the study has evolved to include an examination of three- and four-generation relationships (child, parent, grandparent, and great-grandparent), as well as investigation of the roles nonbiological elders play for children (especially those at-risk).

Purpose of the Foundation for Grandparenting

Through research, program development, education, communication, and networking, the Foundation for Grandparenting seeks to accomplish these goals.

- Explore the social, psychological, and physiological benefits of intergenerational relationships, and especially the grandparent-grandchild bond.
- Manifest grandparent power by creating new roles, programs, and metaphors for useful and meaningful aging.

- Promote the roles and functions of grandparenting for those without biological grandchildren.
- Establish an international community of grandparents dedicated to changing the world for the better.

Selected Findings

Over the years, the Foundation for Grandparenting has gathered information about the roles and functions involved in grandparenting. Here are some of the organization's findings.

- The grandparent-grandchild bond is a separate and unique human relationship; it is second only to the parent-child bond in emotional importance.
- Grandparents and grandchildren have a complex relationship that comprises biological, psychological, intellectual, social, and spiritual dimensions of human experience.
- The grandparent-grandchild relationship is an illuminating relationship that is a repository of unconditional, nonjudgmental love.
- The grandparent function is built on basic truths that may be expressed differently in different societies.
- Grandchildren learn things from their grandparents they can learn nowhere else. Contact with a beloved elder enhances a child's emotional, physical, and spiritual health.
- The roles of grandparent offer a template for elders to live meaningful and useful lives. Some roles are: living ancestor, family historian, nurturer, mentor, spiritual guide, wizard, and crony. Grandparents provide their grandchildren with a role model for the child's future grandparenthood and perception of aging.
- The grandparenting role shifts and changes during the life cycle and responds to differing needs of the growing child.
- Enacting the role of grandparents helps to maintain the mental and physical health of aging individuals and fosters a positive

identity and a sense of usefulness, empowerment, and meaning to later life.

■ Many of the functions of biological grandparents can be carried out by nonbiological grandparents.

A Review of the Work of the Foundation for Grandparenting

1970–1978　Preliminary research

1978　Beginning of effort to implement consciousness-raising projects and programs

Publication of *Grandparents-Grandchildren: The Vital Connection*, Arthur Kornhaber, M.D., and Kenneth L. Woodward, which explained the nature and complexity of the grandparent-grandchild relationship and its meaning for all family members

1979　Establishment of Grandparent's Day in the Schools

1980　Establishment of the Expectant Grandparent Program in hospitals (collaboration with LaMaze)

Establishment of the Foundation for Grandparenting, and conception of the Grandparent Movement, dedicated to creating an international community of grandparents to better the family and society

Publication of more than fifty articles and speaking appearances nationally and internationally to raise consciousness about the grandparent movement

1981　Basic research to support the establishment of grandparent-visitation laws nationally

Hearing before the U.S. House of Representatives after which laws were enacted in all states and are ongoing

1982   Community initiative reaching out to at-risk children

Establishment of Grandparent Connection programs in schools, religious organizations, communities, etc.

Establishment of surrogate grandparent programs and mentoring

1983   Establishment of grandparent classes

Collaboration with universities and individuals to offer courses Curriculum development

1984   Publication of *Between Parents and Grandparents*, by Arthur Kornhaber, M.D., an exploration of the complexities of the relationship between parents and grandparents, and its effect on the grandparent-grandchild relationship

1985   Inaugural Grandparent-Grandchild Summer Camp as a creative project to foster the vital connection between long-distance grandparents and grandchildren

1986   Initial publication of *Vital Connections*, the quarterly newsletter of the Foundation for Grandparenting

1987   Addressing the issue of grandparents raising grandchildren, hearing before the U.S. Senate Committee on Aging

Consciousness raising through media, professional symposia

Consultation and advocacy for the grandparent movement in academic, educational, legal, political, and religious areas

1988   Promoting awareness of grandparents raising grandchildren

Organization of groups with Barbara Kirkland

Initiation of the Grandparent Clinical Project for at-risk and behaviorally disordered children at the St. Francis Academy Treatment Centers

Publication of the book *Spirit*, by Arthur Kornhaber—an effort, among other issues, to explore and explain the spiritual and emotional aspects of the grandparent-grandchild relationship

1990   Collaboration and consultation with intergenerational projects and programs; increased educational effort

1991   The first National Grandparenting Conference in Kansas City, Missouri

Initial conception of a Grandparent University

1992   Exploration of the medical, psychological, and emotional benefits of the grandparent-grandchild relationship at the Mind/Body Medical Institute, Harvard Medical School

Early scientific exploration of differences in the way children communicate with parents and grandparents

1993   Joint conference in Washington with Generations United

1994   Publication of *Grandparent Power* (Crown), by Arthur Kornhaber—a call to arms for the new generation of grandparents to celebrate their identity and get involved

1995   Publication of *Contemporary Grandparenting* (Sage Press), by Arthur Kornhaber—the first comprehensive textbook on grandparenting, complete with new research and theories

1996   Expansion of networking and communication media, creation of website www.grandparenting.org

1997   Conference on Grandparents Raising Grandchildren: establishment of Grandparent Productions to promote grandparenting via film and educational and entertainment television

1998   Public appearances and bimonthly appearances on national television (NBC's *Today*)

Kornhaber's appearances are coordinated with the MSNBC website and linked to the website of the Foundation for Grandparenting

Grandparent Productions debuts two film projects, *Click Three Times* and *Kartenspieler*

1999   Educational initiative to increase efforts in education, communication, networking, and research

Expansion of website www.grandparenting.org to include international advisory board

Educational Conference convened first-time (statewide) conference for Grandparents of Children with Disabilities in New Mexico

Release of *Kartenspieler* in summer 1999

2000–2002   Continuation of the Grandparent-Grandchild Summer Camp

Continued improvement and expansion of the website to enlarge international grandparent community

Development of new programs and products to achieve this purpose

Creation of a cyber environment to replicate, as closely as possible, the traditional familial and community context of lifelong children's and family learning over the Internet

Campaign for increased public awareness by spotlighting individuals who exemplify the ideal of grandparent power

Research into the implications of gay and lesbian parenthood on grandparents

Research into the roles of grandparents with "special needs" grandchildren

Media outreach to promote the importance of grandparenting

Use of "grandparent power" to remediate harmful social conditions (drug abuse, etc.)

Bibliography

American Association of Retired Persons. Grandparent Information Center. Washington, DC; www.aarp.org

American Bar Association (1989). *Grandparent Visitation Disputes*. Rep. No. 89-83439. Washington, DC.

Areen, Judith. (1982) Statement. Hearing before the Subcommittee on Human Services; Select Committee on Aging. House of Representatives. December 16, 1982. Washington, DC.

Baranowski, M. D. (1982). "Grandparent Adolescent Relations: Beyond The Nuclear Family." *Adolescence* 15: 575–584.

Bekker, L. D., and G. Taylor (1996). "Attitudes Toward the Aged in a Multi-generational Sample." *Journal of Gerontology* 21:115–118.

Bengston, V. (1985). "Diversity and Symbolism in Grandparental Roles." In V. Bengston and J. F. Robertson (eds.) *Grandparenthood*. Beverly Hills: Sage Publications Inc. (11–27).

Blackwelder, D. E., and R. E. Passman (1986). "Grandmother's and Mother's Disciplining in Three-Generational Families." *Journal Of Personality and Social Psychology* 50(1): 80–86.

Blau, T. H. (1984). "An Evaluative Study of the Role of Grandparents in the Best Interest of the Child." *American Journal of Family Therapy* 12(4): 47.

Bower, B. (1991). "Marked Questions on Elderly Depression." *Science News* 140(20): 310–312.

Breinig-Glunz, Denise. Personal communication with author regarding grandparents rearing grandchildren.

Brookdale Grandparent Caregiver Information Project. University of California (1992).

Buchanan, B., and J. Lappin (1990). Restoring the Soul of the Family. *The Family Therapy Networker* (November/December): 46–52.

Burton, L. M. (1992). "Black Grandparents Rearing Children of Drug-Addicted Parents: Stressors, Outcomes and Social Service Needs." *The Gerontologist* 32(6): 744–751.

Caren, L. D. (1991). "Effects of Exercise on the Human Immune System." *Bioscience* 41(6): 410–416.

Cath, S. H. (1985). "Of Gifts and Grandfathering." Paper presented at the annual meeting of the American Gerontologic Society, Boston.

Cerrato, P. L. (1990). "Does Diet Affect the Immune System?" *RN* 53(6): 67–70. Chairman Reports. Subcommittee on Human Services. *Grandparents: New Roles and Responsibilities*. Comm. Pub. No. 102-876.

Cherlin, A., and F. Furstenberg. (1986). "Grandparents and Family Crisis." *Generations* 10(4): 26–28.

Cherlin, A., and F. Furstenberg (1986). *The New American Grandparent: A Place in the Family, a Life Apart*. New York: Basic Books.

Cloninger, C. R., D. M. Svrakic, and T. R. Pryzbeck (1993). "A Psychobiological Model of Temperament and Character. *Archives of General Psychiatry* 50: 975–990.

Cohler, Bertram J. (1981). *Mothers, Grandmothers, and Daughters*. John Wiley & Sons, Inc.

Derdyn, A. P. (1985). "Grandparent Visitation Rights: Rendering Family Dissolution More Pronounced!" *American Journal of Orthopsychiatry* 55(2):27–287.

DeWitt, M. (1997). Reaction of Toddlers to Teaching by Parents and Grandparents. Personal communication.

Drew, L. A., and P. K. Smith (1999). "The Impact of Parental Separation/Divorce on Grandparent-Grandchild Relationships." *International Journal of Aging and Human Development* 48(3): 191–216.

Erikson, E. H. (1963). *Childhood & Society*. New York: W. W. Norton.

———— (1982). *The Life Cycle Completed*. New York: W. W. Norton.

Erikson, E. H., J. M. Erikson, and H. Kivnick (1986). *Vital Involvement in Old Age: The Experience of Old Age in Our Time*. New York: W. W. Norton.

Foster, R., and Freed, D. (1979). "Grandparent Visitation. Vagaries and Vicissitudes." *Journal of Divorce* 70 (Fall/Winter): 643–651.

Freedman, M. (1989). "Fostering Intergenerational Relationships for At-Risk Youths." *Children Today* 18(2): 10–15.

Furstenberg, F., and A. Cherlin (1991). *Divided Families*. Cambridge, MA: Harvard University Press. Generations United, Washington, DC (1992).

Golden, R. N., C. A. Pedersen, M. Corrigan, J. Gilmore, S. G. Silva, D. Quade, and H. Ozer, (1992). "Circulating Natural Killer Phenotypes in Men and Women with Major Depression: Relation to Catatonic Activity and Severity of Depression." *Archives of General Psychiatry* 49: 388–395.

Greenburg, J. S., and M. Becker (1988). "Aging Parents as Family Resources." *The Gerontologist*, 28(6): 786–791.

Hayslip, B. "Grandparents Raising Grandchildren: New Challenges for Geropsychologists." *Adult Development and Aging News* (Spring 2001), 5.

Ivester, M. C., and K. King, (eds.) (1977). "Attitudes of Adolescents Toward the Aged." *The Gerontologist* 17(1): 22.

Jendrek, Margaret P. (1993). *Grandparents Who Parent Their Grandchildren*. AARP/Andrus Foundation.

Johnson, C. (1983). "A Cultural Analysis of the Grandmother." *Research in Aging* 5(4): 547–567.

Joseph, A. M. (1968). *The Indian Heritage of America*. Bantam Books.

King v. King (1992) 8:28. S.W. 2d 630 (Ky). Cert. Denied 113. Ct. 378.

King, V., Elder, G. H. (1999). "Are Religious Grandparents More Involved Grandparents?" *Journal of Gerontology* 54(6): S317–S328.

Kennedy, J. F., and V. T. Keeney (1987). "Group Psychotherapy with Grandparents Rearing Their Emotionally Disturbed Grandchildren." *Group* 11(1): 15–25.

Kennedy, J. F., and V. T. Keeney (1988). "The Extended Family Revisited: Grandparents Rearing Grandchildren." *Child Psychiatry and Human Development* 19: 26–35.

Kornhaber, A. (1982). "The Vital Connection Between the Old and the Young: The Birth of the Intergenerational Movement in America." Address to the Administration on Aging National Meeting.

————— (July 1983). "Grandparents Are Coming of Age in America." *Children Today*. July 1983.

————— (February 1983). "Grandparents: The Other Victims of Divorce." *Reader's Digest*.

————— (June 1984) "America's Forgotten Resource: Grandparents." *U.S. News & World Report*.

————— (1985). *Between Parents and Grandparents*. St. Martin's Press.

————— (1986) "Grandparenting, Normal and Pathological." *American Journal of Geriatric Psychiatry* (October).

————— Grandparents As Clinical Collaborators. *Vital Connections*. Spring 1991.

————— (1986). Proceedings of the World Congress of Child Psychiatry. "Grandfathers; From Warriors to Wise Men." Paris.

————— (1987). "Are Your Children Problem Parents?" *Grandparents* 2 (Fall).

————— (June 1989). "Grandparents and Infants." *French Journal of Child Psychiatry*.

————— (1989). "Infants and Grandparents." *Infant Psychiatry*. Yale Press.

————— (1988). "The New Social Contract." *Grandparenthood*. Sage Press.

————— (1989). *Spirit*. St. Martin's Press.

————— (1990). "Les Grands-parents." *Le Monde Du Bebe*. Presse Medicale Paris.

————— (January 1992). "Talking to God." *Newsweek*.

————— (Spring 1993) "Raising Grandchildren." *Vital Connections* XIV.

————— (August 2001). "The Grandparenting Instinct," on www.grandparent ing.org.

Kornhaber, A., and K. L. Woodward. "Bringing Back Grandma." *Newsweek*, May 1981.

————— (1985). *Grand-Parents, Petits-Enfants*. Le Lien Vital. Paris: Robert Laffont.

————— (1981). *Grandparents/Grandchildren: The Vital Connection*. Doubleday, 168–170.

Lowinsky, N. R. (1996). *Stories from the Motherline*. New York: Jeremy Tarcher.

Matthews, S. H., and, J. Sprey (1984). "The Impact of Divorce on Grandparenthood: An Exploratory Study." *The Gerontologist* 24(4)1–7.

McGoldrick, J., J. K. Pearce, and N. Giordano (eds.), 1982. *Ethnicity & Family Therapy* (84–107). New York: Guilford Press.

McGreal, C. E. (1985). "The Birth of the First Grandchild: A Longitudinal Study of the Transition to Grandparenthood." *Dissertation Abstract International* 46(2): 675B.

Minckler, M., and K. Roe (1993). *Grandmothers As Caregivers*. Sage Press.

Minkler, M., and E. Fuller-Thomson (1999). "The Health of Grandparents Raising Grandchildren: Results of a National Study." *American Journal of Public Health* 89(9): 1384–1389.

Oliver, J. E. (1993). "Intergenerational Transmission of Child Abuse: Rates, Research and Clinical Implications." *American Journal of Psychiatry* 150: 1315–1324.

Pashos, A. (2000). "Grandparental Solicitude." PubMed. PMID 10785346. Institute of Human Biology. University of Hamburg (Germany).

Patterson C. J., S. Hurt, and C. D. Mason (1998). "Families of the Lesbian Baby Boom: Children's Contacts with Grandparents and Other Adults." *American Journal of Orthopsychiatry* 68(3): 390–399.

Pearson. B. (1981). "Child Custody: Why Not Let the Parents Decide?" *Judges Journal*: 20: 4.

Peterson, C. C. (1999). "Grandmothers and Grandfathers Satisfaction with the Grandparenting Roles." *International Journal of Aging and Human Development* 49(1): 61–68.

Roberto, K. A., and J. Stroes (1992). "Children and Grandparents: Roles, Influences and Relationships." *International Journal of Aging and Human Development* 34(3): 228.

Rosenthal, C. J., and V. W. Marshall (1983). "The Head of the Family: Authority and Responsibility in the Lineage. Paper presented at the annual meetings of the Gerontological Society of America.

Saltzman, G. A. (1992). "Grandparents Raising Grandchildren." *Creative Grandparenting, Inc.* 2(4).

Select Committee on Aging. House of Representatives. December 16, 1982. Washington, DC.

Somary, K., and G. Stricker (1998). "Becoming a Grandparent: A Longitudinal Study of Expectations and Early Experiences as a Function of Sex and Lineage." *Gerontologist* 38(1): 53–61.

Spruyette, N., et al. (1999). "Grandparents: The Experience of the Relationship with the Oldest Grandchild and Their Psychological Well-Being." *Tijdschr Gerontoligica Geriatrica* 30(1): 21–30.

Stone, E. (1991). "Mothers and Daughters." *Parent's Magazine* 66 (5): 83–87.

Stotland, L. N. (2001). "Gender-Based Biology." *American Journal of Psychiatry* 158(2): 161.

Strom R., and S. Strom (1992). *Achieving Grandparent Potential*. Newbury Park, CA: Sage Publications.

——— *Becoming a Better Grandparent*. Newbury Park, CA: Sage Publications.

Timberlake, E. M., and S. Chipungu (1992). "Grandmotherhood: Contemporary Meaning Among African American Middle Class Grandmothers." *Social Work* 37(3): 216–222.

Thomas, A., S. Chess, and H. Birch (1968). *Temperament and Behavior Disorders in Children*. New York: New York University Press.

Turtletaub, S. (2001). *The Grandfather Thing*. Los Angeles: Tallfellow Press.

United States Department of Commerce, Bureau of the Census (1990). Statistical Abstract of the United States. Washington, DC: U.S. Government Printing Office.

Victor, R. S. Statement. Hearing before the Subcommittee on Human Services,

Wiscott, R., K. Kopera-Frye (2000). "Sharing of Cultures: Adult Grandchildren's Perceptions of Intergenerational Relations." *International Journal of Aging and Human Development* 51(3): 199–215.

Index